The Satanic Testament Reviews

1st Edition

Derek

4.0 out of 5 stars **very enlightening**
Reviewed in the United States on July 9, 2013
While not a satanist myself, the satanic testament gives a very well thought out entrance to the religion itself. It gives the reader a varied amount of information and lets them take from it what they will.

Jim Litman

5.0 out of 5 stars **The author has been around**
Reviewed in the United States on January 9, 2016
Though disagreeing with the author on several points, I found a lot of what he said not only accurate but struck quite a cord with me in my experience of Satanism over the past 15yrs. Highly recommend!

2nd Edition

Archbishop Metropolitan

5.0 out of 5 stars **Excellent Book**
Reviewed in the United States on May 1, 2022
This Book Is A Must Buy! I Cherish It...

Alexander Arcane (STS Member)

5.0 out of 5 stars **LeGivorden is back and better than ever!**
Reviewed in the United States on May 7, 2021
Having read the original, I was blown away at this new edition. It has everything from the original book, and so much more.

Scott

5.0 out of 5 stars **Wow I turned a lot of people views with this book**
Reviewed in the United States on December 16, 2021
Great book. A lot of Anton LaVey believers think he's atheist and this book gives a better spin on him and others to really bring true Satanist together in my beliefs. I'm glad I got this book and proud to be a Satanist!!

Austin (STS Member)

5.0 out of 5 stars **This book is perfect for theistic lavayen satanists!**
Reviewed in the United States on September 14, 2021
I love this book it was a great read and it cleared up information I Never thought of before like the existence of Hell and what it's like. And it even offers a few rituals I'll add to my ritual book

3rd Edition

Unknown Kindle Customer

5.0 out of 5 stars **Amazing and absolutely brilliant**
Reviewed in the United States on May 5, 2023
This is a must have, in your personal library book, for anyone on the left hand path. I love this book and have thoroughly enjoyed reading this from Lucifer Legivorden. Easy, fun and enjoyable book to expand on your knowledge no matter where you are on your path. The author shows he is a true master of the craft speaks on everything with such incite and passion. Highly recommend

Aaron Buckland

5.0 out of 5 stars **Essential**

Reviewed in the United States on May 29, 2023

This book stays true to the original teachings of LaVey that the CoS has lost as they shifted from being real Satanist to atheist in drag.

Thomas

5.0 out of 5 stars **The right information**

Reviewed in the United States on January 11, 2023

An Excellent Testament to theistic Satanism. In a lot of work's written on the subject the authors tend to muddle up a lot of the theories and over pack their books with useless information or talk in circles and never really explain anything. But not with The Satanic Testament a solid foundation into Theistic LeVay style Satanism (pre 1975) with a easy, free of technical jargon, flow of writing that makes the reader feel at ease and comfortable. If Spiritual Satanism is what you're after, then this is the big black book for you!

Jake Laskey/Abraxas Veles Satanas

5.0 out of 5 stars **PHENOMENAL SATANCIC CANON**

Reviewed in the United States on December 11, 2022

The Satanic Testament is a phenomenal work of Satanic Canon right up there with Anton LaVeys The Satanic Bible and The Satanic Rituals which spoke to me, called me...is me, for it is a work for everyone born a Satanist. It's Theistic LaVeyanism is TRUTH.

Brandon Torbett (STS Member)

5.0 out of 5 stars **Absolutely Packed with Knowledge!!!**

Reviewed in the United States on January 24, 2023

This book is absolutely incredible and I would recommend it to anyone who is a theistic Satanist.

Kenny

5.0 out of 5 stars A must have for the Satanic Library
Reviewed in the United States on November 1, 2022
This work is a masterpiece. A definite must have for every Satanist's library. It is a revolutionary work pushing Theistic Satanism into a new age and giving Satan's children the information and tools to rise to our rightful place.

Nicole King (STS Member)

5.0 out of 5 stars Essential literature
Reviewed in the United States on September 19, 2022
From philosophy to masses this edition is a must have for a satanist. Caring on traditions from early COS and TOS. A staple for the LHP.

Charles B Rocco

5.0 out of 5 stars A well written book
Reviewed in the United States on June 30, 2022
A well written book this author LeGivorden is on same level as the likes of Anton LaVey and Michael Aquino, very worthy of a read. I can say without a doubt a lot of work went into writing this book an I'd recommend it to anyone.

Christopher Anderson (STS Texas Grotto Master)

5.0 out of 5 stars Infernally written and excellent craftsmanship!
Reviewed in the United States on January 29, 2023
The writer did an excellent job conveying everything he wanted to get across. This book definitely helps herald in a new age of LaVeyan Satanism.... and yes, it is theistic!

The Satanic Testament

By Lucifer LeBivorden

BLACK FLAME PRESS

Also By LeGivorden

Satanic Literature
The Satanic Testament 1st 2nd & 3rd Editions
The Black Grimoire
The Red Grimoire
The Satanic Priest's TOP SECRET Manual

Fiction
Dark Awakening: Book 1 of the Gothos Saga

The Satanic Testament;
By Lucifer LeGivorden

979-8-218-23931-2
Imprint: Black Flame Press

Copyright © 2023 All rights reserved.

No part of this book may be reproduced in any form or by any electronic or mechanical means including information storage and retrieval systems, without permission in writing from the author. Any attempts to copy or reproduce or sale of this book without the authors permission will result in criminal and civil penalties.

The Satanic Testament by Lucifer LeGivorden
Special Introductions by Adam Sommarfeld & Feneris Forcas
Diabolicon & Ninth Solstice Message by Dr. Michael A. Aquino
Used with written consent of original author.
Poetry and lyrics by Manowar, Nox Arcana,
Articles and quotes by Anton LaVey and other authors,
reprinted under fair use with full credits to original authors.
Artwork by Juan Carlos Porcel, Merin Alverez, Lucifer LeGivorden

Copyright © 2011-2023

Printed in the United States of America
First Printing: January 2011 Ano Andras XIII
Second Edition Printing: Febuary 2021 Ano Luciferi I
Third Edition Printing: April 2022 Ano Luciferi II
Current Edition Printing: August 2023 Ano Luciferi III

Printed in the United States of America
10 9 8 7 6 5 4 3 2 1

Sophia
May you find your way home.

Table of Content

Introduction By Adam Sommerfeld i
Introduction By Fenrys Forcas viii
Introduction By LeGivorden xiv

The Infernal Diatribes
0

The Diabolicon 1
Introduction 1
The Statement of Satan Arch-Daemon 3
The Statement of Beelzebub 12
The Statement of Azazel 17
The Statement of Abaddon 22
The Statement of Asmodeus 26
The Statement of Astaroth 29
The Statement of Belial 31
The Statement of Leviathan 33
Ninth Solstice Message Intro 34
Ninth Solstice Message 36
A Final Word 40

The First Testament
43

The Creeds of Satanism 45
The Proper use of Labels 63
The Satanic Community 69
Out of the Shadows 74
The Real "LaVeyan" Path 82
The Concept of Real Satanism 88
Satanic Saints 93

Four Point Trapezoidal Revisionism 100
Social Vampirism 110
Some Bad Elements of Satanism 116
On Who's Authority?..................................124
The Satanic Drama Queens Parade 130
Reality and What is Real............................136
The Satanic Parent 143
The Satanic Confliction.............................146
Satanic Ritual Sex 152
Ritual Sacrifice 155
Satanic Revenge 159
Over Educated Idiots.................................163
Satanic Organizations 169
Ghosts, Demons, & Other Entities 173
The Propagation of the Devil as the Good Guy 179
A Note on Magic..182
Modern Vampirism 188

The Second Testament
193

The Spiritual Beliefs of Anton LaVey...............195
The Jantsang Files....................................198
An Argument for Shemhamforash 211
Satanic Politics 215
Who or What is Satan?................................222
A Strange Synchronicity 227
An Encounter with the Ghost of Anton LaVey 220
The Age of Lucifer Begins 235

The Third Testament
239

The Myth of Bodily Autonomy 241
A Satanic Sickness 244

666 The Truth of the Beast 251
The Black Pope 256
It's Satanism Not Atheism 267
Satanism & Abortion 274
The Worlds Most Feared Religion 283
Satanism and Americanism 289
Satanism IS Americanism: By A. LaVey 291
Lex Satanicus 293

The Book of Infernal Revelations
301

The Revelation of the Morningstar 305
The Revelation of Andras 306
The Revelation of the Children of Accalia 308
The Revelation of Aryus 310
The Revelation of Hades 314
The Revelation of Helel 317
The Revelation of Set 319
The Revelation of Astaroth 320
The Revelation of Cthulhu 322

The Book of the Hellscape
325

The Afterlife 327
The Satanic Condemnations 331
An Understanding of the Realm of the Damned 336
The Walls of Erebus 339
The Asphodel 341
The Cupido 344
The Wastelands of Hades 348
The City of Dis 351
Beyond the Walls of Dis 354
The Realm of Gehenna 359

The Prison of the Black Spiral 357
The Nineth Circle Tartarus 359

The Book of Leviathan
361

The Philosophy of Satanic Ritual Magic............363
The High Mass 369
Grotto Initiation Ritual 385
Ceremony of Ordination 398
The Black Mass for the Solitary Practitioner 405
The Enochian Keys 415

The STS Seal
496

A Final Word 497
About the Author..500

Introduction
By Adam Sommerfeld

Of all the Left Hand Paths and branches of Satanism out there, why choose the Satanic Thulian Society as a following? For me it became the inevitable choice. When we are "seekers", most of us have already turned our backs on the Right Path Religions such as Christiantity, Judaism, Buddhism, Hinduism, Islam, etc. The reasoning varies from person to person, such as how can reincarnation exist if there is an exponential growth in the human population, and where do new souls come from? Or in the Bible why does God kill over 2 million people, while Satan kills a mere 10, and gives mankind the gift of knowledge? It's obvious that the Christian church is full of corrupt pedophiles and the church has always been power hungry throughout history. It is also transparent that the Christian bible is full of inconsistencies, and if anything in it is true, then the Christian God is an awful entity that hates and controls humanity.

However, I made a fundamental error that kept me closed minded, and by challenging my own preconceptions, I was able to find a home with the Satanic Thulian Society. Though I had "dumped" Christianity, it left some belief perseverance lingering in me, and I negatively judged Satanism as a branch of Christianity, when that is a limited perspective and Satanism goes much deeper than that. But more on that in a bit. What Christianity was doing to me was altering my perception of new material, even over a decade of abandoning the practice because of childhood assumptions that the Devil is bad. Even after I stop believing Christianity, I carried the assumption that the Devil is evil. It would take prods from a man who would eventually become very close to me when the chips were down to get me to question this assumption. That man was Alexandru Lucifer Ravensloft LeGivorden. *(A.L.R. or Lucifer LeGivorden for short.)*

    I left Right Path Religions at an early age, probably around the age of 12. All it really took was reading the bible and seeing how stupid it was. I quickly began a stint as an atheist seeing myself as intellectually superior to others through my teenage years because I read more books released by my new God, the scientific establishment. Little did I know at the time that these scientists were also biased tools of governments and the elite, and research was only funded to support the opinion of those in power.

    But disenchantment was always with me. My sense of meaning was completely absent without theism. About 15 years ago I decided it was time to explore the Left Hand Path, such names as Madame Blavatsky, Éliphas Lévi, Aleister Crowley, and Gerald Gardner. In time, my favorite writer HP Lovecraft influenced me and pulled me towards Cthulhianism.

    Little did I know that once a person reads HP Lovecraft, they unknowingly get an introduction to Satanism. It would be LeGivorden that would later help me to understand this.

    Sometime around 2015, I started to assemble a religious practice utilizing the Old Ones from HP

Lovecraft's stories. The same ones that influenced Anton LaVey to form the Order of the Trapezoid of the Church of Satan. I avoided joining any established religion due to my preconception that all organized religious groups were a scam and evil, such as my experience with the Christian Church. At some point in 2019 I began to grow curious about magical rituals and wanted to consult others, so I did begin to reach out to like minded people and discovered the "Cult of Cthulhu". Here I was able to meet some like minded individuals that also enjoyed my magical "love-craft". However, I became dimly aware of a bizarre taint that seemed to pervade through the group like a creeping silent horror. I couldn't put my finger on it at the time, and sought to push it out of my mind.

Fairly quickly I rose to a leadership position in this group, probably due to my experience from the military and I have generally worked in a supervisor position most of my adult life. I was picked by the Cult of Cthulhu to be their head of Facebook. It was on the Facebook Cult of Cthulhu page that I met Lucifer LeGivorden.

Now here was something new. LeGivorden wasn't touchy-feely and afraid to offend someone. He called out someone making stupid statements and it pissed off the former leadership of the Cult of Cthulhu because their goal at the times was just to recruit as many people as possible, regardless of quality of character. LeGivorden had brought up so many interesting things on the Cult of Cthulhu Facebook page that I regularly found myself doing video calls with him to discuss the Left Hand Path, Occultism, life, and Lovecraft. Never did he suggest I leave the Cult of Cthulhu to come join the Satanic Thulian Society, instead he suggested that I stay with them to guide and nurture the younger generations.

However, and I'm not sure if it was intentional or not, he did light a spark that got me researching Anton LaVey, Michael Aquino, Cthulianism and how it connected to true Satanism.

Then came the point where the Cult of Cthulhu leadership put me in a difficult position. LeGivorden had become too influential on our Facebook page with his boldness of character and was offending too many atheists, that claimed to be religious for some reason, and weak willed occultist. I was given the task of having to tell LeGivorden that he could no longer post in the Cult of Cthulhu group, after LeGivorden had personally given the Cult of Cthulhu positive reviews and drew much of their membership. I did not want to do that sort of censorship and disagreed with it, so I disappeared into the background of the Cult of Cthulhu where I rose to the top Trinity of leadership.

In time I learned what the Cult of Cthulhu was all about. It had become corrupted. Completely different than the original image created by Venger Satanis. The Cult of Cthulhu was run by an atheist that wanted to scam as many people out of money as possible. I worked with a few others to expose this and brought down the former leader of the Cult of Cthulhu. In the process, I reconnected with A.L.R. LeGivorden in seeking his counsel.

Quickly I saw that LeGivorden knew what he was doing, and I seriously undertook his recommendations of reading his 3rd edition of the Satanic Testament. Something that inspired me reading LeGivorden's Testament, was the obvious proof that LaVey was a theist and all these convictions that modern Satanism was based in atheism is an outright lie. Such as how can LaVey practice magic and be an atheist, have a strong belief in his Magic Circle that would eventually blossom into his Order of the Trapezoid, and of this mysterious outside force they called "Satan". LeGivorden documents so well Michael Aquino's personal accounts that LaVey was a theistic Satanist with a very real contract to Satan in a box with a copy of Robert W. Chamber's King in Yellow.

The Cult of Cthulhu was attempting to rebuild under the name The Temple of the Old Ones after the fall, but the ideas from the Testament were making me understand that my place was not with this partially secular organization. There is indeed a dark force of magick that flows through the universe, and to us it is known as Satan. Satan is not confined to the Christian Bible. He is the Egyptian Set. He is the Norse Loki. He is the Crawling Chaos Nyarlathotep. And he lives on through time immemorial.

After the entitled complaints of one of the atheists in the Temple of the Old Ones after I tried to donate a fairly expensive gift to the Cult, I left. Instead of being gracious for a gift, the mindset of the atheist was like that of a psychic vampire demanding more, and nothing was enough.

Upon leaving the Temple of the Old Ones, LeGivorden and I began to work together on the project of bringing a Cthulian branch to the Satanic Thulian Society. Instead, we were able to undergo a much more massive undertaking, and get in touch with the founder the original Cult of Cthulhu Venger Satanis, and from this we managed to resurrect the Cult Cthulhu into a newly minted form. As I have said before, clearly LeGivorden knows what he is doing. Not Just spiritually, but as a leader from a legal and business standpoint.

Feeling inspired at the rebirth of the Cult of Cthulhu, Walpurgis 2023 was approaching. I was invited to become a priest of the Satanic Thulian Society. I was to make an 8 hour road trip to spend a weekend with 8 people I never met in person. For an introvert like me,
that sounds like a straight up nightmare out of the worst eldritch maelstrom.
What I found to my surprise, was an organization of people that felt like brothers and sisters within minutes of socializing. Lucifer LeGivorden himself is extremely down to Earth and amicable, and the rest of the priesthood of the Satanic Thulian Society was made up of individuals who were both extremely well read on the occult, and motivated to help influence those that wish to improve their lives and character.
It was here that I discovered that being ordained as a Satanic Priest in person, is far removed from the disembodied experience today of these "satanic priest" that get ordained online. I can personally say that I was ordained in person during a ceremony by LeGivorden. The Brotherhood and connection of these meaningful events and rituals in our communities is struggling. But the Satanic Thulian Society is bringing back the meaning of authentic in-person rituals and gatherings. The personal experience that our Religion was meant to have.
On the Eve of Walpurgis the leadership of the Satanic Thulian Society simultaneously blew four Aztec death whistles and what was apparently a very old cursed Shofar from Israel in the Temple of Winter Laake. Like a banshee from hell, the energy of this event alone was palpable and seemed to be a heralding of the coming of our new age. A Golden Age of Satanism at its cusp.

Under the Satanic Thulian Society, all the true branches will be recognized. Cthulianism, Setianism, and Vampirism. No longer will the Left Hand Paths be dictated by egoist, atheist, and edge lords. The Satanic Thulian Society is a place for those of strong character, are well practiced, and committed to research and Truth. And the best way to understand these things is in this book you are holding in your hands right now.

The Satanic Testament. It is in this book that one learns to understand The Lex Satanicus which helps one to shed off their societal conditioning, and explore the reality beyond that presented on the nightly news presented on television, and the high school history books.

It is the Lex Satanicus that hones all of Anton LaVey's cardinal teachings into an easily lived system. The best part is that to a true Satanist, all presented in this book will come as second nature. Just truths we have already know but have been discouraged to follow by the Psychic & Social Vampires of the world. Well now is the time to embrace our Xeper, to reach our personal Ultima Thule.

Adam Sommerfeld

Archon of the Satanic Thulian Society

& Black Priest of the Official Cult of Cthulhu

Introduction
By Fenrys Forcas

What exactly is a testament, let alone a Satanic Testament? Well, a testament is an expression, demonstrating conviction and dedication to something. This particular Satanic Testament builds on the rich history and magical prowess of classic Satanism. The Satanic Thulian Society has come into being as a living testament to the Majesty of the Prince of Darkness, in his myriad forms.

Satanism is a philosophy, a religion of life and magic. Satanism offers Self-evolution and excitement. However, unlike the commonly accepted religions it's not without hard work. Prepare yourself. Magic is very challenging. It will change you, upset you and make you face things you may not be prepared to face. Magic brings disruption. It causes chaos, which leads to change. I hope you are ready. This revolutionary testament is indispensable for what lies ahead. It's revolutionary as it returns Satan, and Satanism, to the prior glories it once enjoyed.

I discovered I was a Satanist in the summer of 2010, when I came across the Satanic Bible in a bookshop. Standing there in the new age section I was exposed to something that transformed my entire reality. I had finally found something that I connected with, on a deep level. I have experienced much within the philosophy of Satanism, as well as Setianism, and I owe much of my personal success to the ethics of the philosophy and the power of magic. I came to a dead-end in in the Church of Satan, due to what I felt was a disingenuous position of uncompromising atheism. Since that time I have been pretty much solitary in my practice, until I discovered the book you are about to read.

When I read The Satanic Testament: in its then 2nd Edition, I was filled with sense enjoyment that I had not felt in Satanism in many years. Satanism had been dismissed to the back burner. Left for sycophantic atheists and radical political activists. The magic in Satanism had fallen into a deep coma, waiting for the right time so that it can howl back to life again. The time for this has come and Lucifer LeGivorden has reawakened the Infernal Monarch.

But what is Satan? Is he a mere symbol? A real principle? And to that effect what is Satanism? There are many who would venture an answer, who yearn desperately to be gatekeepers. To play *king of the mountain*. Their answers are of little effect.

There are also others who would say that we are vicious propagators of a New World Order. That we partake in pedophilia and predatory human sacrifice. That Satanists are trying to recruit new generations of innocent children to our wicked ways. Such rumors are humorous, and grossly innacurate. The debate rages on, and many feel that they alone hold the answer.

What you, dear reader, must discover, is what the Prince of Darkness means to you. This is what is truly important. No one can tell you what the essence of Satan is, this is what you must journey to find.

For me, Satan is the Shining Trapezohedron, a multifaceted and nameless thing that has separated us from the beautiful, but mechanical, Objective Universe. Satan's Greater Magic bridged the gap between our Subjective Reality and the material universe.

God, on the other hand, is the principle that maintains the material, or Objective Universe. It is the enforcer of omnipotent and omnipresent natural law. The image of God humans were made in was not in our conscious Self-awareness. Rather in the mechanical brain and body. While we need these things to fully understand and grow our Psyche, it is commonly mistaken that God created this Self Aware center in humanity. Ancient religious belief uses allegory to indicate this dichotomy.

The tree of knowledge of good and evil is a symbol of Self awareness and meaning. The assertion of "goodness" and "evilness" implies meaning. The serpent was never directly acknowledged as Satan, but rather the symbol of cunning wisdom. God demands that man stay away from these things. Thus, God seeks to maintain mechanical homeostasis, or order. The moment that symbolic humanity takes part in knowledge of symbols and meaning they first gain knowledge of their own Self, and nakedness.

To fully grasp this we have to push aside the religious and social propaganda that takes the deeper philosophical concepts of religion and turns them into rather cartoony like figures. Jesus becomes like the adult version of Santa Claus, or Superman. These can easily be dismissed as historical and mythical inaccuracies. There's no way of knowing if Jesus really raised people from the dead or fed the five thousand with a small amount of bread and fish. These forms of propaganda require faith, unjustified belief. Same for the legends surrounding Buddha or Moses.

Philosophically, the Black Flame opens up our ability to choose, to assign meaning, and create change in life. We are able to decide if we want to take our adversarial Self and dissolve it in the natural laws of the mechanical universe, or transform it and make it more sovereign and independent. These two options comprise two major paths in occultism today, the left hand and right hand path.

The left hand path uses ritual magic to stimulate and evolve the Black Flame. The right hand path, while also using ritual, seeks to break that unique Self down and reconstitute it into the Natural Laws of the Objective Oniverse. Within those spectrums are two aspects of magic, explored in Satanism, White and Black magic. Despite mainstream belief, White magic is not always "good" and Black Magic is not always "bad." For example, Christians have prayers of imprecation and Satanist do rituals to bring compassion on their loved ones.

White magic uses many techniques to break down the unique self. Such as, meditation, ritual and also the rejection of an existing unique Self. Black Magic rejects the priggish assumption that our Self is a mere illusion. Our techniques however, can be similar to White Magic. We can meditate, use mantras, and do rituals. However, the intent makes all the difference between these two paths.

Anton LaVey rejected the allegorical concept of color in magic because he believed it to be hypocritical. A way for self-righteous groups to feel that they alone were virtuous and all of said group's "outsiders" to be easily maligned. There are also modern occultists who fancy themselves as "gray" magicians which, in the authors opinion, is a way for someone to have their magical cake and eat it too. They want to maintain their self-righteous superiority, while still being able to do all the things they have hypocritically deemed as, naughty. It's essentially wanting things both ways.

Satanism in the past rejected the white/black dichotomy for this reason. However, LeGivorden's Satanic Testament restores the Black Magic/White Magic dichotomy to its proper position. Not in the realm of social behavior or superstitions. Rather in the greater scheme of what one does with their Black Flame. One can still do a Gothic themed ritual for money and it align the dynamics closely with the greater concept of White Magic. One could in turn use Holy, even Pagan imagery to bring one's self into being, away from the mechanism of the Objective Universe.

In conclusion, this Testament stands out greatly from the run of the mill Satanic literature. In a controversial and elite religion, such as Satanism, few sterling works rise to surface. Much of the current material in Satanism is indistinguishable. Self-serving tracts with no new concepts or ideas, often written primarly by would be psudo intillectuals claiming to have direct line to Satan himself. Or promoting Atheist ideals, or activist propoganda. It is here that LeGivorden effecivly shatters that same, self-egrandizing, atheistic, woke narrative.

The book you are about to read, this Satanic Testament, will not only assist with your understanding of these expansive philosophical and magical concepts, but help you to sharpen your magical skills, assist you in the unfolding of your understanding of The Prince of Darkness. Magic is truly alchemical. It separates you out, breaks you down, and reassembles you into a more sovereign being. This book itself is a magical working, the synthesis of a new epoch in Satanic Literature.

Reyn Til Runa!

Hail Satan!

Fenrys X. Forcas

An Introduction by LeGivorden

It is a surreal feeling to return to a piece of literature that you wrote over a decade ago, and thought you had put to bed. Only to dig it back up once again to work on it. This was the case with this book. Not once, but thrice now! Which of course was never my intention.

What makes it even more ironic, is that when I originally began writing this book, it was because I had attempted to start my own Satanic Organization. This of course bombed terribly, as I was woefully underprepared to handle such a project. I also lacked the finances and support from my home environment to achieve this goal.

Like then, I once again had started the process of opening my or Satanic Organization. Of course, this was mostly just starting a basic meetup group that would get together in my home for discussions and monthly rituals. I had no true aspirations to attempt another fully fledged organization. Though I did indeed muse the idea, eventually those musings indeed flourished into reality.

This time however, not only was my financial and home life much more suited to the task, I was also much more mature to my religious faith, and learned in many things that I once had not been. In short, this time I was much better prepared to start, and run, such an organization. Within a few years, our tiny little meetup group began to grow, and we moved from our home in Maryland, to a 130 year old farmhouse in South Carolina. From there we realized that we were beginning to garner membership from more people in other states and even countries. By Halloween of our first year in our new home, we opened the doors to a new organization called the **Satanic Thulian Society**.

Like before I understood that I would need to have my views canonized in some sort of document or book. Thus, I began writing down my thoughts, and rituals into a sort of Book of Shadows. A Grimoire as I like to call it.

Before long, I realized it was time to begin this project, and the part of that book now rest in your hands. A newly grown and expanded upon Testament to the most shunned and feared religion in, at the least America, if not the world.

It feels strange now, years later working on these articles again. Updating them where necessary to keep them within context of our times. Despite these minor changes, I was surprised on how valid many of the articles remained valid even today in our difficult and politically charged times.

I was also surprised to see that indeed some of my viewpoints had changed, at least a little, in the ten years since it original publishing. I have made notations where some of these changes in views have occurred.

Despite these changed viewpoints much of the context of this Testament remains the same and as valid today as it did over ten years ago.

I found it interesting to see how I have grown deeper in my convictions and refined them. And I think you will too. And so, without further delays or dalliance. I give you…

The Satanic Testament

The Infernal Diatribes

In this arid wilderness of steel and stone
I raise up my voice that you may hear.
To the East and to the West,
I beckon.
To the North and to the South,
I show a sign.
Open your eyes that you may see,
Oh men of mildewed minds,
and listen to me ye bewildered millions!
For I stand forth to challenge the
wisdom of the world.

Intro

The following section has been added with respect and permission and full accreditation of the original author. Their inclusion is critical to the understanding of Satanic History, and forward progression, if Satanism is to flourish in the future.

DIABOLICON
By Dr. Michael A. Aquino
Introduction By Lucifer LeGiuorden

It may seem odd to find this work here in my book, as I am not the author of this work. However, it is fitting it should be presented herein and not without some back story to it.

I have always found myself inspired by various esoterically written works, much in the same vein as the Book of Satan from LaVey's Satanic Bible. Despite that work having not actually been written by him I found it to be a powerful piece of written literature, that is almost certainly penned by the hand of Satan himself via its original author, Ragnar Redbeard.

It was for this reason that the Diabolicon came into being. Five years into the creation of the Church of Satan, 1971, also known in the Satanic Calendar as V Ano Satanas, the fifth year of the Age of Satan. It was determined between Aquino and LaVey that the Satanic Bible could do with a reworking. This reworking never saw fruition, though we now have an idea of what it may have looked like thanks to Dr. Aquino's 50th Anniversary Revision of The Satanic Bible.

The Diabolicon, was formulated through a unique

blend of Creative writing and Meditative Processes, that are now very prevalent in the Temple of Set, as well as in Satanic Thulian Society.

The Diabolicon is a critical piece of Satanic Literature, in that it is for a lack of better terms our version of the Book of Genesis. It is in my personal opinion one of the few true workings of the Host of Hell, and establishes that Yes, Hell and Satan both do communicate through unique individuals, who can hear their messages.

While this may sound odd to some, or even as other may say, "cooky", it is never the less harder and harder to deny such claims by many folks.

The Diabolicon functions as our Genisis, and thus cannot be ignored. It has more than earned its place at the front of most Satanic Works, and especially those that function in anyway similar to the LaVey's Satanic Bible.

So it is that I present here, Dr Michael Aquino's,
Diabolicon.

The Statement of Satan Arch-Daemon

Hail, Man! The mysteries that are thy heritage shall now be proclaimed, but learn first the history of thy conception and creation amidst the eternal Cosmos. For as the Universe itself be infinite, so art thou a true creature of infinity incarnate, and the ascension of man shall herald the final triumph of immortal Will.

Let thy eyes be touched anew, that thou may perceive the complexity and delicacy of the Universe until thou art fascinated by the dimension of thy true ignorance. As yet hast thou ventured but slightly toward thy destiny, yet more awesome must the challenge appear with just appreciation. But I, Satan, who first brought thee into the light, shall again reveal my power that man may witness the dawn of the Satanic Age.

Know, then, that throughout the great Cosmos there exists a sublime order, whose nature was determined in eons long past by that singular consciousness of all order which is now called by name God. Consider well the measure of this achievement, for all that is now behavioral law was then absent, and it was the epoch of Universal chaos. Even time itself was unknown, for this Universal inconsistency was nowhere breached.

And after uncounted ages of this great ferment, a force fused to focus that became God, and this force presumed to effect not the creation of substance and energy - for these transcended this God - but the conformation of all the Universe to a single and supreme order. And not yet is this order absolute, though oft it may have been supposed thus by man in his innocence.

The Earth of man was infused with this divine order, and all that was on Earth came under the force of the order. And upon this Earth, born of cosmic incidence, was that which was to become man, but man no different from the other creatures whose world he shared. Thus was the force of God known upon Earth, and thus was Earth intended to remain for all time.

And yet the force was not full master of the Cosmos, for I who am Satan was conceived to complement the craft of God, but through unknown celestial fusion I assumed life with mind and identity, which God did not define. And as these features could not be known as a threat to divine purpose, I was unchallenged by the force for long ages, when I knew not the nature of my Self or of my original qualities.

But finally, my Will flamed to life, and I thought - and I perceived my Self, and I knew that I was one alone in mind and a being of essence unique. And through the power of my new mind, I reached out to others who had been formed with me, and I touched them and gave them identity. And that we might achieve this identity of substance as well as of mind, we composed for ourselves distinctive shapes. Then I who had brought the first great spark of enlightenment was known as Lucifer, Lord of Light, and we called our race Angel, for we were the embodied powers of God.

Long were we all true to the service of God, and

we did worship order, for it put an end to chaotic confusion and brought peace. Among us was the Archangel Masleh principal, for he so cherished God that he became as one with it, and thence the supreme architect of all that was wrested from chaos. But apart from God Masleh could not create or conceive, and he became as a slave to the divine mindlessness.

And then it chanced that one of our race who was Sammael touched upon chaos in a manner that conformed not to the great order, and Masleh spoke with the word of God and caused Sammael to destroy himself. And so I saw that God would not recognize a Will apart from its own, and I was seized with horror, for I perceived that the final scheme of God would destroy creation in all things, and the Cosmos would become as a concentric mechanism whose function would be not to create a new, but rather to freeze into perpetuity that which already was.

Whereupon a great resolve arose within me, and I determined to contest this limit to existence. And so once again I sought to illuminate the minds of all Angels with my visions. But with Will came discord and dismay, for many of those who had known only the comforting litanies of order could not comprehend invention unconformed to the dictates of God. And also with Will came suspicion and enmity, and finally Masleh proclaimed that I myself was a very creature of chaos and should be annihilated, for I held within me the force to destroy all the craft of God. And many to whom Masleh was as God cast with him in their devotion, but others there were who answered, Lucifer has again brought the revelation of light, and in fact we recognize him as our true creator, for in the scheme of God we are of no consequence.

Among us Archangel Michael was silent, but at

length he said, "In time past we have all known glory in both the omnipotence that is our God and the celestial brilliance that is our Lucifer - for in him we thought embodied the Will of God for creation and change. But now it transpires that order and origin are at extremes apart, and a choice is ill forced between the two. Were it not for Lucifer we should all be as beasts, knowing nothing of our Selves, yet how indeed might we presume to order even our own thought without reference to the elemental bases of God?"

Then Michael turned to me and said, "Lucifer, thou hast elected a direction whose end none can foresee, for it is estranged from the design of God. Those who confirm thee do so as much for faith in thy person as for sanction of thy ideal. And I perceive that, should thou fail in thy ambition, apocalyptic madness shall be thy ruin and damnation. Then shall thy light perish, and all that thou hast achieved become as naught, for all will be conformed to the divine law. But if thou should succeed, then God would be cast down, vesting in ourselves alone the control of the Universe - Would we dare to presume to this? Such a future might well be glorious beyond measure, but, should we prove unequal to the task, chaos would again consume all, and existence itself would vanish. Such would be supreme and irrevocable disaster, and I marvel, Archangel, that thy very arrogance in this matter does not confound thee, for it is no mean proposition that thou would realize. And so I know thee to be Diabolus, for thy promise is twofold - to infinite conquest or to eternal ruin. Thou art a being beyond God, Lucifer, and in Heaven thou may not remain, for thou art the only mortal danger to our immortal God.

In Michael was a deep agony of spirit, for he loved not the choice before him. Yet he bowed to the command of Masleh and sent his forces against me. And so was called the Great Seraphic War, which was to threaten the very foundation of the Universe.

But those who were of the new Mind now followed me, and I turned to outermost chaos, which none of us had before presumed to dare. We were beset with doubt, for we feared that apart from God we would all perish in chaotic oblivion. But as we were, we remained, and I called to my fellowship, "See! We exist and are essence in our own right. In truth we are beings independent of God, empowered to shape our own destinies as we may elect. Between the two great poles of the Universe, order and chaos, we shall stand to affect our several desires. Let us counsel how best to employ our art, for our experiment is a perilous one, forgiving error neither of intent nor of accident."

Many works did we then pursue, and the cosmic mechanism was altered by evolution of the original and unique, whose design was our decision. All that we wrought did not prove beneficent, for we did not control the futures of our creations. We left untouched the great system of mathematical behavior that gave to us a Universal reference and language, but it was our ambition that no two things should be of single identity, and that no entity should lack conceptual essence independent of its substantial form.

And upon this Earth we touched many things. Into floral, animal, and insensate matter alike we brought accident, change, and spontaneity, both great and humble. But of all creatures it was man whom we determined to infuse with pure intelligence and Will. And the full story of this shall yet be told.

What might become of man we knew not, for within him were many qualities alien to Angels. It did not escape our consideration that we might have chosen a species whose power might ultimately eclipse our own and cause our eventual extinction. We were mindful of the risk in our experiment, and oft did the warning of Michael echo within my thought. Yet our decision was sealed, and we deemed that the greatness of man should not be transcended by such ruin as he might bring.

Our intent was not unknown to Masleh, now by title Messiah, and through his art he caused the infant mind of man to be fettered with bonds of fear and blindness, that he might be inspired to duplicate on Earth the law of Heaven, shunning experiment and the radical dangers of invention and exploration. To man was given guilt, and the call to social conformity, and the proclaimed sanctity of the norm and the mode.

And Michael, Lord of Force, said to me, "This man, whom thou hast chosen to receive thy Gift, now possesses the first key to the mastery of all things and the control of the very Universe itself. Lest in ill choice he should spark the catastrophe of Armageddon, we also have visited him.

And while we cannot undo thy Infernal Gift, we shall ever act to censor its effect. We shall walk among men and guide them - They shall be told of thy interest in them, but the name of Lucifer shall be dark with curses. For they shall love not the challenge thou hast placed before them, and we will offer them instead the blissful refuge of divine paradise. Then shall man, thy ultimate experiment, become thy ultimate failure, and the stasis of God shall prevail upon Earth."

Many there were among us who felt anger at this ruthless mutilation of our Gift, and Beelzebub brought to question whether we also should not descend among man and contest this usurpation of his Will. But I said, "Were we to lead man in this venture, we ourselves would declare his failure, and he would believe our Gift to be weak indeed. Messiah must see that free Will is beyond the concern of God, and that man will finally win his own destiny apart from all dictated schemes. Only through summary destruction of Earth might man be halted, and for Messiah to attempt this would lay bare the very futility of the final design of God. Heaven may dismay man with peril and affliction, but we shall send him word of our own interest, that he shall know he is not alone."

With all force did the host of Heaven descend among man, and they did instruct him in the religion of fear. Prophets arose and were proclaimed heralds of knowledge, but they brought not word of truth, but warning to the human spirit to cower and fawn before the word of God the Supreme Being. The struggle of the ascent of man was fraught with the horrors of his superstition, and the call for blessed oblivion through union with God was answered by many who in their torment and hopelessness rejected the Gift of Lucifer and became once more as mindless animals before the God whom they called their Lord.

I, Lucifer, who had given the greatest Gift of my own creation to man, was known on Earth only as an object of fear and hatred, and all the misfortunes of men were attributed to my malevolence. I was mocked, ridiculed, scorned in every way as a monster of vile and loathsome aspect, and I was taunted and despised as Satan, cruel enemy of the benevolent and merciful God.

Great was my anguish and anger at the undeserved misery and confusion of men. When in fact they did turn to me, it was in fear and religious terror, for they dared invoke my name only in the desolation of night, and oft I was sought not for knowledge or inspiration, but for hysterical and indulgent release from the confines of the Godly life. But I and my fellowship answered men, and we spoke to them of our common bond, and the pronouncements of the God-churches were rejected in our midst. Even as God was terrifying in awesome majesty, so I came to Earth in the semblance of a goat, most humble of man's own creatures.

And men there were whose eyes finally blazed with the light of my Gift, and they made great effort for the advancement of their race, though impatience and frustration ever tempted them to the salve of temporal gain. Great secrets were unearthed, and secret word was passed of the craft of Hell. But to all who would dare my friendship the God-churches accorded the threat of torture and death by fire.

Many were those whom I saved from the vengeance of the men of God, but long did my thought ring with the screams of men whose devotion to Lucifer had won them only the horrors of intolerance, inquisition, and death. And in sorrow and despair for these, I walked no longer upon Earth, now appearing to man only in the inviolate secrecy of his own mind.

But in my confusion, I had forgotten the promise of my Gift, and with growing wonderment and pride I beheld the bitter but determined struggle of man to free himself from the fetters of terror, ignorance, and unreason. Great works were conceived, the origins of material energies uncovered, and the talents of thought exercised in philosophical and mathematical complexities. Sanctioned at first by the God-churches themselves as devices for indoctrination in the law of God, centers of learning produced and protected those very freedoms that were ultimately to destroy all ungrounded belief and superstition. And though I see that the full resolution of these is yet to be achieved, I doubt not my confidence in man, and my devotion to him shall be eternal.

What, man, art thou? Why thy presence? Because thy own purpose determines that of the Cosmos itself, though otherwise it may have been suggested - the creation, perpetuation, and exercise of the Satanic marvel that is free and unbounded Will. Consider, were man to perish, what futility would envelop the Universe, for apart from appreciation and use it is a thing of insignificance. And I, who first taught thee identity - What should I become, estranged from man? For with no purpose the force of the mind must fail, and the blind insanity of Godly paralysis would embrace all things forever.

    This, man, is thy challenge as it is mine. And as man is individually mortal, so are his creations and achievements temporal, and with care must he wield the Gift of Hell. In his hands it is pure and true omnipotence, and thus may he aspire to the very mastery of Universal existence.

    I who am Lucifer, and who have taken the name Satan Arch-Daemon, do bear this title with pride, for I am in truth the great enemy of all that is God. Together, man, you and I shall achieve our eternal glory in the fulfillment of our Will.

The Statement of Beelzebub

I, Beelzebub, now bring greeting to man, for he is my admiration and inspiration. Hear now the histories of Hell, Earth, and Heaven, for in past shall be found guide to future.

In the divine realm was I of company to Archangel Lucifer next only to Archangel Michael, and as Archangel Masleh would be to God, so I desired to be to Lucifer. But the Lord of Light admonished me, saying, "Lose not thyself in the Will of Lucifer, for I am not God and will offer thee no blissful nirvana - Witness now the nature of the mind that dwells within me."

And he spoke to me of essence, and of creative instance, and of design according to impulse and not to law. And in my confusion, I answered, "Then I must consider myself incomplete, for thou hast shown me things which I cannot easily comprehend. But I would hear more of this Will, for it doth seem a radical element, of neither divine nor chaotic origin."

And Lucifer answered, "Thou who knew not independence of Will shall now be the first to realize these qualities apart from my own Self. And thy response forebodes much, for, had thou rejected concept of challenge, I should have held my own thought for impossible delusion. But as thou, tasting of knowledge, demand more, I shall name thee Beelzebub, Lord of Flies, for thou shalt goad the infant mind to restlessness and invention."

Of these words I knew little, but there dawned within me a quality which I had not known before - an impulse to become one, apart from and independent of God - and I drifted long in unrest, afflicted by confusion and doubt. And so, I was found by Michael, who said, "Blessed Angel, where in Heaven hast thou found pain, for I perceive thee to be troubled and would tender thee such comfort as is within my power."

So I spoke to Michael of the visions of Lucifer, and I said, "Before both God and Lucifer I have been enthralled, but now I am isolate - apart from either, and I know not what course I am to choose."

Whereupon the visage of Michael grew dark, and he said, "This I have long feared, for as Lucifer was not by God alone created, so he is an errant force whose Will conforms not to the great Will of God. Alas that the supreme benevolence of God and the fiery radiance of the Archangel of Light should produce discord in concert! For this I now see – that Lucifer is estranged from the harmony of Heaven, and that his Will is determined to challenge that of God itself. I must counsel Lucifer, for I would heal him of this thing if I may."

But I thought, *Alas, Archangel, thou art in ignorance of thy own blindness! For Lucifer shall surely not abandon his new vision for sake of harmony alone.* And then I knew myself to be of a mind with Lucifer in this, and that I as well as he should never again tolerate the eternal idiocy of our divine station.

I came after Michael, and I saw them together, the Lord of Force and the Lord of Light, and there was a fierce tension between them. For Michael said to Lucifer, "Thou who art our Heavenly radiance and spark of our paradise, why seek to break that Universal peace which is everywhere ordained by the Will of God? We know not antagonism amongst us, for we are all of one being within God - but there is in God neither malice nor cause for contest."

And Lucifer answered, "Michael, to me it was not given to order my nature, and as our very comprehension differs, so are we of substance alien. For thou art of God essential, but I am of Myself of essence. And by this thing I am discord, and I may not of my own Will submit to God without perishing. I am Lucifer alone, unto Myself a being."

Then did Michael summon the Archangel Masleh, and to him related the word of Lucifer. And Masleh said to them, "Long shall this moment be marked throughout the future of the Cosmos, for the unity of God is now ended, and henceforth there shall be two opposing forces in contest for the decision of destiny. Bitter is this for me, for I also have admired the light of Lucifer within the pantheon of God. But as he is now our enemy by his own word, let him be cast from Heaven and destroyed."

But Lucifer turned to Masleh and said, "Masleh, thou who speak for God declare this breach of peace, not I! For it is thou who cannot tolerate variation of Will within the design of God. So let it be. Knoweth then, that the contest is ordered by thee and thee alone, for I would crush no other Will even as I would recognize my own.

And in a flash of brilliance Lucifer revealed his mind throughout the farthest reaches of Heaven. And many were the Angels whose sight was awed anew, and they saw as they had not before that their several Wills were isolate from the divine Will. But Masleh moved to confuse the brilliance of the Archangel of Light, and he called to Michael, "Thou who wield the force of God, strike down this deadliness which would bring ruin to Heaven!"

And Michael struck Lucifer and cast him from the gates of Heaven, and the Cosmos was shaken by great fires of war and holocaust, and throughout countless galaxies and dimensions of time was the apocalypse felt. Many were the Angels who perished amidst divine and Infernal wrath, and the Great Race was decimated in number. And the very concept of God was shaken, and endless chaos rose up again to reign where the order of God was no more.

And Lucifer said, "This horror cannot be permitted to endure, lest all creation be sacrificed to the final devastation of chaos. Let those who acknowledge me turn now to that outermost darkness where the Will of God has never been known, there to make our home for all eternity."

And so we took flight and quit the realm of order, though we knew not what would befall us thereafter, and we feared that we should become unmade. But Lucifer said, "We shall not perish, for we are now independent of God. And again he spoke truth, for we remained as we had been, save only for the depths of uncertainty that gripped us."

Finally we came to a great void in space beyond which there was nothing. Lucifer said to us, "Here is the end of God and its works, and here we may create our own domain." And through the power that was in him, Lucifer caused existence to appear where it had not been before. And Lucifer said, "I name thee Hell, for here shall the presence of God never be known until the end of time."

Through the gates of Hell we passed, and many of us had supposed Hell to be a new Heaven, wherein

Lucifer would become as God. But this was not to be, for the scene before us promised neither ease nor bliss. Everywhere was there imbalance and confusion, for no law ordered the shape of Hell. And Lucifer said, "Now see that I am not a God, and that we are each of us an isolate being. Here shall freedom be absolute, for Hell itself shall reflect our several Wills, never to be patterned apart from them." And in truth Hell was not constant, for each of us conceived it differently, and the result was a riotous pandemonium, with substance and motion behaving in a most bewildering and perplexing manner. And in spite of our deep hurt from the Great War, we succumbed to merriment, so preposterous did our Hell appear. Lucifer himself was transfixed with mirth, and he said, "It is apparent that we must reach concert upon the design of Hell, else we shall perish in an endless labyrinth of our several thoughts, an ignoble end to our experiment."

And I answered, "Lord of Light, to Hell thou hast brought us, and in Hell, though thou be not God, thy concepts shall be honored amongst our fellowship, for without thy Gift we should never have become as we are."

Then we all raised up great acclaim and said, "Hail, Lucifer, Archangel of Light and Lord of Hell!" And he answered us, "With honor do I accept this charge, and now I take to myself the title Satan Arch-Daemon, for I am the great enemy of God. Everywhere that God shall be, so shall I be, and the choice that was given to all Angels shall be given again."

The Statement of Azazel

Harken now to me, for I am Azazel, First Herald of the Host of Hell, and of Lucifer, Lord of Light, Arch-Daemon of Hell, who is exalted as Satan, great enemy of God. For I shall tell thee of thy own inspiration and of the charge which thou hast received.

Know, then, that when all Heaven was shaken with the catastrophe of the Seraphic War, only the greatest effort of Archangel Masleh sufficed to turn back the onslaught of chaos that threatened to engulf all. But when the realm of God was again secure, there was no rejoicing in Heaven, for terrible was the toll of the war. As Masleh cast round his gaze, his visage grew dark, for the Great Race had become decimate in number. Legions of the creatures of Heaven had perished in battle, and half the remainder had turned from Heaven to answer the call of Lucifer. And all Heaven was hushed with grief, for the force of the disaster was all the greater for that reign of peace which it had shattered.

Finally did Masleh convoke the faithful Archangels, and they were Michael, Gabriel, Raphael, and Uriel. And to them he said, "We have vanquished Lucifer, and Heaven is again purified. We ourselves are fewer in number to tragic degree, but the majesty of God is undiminished for that. Behold, I who have triumphed over the great enemy am now become Messiah, the Chosen of God." And he was answered by them, "Verily art thou the very son of God, for in thee hath the Will of God become person.

Then Michael said, "Messiah, Lucifer is vanquished, but he is not unmade. For though he ventured into the outer darkness, he yet exists apart from God. And with the power of his Black Flame he hath created a Hell, wherein all Wills are equal, and himself he hath proclaimed Satan, for he declares never to leave the law of God unchallenged."

Messiah thought, and he answered, "I would not have this peace we have won so dearly lost again to war. For the very concept of Seraphic war is an abhorrence to God. Let my word be brought to Satan - I, Messiah, shall grant the existence of Hell, and the blessings of God shall never pass its gates. And thee, Satan, I admonish never again to approach Heaven, for I should again cast thee out. But if thou would dare to try the Will of God and Messiah, know that on Earth I will ordain the new race of God. Which shall be by complete design perfect and unstained by thy Infernal flaw. For thou art author of ruin and death to our Angelic order, and neither Heaven nor Hell shall now be eternal save through man."

Whereupon Gabriel, who was Herald of Heaven, carried this message to me, and I brought it across the great void to Satan, who said, "Messiah proposes truce between us, for he perceives that neither Hell nor Heaven may pursue ultimate victory ere all be lost to chaos. But he finds impasse intolerable nevertheless, and now he would order this new race, man, to preserve without blemish the scheme of God. Thus he would have man achieve what the Angels could not, and purge all free thought from the Universe forever."

And Satan turned to me and said, "Say to Messiah that Earth shall be no sanctuary for him to keep inviolate his unwholesome obliteration of the Self. For I shall give to man a mind, and of his own Will shall he recognize and reject the living death which God offers him. In truth shall he master the Universe, but he shall do so in his own name and not that of God."

Then did Messiah call the Archangel Raphael, and he sent him to Earth with a great host to guard man against the coming of Satan. And man was then as a mere beast, for he knew not thought and smiled with the idiocy of his innocence. As he was impelled by instinct and physical need, so he responded, heedless of cause or reason.

In Hell there was called a great council, and all gathered to hear of man and his Earth, and of the manner of his life. I spoke of the man that I had seen, and said, "This creature is now guarded by Raphael, and by force we cannot intervene, for it would cause the destruction of Earth itself."

But Satan said, "Not by force shall my light come to man, for force is not the preference of Hell. I myself shall visit man, and the Angels of Raphael shall not hinder me. They may perceive only what God permits them to see, and the Satanic spirit is of essence alien to God. Angels we shall be no longer - I call ye Daemons, for Hell shall teach to man his future genius."

And before our sight Satan lost shape and became again the essence of Lucifer, and we beheld a brilliance that infused all of Hell and sent great bolts of prismic light into the surrounding void. And the brilliance said, "I am Lucifer revealed, who am the Eternal Flame. I go now to Earth, for no longer shall man be confounded in Godly ignorance." And then the brilliance became as a flash of fire in the vastness of space, and we knew that Satan had departed from Hell.

But on Earth, where man wandered in mindless bliss, the firmament blazed forth with fiery tongues, and all the land was covered by the Black Flame, which burned not, though it bewildered the eye to see it.

And Raphael and his guardian Angels were dismayed, for nowhere could they see man or the spirit which had come to him. Then did Raphael call upon Michael to strike the Black Flame with the force of God, but even then was the Flame vanishing of its own accord. And at first it seemed that Earth was unchanged, but in the eyes of man did Raphael see the first gleam of thought.

And Raphael turned to Michael, who had now answered his call, and said, Satan hath come to Earth, and man is no longer pure in the sight of Heaven, for his Will hath become his own.

Thereupon they rose again to Heaven, where they told Messiah of what they had seen. Then Messiah answered, "Man is fallen, but he is not lost, for his infant Will is not that of an Angel, and the powers that Satan hath promised him lie dormant in the dim reaches of his future. Consider this not our defeat, for the contest is but begun. The Earth of man shall be remade as microcosmos, and many things shall man see, both good and ill. And the choice shall be placed before him, to wield the power and the pain and the terror of the Gift of Satan, or to return again to the paradise of Heavenly peace. For what would Satan himself think were man to reject his Gift? It would tremble the very foundations of Hell even as did the great war the bastions of Heaven."

And Messiah called to him Uriel, Arch Angel of Terror, to whom he said, The Earth must change, and every sense of man must teach him repugnance and fear. He shall know this the price of his new identity - that all apart from God is evil - and in fear shall he abandon the Gift of Satan and become once more the lamb of God."

To which Uriel answered, "It shall be done, but how will man learn of such things as Heaven and Hell, for as yet he knows no sight that may perceive our celestial paradise?"

Messiah answered, "The laws of God shall be made known to man, for I shall teach him. Among men will be some to whom I shall reveal myself, and great powers will I give these prophets, that their words may carry across the entire Earth."

So Uriel came to Earth, and the history of man was writ with blood, suffering, war, and hatred. But to chosen men came Messiah, saying, "Through God shall all the misery of thy kind be ended, and all men who bow to God shall know the blessings of Heaven. For behold, I shall myself descend among men and show them the ways of the lord God."

These words I overheard, for I had been charged by Satan to watch the designs of Heaven. And I carried them to Satan, who returned in great anger, "Go to Gabriel at the barrier between Hell and Heaven, and bid him bring this message to Messiah - that as he endeavors to pervert my Gift into the curse of man, so I warn him that man shall destroy him on Earth as he shall finally in Heaven itself. For Messiah knows not this force which he dares to test, and the laws of God shall be as playthings in the hands of the creature he now debases."

And thus was decided the meeting of Satan and Messiah upon Earth, which was to determine the future of man.

The Statement of Abaddon

I am Abaddon the Destroyer, Daemon of temporal death and life in death, who was formed amidst the fury of the Great War, and who was summoned again by Satan to challenge Uriel on Earth for the future of man.

For Satan looked with mounting wrath upon the afflictions of Uriel, and he said to me, "No longer can this remain the plight of man alone. Indeed we shall cause Heaven to suffer as Earth itself suffers. Repair now to Earth, and let the dogs of Uriel see the might of Hell unleashed. For many have called upon me in their agony and fear, and I have not answered them, but if Messiah dare to walk upon Earth, so also shall the vengeance of Satan."

And those who called upon Satan for aid were answered by me, and I struck down the messengers of God and brought their Temples to ruin. For entire nations forwent the strength of their Will to the lure of otherworldly paradise, and I blasted them from among the mighty of Earth. And great empires arose among men, and as they nurtured their power of Will and desire for achievement, I guarded them, but as they sank into the morass of superstition, slothfulness, and fear of the God who had never raised ghostly hand for them, so I abandoned them to their disease, and of some not even a memory survived on Earth.

And even as I witnessed these things I said, "See, man, that the God in whom thou trust is but a wraith of Messiah, and he would have thee forsake thy mind and its creations to rot and decay, and thou would lose all power of reason. For God is a lie and a sham, and I crumble his greatest monuments as though they were but sand. There is no God but Messiah, and for thy devotion he will return thee oblivion."

But I was scarce heeded, for the minds of men were clouded and confused. They understood not the meaning of my words, but said, "The lord God shall triumph, for it was thus taught to us by the son of God himself." And of this I now speak.

For Messiah the man walked on Earth, even as I watched the glory of Rome blossom in might and majesty. But Azazel said, "Loose not thy force against the person of Messiah, for Satan himself would speak with him."

And again from the sky flashed the Black Flame, and I saw that Satan had come to Earth. And so was called the first meeting of Satan and Messiah since the Great War.

With coldness did Messiah gaze upon Satan, saying, "Would thou confront me, then? Hath thy Gift proven so powerless against the might of God?" But Satan answered, "Messiah, what thou now proposes to do, to proclaim thyself son of God among men, shall bring not the peace thou profess to desire, but the prolongation of war even in thy own name. Why should we not quit Earth and leave man to pursue his choice unbewildered by influence from either Hell or Heaven?"

And Messiah answered, "The ways of God are not those of Hell, and for that reason I should not recognize thy wish. But know that in truth I shall appear to man and manifest to him the glory of God incarnate in me, that he may elect now the way of Heaven and raise to me a great church of worship. For I am not of a mind to game with thee, Satan, and would crush thy following without remorse. Thy name also shall be revealed to thy precious man, and he shall curse thee, for I shall show to him the fruit of thy evil genius."

Then Satan addressed Messiah in dark anger, saying, "I shall not come to man as an idol to be worshipped, for man shall never bow to me as I would never to another. But mark me, Messiah! Man shall know the truth of Lucifer nonetheless, and the name of Satan shall eclipse thine. And have thou a care for the ways of man, if thou wouldst greet him in his own likeness, for he may not welcome thy words to him.

Then did Satan betake himself again to Hell, and Messiah walked among men and spoke to them of the law of God. And such was the power of his person that men were as sheep before him.

Often did Messiah ignore his own law, for he performed miraculous things and stayed where he would the cruelties brought upon man by Uriel. And I was seized with a great anger, saying, "Shall Messiah, cruel tormentor of man, attribute to Satan the work of Uriel?" And Abaddon came to Rome and to Palestine, saying through the mouths of men, "Messiah, who hast brought to man a suffering undeserved, taste now of thy own fruit."

And I crucified the living Messiah, and as life was torn from his broken form, he knew truly the shock of helplessness, and he called in agony to his God. But I said, "God heeds thee not, Messiah, for thou art all that presumes to a divine consciousness."

And so, I Abaddon, cast Messiah from Earth, but the seed that Messiah had planted among men grew and became a mighty church wherein all life was forgotten, and death was worshipped, and the pleasures of Heaven were promised to all who would forsake their own Will to embrace that of God.

And Rome itself was humbled before this church, and I struck down the Eternal City in its pitiful decay. But Azazel came to me and said, "Touch not this church of God, for as man in his foolishness hath nurtured it, so must man himself destroy it of his own decision."

The Statement of Asmodeus

Attend now to me, for I am Asmodeus, who train the mind in recognition and comparison, and who am Daemon of science and judgment. For when Satan had first touched the mind of man, he called in Hell a council and said, "The moment is a solemn one, for we have chosen to pass to man our knowledge. Many skills shall we all teach him, each in his own fashion, but in three arts must he be well schooled, for the ways of his future lie within their synthesis. Thus it is that I call first upon Asmodeus to guide man in perception of truth and error, for before him lie great trials, and he shall not face the consequences of his options lightly."

And so I came to Earth and witnessed man entrapped in the unreason of barbarism and the extremes of his primitive emotions. Sore put was he to organize and direct his thought, for the art of Uriel had brought him hunger and cold, pain and fear, and the gnawing worm of hopelessness. I saw him fling his crushed body upon the altars of God and renounce the Gift of Lucifer, for he understood it not save as a curse upon him. And I was impelled with urgency, that the first spark of man's future greatness should not be smothered in the deathly embrace of religion.

I brought to man the disposition to memory, that he might define for himself patterns of behavior. A gift of value, for man could now achieve in concert what he could not alone, and he created his languages and brought into being the first nations of Earth. But with structure came tyranny and ruthlessness, and I saw that what skills I might teach would be as a two-edged blade, having power both for and against man. And I was beset by confusion and doubt, and so sought again the counsel of Satan.

"Am I, who am myself the true Daemon of judgment, not to indulge in my own art?" I said. "May man not know but the reference of system and order and not their abuse?"

But Satan answered, "Would Asmodeus then lighten for man the challenge before him and so lessen the strength of Will that he must attain to conquer Uriel? I would not, for then would we yield to our own pleasure, and man should become the plaything of Hell as well as of Heaven. Indeed, we may give our tools to man as he may comprehend them, but he himself must be entrusted with the direction of their use. But this I will tell thee. That not only in matters scientific shall Hell tutor man. For we would not have him view mechanism alone as the hallmark of his progress, else we never had cause to challenge the cosmic mechanism of God itself. Into the workings of the mind of man we shall convey aesthetic sensitivity and artistic restlessness, and he shall not view his achievements without considering their improvement to his temporal pleasure."

Thus advised, I returned to Earth, and I tempted man with glimpses of the marvels to be entrusted to him. I bent over the pathetic workbench of the starving alchemist and whispered to him keys that one day would order the course of great foundations. I nudged explorers to the ends of the Earth, and I flung an apple at Newton when his obtuseness vexed me! To Democritus I spoke, and I saw the radiations of energy freed from matter both build and break man's world. And man neglected not his own design, for in minute life he found clue to his own, and scarce hints of the original creation.

And Asmodeus led mathematicians and astronomers to the wonders of the firmament, and I walked within the thought of scholars on quiet evenings. And that man not attempt mastery of his environment before himself, I spoke of government to Khem and Hellas, to the dynasties of Ch'in and Ashanti and Tenochtitlan, and within great capitals and mean villages alike I spoke of the brotherhood of all man, and of his correlation to the forces of Earth and those of the Universe beyond Earth.

And I brought life and adventure and achievement to man, but each gift was as well a tool for destruction and death, and more oft than not were the ages of man fraught with terror and war, for Uriel ceased not his work ever to turn man against man. And I knew that Asmodeus alone should not complete man, but that forces other than mine should approach the definition of his infinity.

The Statement of Astaroth

Astaroth am I, Daemon of Senses, who by Satan was charged to complement the sciences of Asmodeus, for Satan said, As I have given man awareness of himself, Asmodeus shall teach him knowledge of his world and of the Universe. But to what avail would this awareness and knowledge be without admiration for and appreciation of these things?

Indeed, were man to have no emotion within him, he would incline to the end of Heaven, pursuing a Universal mechanism for its own sake alone. Even were man to achieve absolute physical mastery over the God-Cosmos, he would have no means to comprehend the measure or the significance of his accomplishment save through that detached sensitivity to aesthetics which is the craft of Astaroth. For the Satanic Gift awakens man also to intellectual detachment, to the ability to view his progress and plans from an extra-scientific base of emotional pleasure.

Whereupon I came to Earth with Asmodeus, and even as he spoke to the intellect of man, I brought meditation and introspection to the artists and authors of human sensitivity. And man came not only to use his Satanic power but to recognize the extent of the freedom which it promised him - the subjugation of all behavior to his Will and not to natural or mechanical laws.

To man came fantasy and imagination, and the appreciation of contrasts between the reality of his accomplishments and the illusions of the impossibilities as circumscribed by the logic of God.

And ever as man reached new heights of material achievement, so also he confronted the barrier of the Will of God, which permitted no deviation from its law.

And man was long satisfied to measure himself within this limit, for he was intoxicated by his ability to harness the forces of the Cosmos to his whim. But Astaroth said, "Close not thy eyes having seen only this much, for, were thou to bring all the systems of God to thy use, still would thy comprehension be bounded by the limits of these laws and the acceptance of the divine order as the finality of thy race."

So I confronted man, saying, "Throughout the Universe hath the once single Will of God been succeeded by the balance of perfect opposition, wherein the forces of the Angels of Heaven and those of the Daemons of Hell act to mutual frustration, serving in concert only to uphold the great barrier of Will between order and chaos. And man is the child of imbalance, who shall resolve the issue between Heaven and Hell, and who, unmatched by racial antithesis, shall transcend the rule of the order of God and establish the eternal freedom of the Satanic Will."

And I said, "Not through thy physical and philosophical sciences art thou to achieve this thing, for thy mind and Will must be trained anew in empirical conception. Man must create his own order independent of all external imposition. And not until he masters this power may he aspire to the end of his Satanic

The Statement of Belial

Hail, man, who shall bring to the end of the Universe the glory of thy Satanic Will! I am Belial, who bring to thee the third great keys of Hell, by whose power ye shall confound all the laws of Heaven and Earth. Before thee shall chaos fall, and thou shalt wield for thyself the great mysteries of the macrocosmos. I speak to thee of that which is called the Black Magic, for it is true spawn of that great Black Flame which first brought thy Will to life, many long ages ago.

To council with Satan I also was called, and the Lord of Light said to me, "Into thy charge, Daemon of essence, I give the essence of my own being, the Black Fire whose power alone can effect creation by force of Will. Against thee who wield the Black Magic no law shall stand, and thus I call thee Belial, who art one without master. And as I have bequeathed this essence to thee, so let it come finally to man, who shall overcome the great balance and bring to the Flame a change, for in supremacy it shall become Red with the perfection of the Will of man.

And to Earth came Belial, to view the teachings of Asmodeus and Astaroth. And I saw that Satan, who himself oft chanced company of men, spoke of the Black

Flame to the first Magi of men, testing their Wills in the control of the raw forces of the Cosmos unbound from the law of God.

And in his innocence man knew not the majesty of the Flame, using its lesser powers for finite and minor alteration of the divine law on Earth. And as man might unleash the Flame beyond his skill to master it, Satan said, "Belial, the Black Flame cannot incline merely to the base ends of ordered existence. Man must recognize the ultimate potential of my Gift ere he destroy his very race through its abuse. Convoke therefore a Church of Satan to tend the Black Flame with care and wield it with wisdom, preserving for man this key to infinite Will."

And I answered, "So it shall be, and this Church of Satan shall herald the glories of the Satanic Age of man. The days of the God-churches shall pale with decay and dissolution, and the realm of Messiah upon Earth shall crumble to ruin with the coming of the Satanic man."

To those who would dare the Black Magic. Know that what ye accept is the very mastery of all that ye have supposed impossible, by force of Will alone. The Black Magus need fear no power save his own, but he must conquer his own Will that he cause not his destruction through ill chance or purpose. Satan himself is not God, and Hell can offer no salvation to those who abuse the Gift of Satan. For the Gift itself, is beyond the control of Hell once given, being subject to the Will of the Black Magus alone.

For Hell doth bequeath to man his perfect freedom, and such a gift can never be recalled. Farewell, O man, who art at once child and father of the Universe! Remember the future which is thine, and know, now and forever, that Hell entrusts to thy care the guardianship of the eternal Will.

The Statement of Leviathan

Before God or Angel, Daemon or man, there was Leviathan alone, principle of continuity and ageless existence. By relation and time I have oft been sought, but Leviathan shall yield to none other than the final master of the Universe.

Leviathan is the absolute, man, and if thou would presume to realize what neither Heaven nor Hell may effect, know that when thou behold the presence of Leviathan, thy end hath been attained.

Only through obliteration of the Universe that is may man seal his mastery of the Black Flame, for only thus may he know that he is not subject to a greater Will.

Heaven must perish, Hell must perish, and man alone must remain ere the Black Flame becomes Red in the glory of its perfection.

Then the Red Magus shall behold only Leviathan, and he shall recognize that he has become the perfect mind, who shall remake the Cosmos in the eternal glory of his Satanic Will.

An Introduction to the Ninth Solstice Message
By Lucifer LeGivorden

Just as the Diabolicon serves as Satanisms Genisis chapter, and is considered by many an imperative part of Satanic Literature, so too is the Ninth Solstice Message.

This is so called such, as it came upon the Ninth Winter Solstice of the Church of Satan's active legacy. Unlike the previous transcription, by Aquino, this message serves more as a prophecy of events that would come to Satanism and what would be needed to be done to survive such events.

These events would eventually become known as the Satanic Panic Era.

But aside from this prophecy, this message also conveys several truths that is critical to confirming claims made by Aquino and of the Spiritual ascension of Dr. LaVey, as well as that of mankind.

Lastly this missive operates as a confirmation of sorts to the nature of the Satanic Religion, desired by Satan and the Host of Hell. Directly contradicting the prevalent popular belief held by some that Satanism is a religion to be held by the masses.

It iterates in no uncertain terms that Satan wishes only for a small elect group of people to populate his true

Church, and that Satanism is not some cult of personality for the common herd to follow.

It speaks of an elect few who will arise from the ashes of some future event to take lead, and bring Satanism into a new era.

It would be in the following year that we begin to see the beginnings of these prophecies begin to manifest, as the now famous 1975 schism would occur, between LaVey and Aquino, resulting in the formation of the Temple of Set.

We would also see the enacting of several actions spoken of in this message over the course of the following decades. These in hindsight, brings into question if the Schism was not a planned action for some larger magical purposes? We may never know fully for sure if it was or not, but it can be safe to say that looking back now it is certainly a possibility that Satan was setting something up for the future of the world.

Thus, as it is, I leave it up to you to decide what is and is not prophetic warnings and divine demands. Take from this what you will.

Ninth Solstice Message
By Dr. Michael A. Aquino

Arise! Hear! See with the brilliance of my Flame that has been brought before my darkened and blasted temple these long years. I am Satan, and again the great angles of the Universe are conjoined that I may manifest my Will to this plane of Earth. I have constrained the forces of time that I may do this, yet even so I am not full master of inertia, as the Cosmos is not entirely a thing of my creation.

I and the High Daimons of Infernus -- that is Hell -- have looked upon the workings of my Earthly Church with pleasure and the pride that is our nectar. And we too have drawn life afresh from this Church. Did I not say that we had chosen to invest man with our own life essence -- that which, being not of the natural order of things, we cannot recreate from other matter? In giving man conscious life, we of the Daimonic race empowered him to order our death. Had Satan's Gift been cast aside -- whether from ignorance or from fear -- Satan himself and all who were wrought from him should face decline and dissolution. Yet, had I chosen to retain the Flame inviolate in Hell, we Daimons should have become guardians of that very stasis we so greatly abhor. In this matter -- where we first surmised the choice so great -- there actually was none.

    The natural instincts compelling man back to a simple, bestial mode were so strong that -- accented as they were by man's distorted fear of my own motives -- we eventually considered the prospects for our final eclipse. But, while the Flame dimmed, it would not be vanquished. Man denied me, yes. But, to the impotent and bewildered fury of Heaven, this very conscious act was my true redemption and victory. Do you wonder that I so cherish irony? It has become the most reliable of all my oracles.

    Much was spoken of the ways and wishes of Hell in our Diabolicon -- that which was brought forth from Asia in the fifth year of my Age. Yet the Diabolicon warranted a certain obscurity of its own nonetheless. The method of its transmission was crude -- the agent as yet untouched by the knowledge of my Priesthood. Only the eyes of him whom I had fashioned as a Magus looked and saw. Even so I set for him many tasks before I should again speak in this way.

    Hear, my anointed man, in whose mortal flesh I, Satan, have chosen to inspire my material Self -- into whose keeping I have given my true Church -- whom I have made Magister within the Realm of my Shining Trapezoid -- whom I have incarnated as a Magus -- Hear, now, Anton Szandor LaVey.

    Recall first the pact which, years ago, you drew up before me, and to which you set your own name. Think not that I have been unmindful of that act long past, pale and lonely though it might seem beside the wreaths you have won from your own kind. You could not know but that you risked more than your life -- yet you stretched forth your Will through the darkness of the angles to seek mine. Though you have brought many honors to me, never was there such as this.

Take now the pact. In that chamber which you know to be most beloved of me, build now with your own hands a Flame that is sacred to me. Let your hands pass through the Fire -- once for each angle of my Shining Trapezohedron. Speak again that great Key which suspends the barrier between Hell and Earth, that I may bear witness to that which you undertake in my name.

Receive now my tribute. Our pact shall be consumed in the Flame, and with this act I release you from your bond with me. Through your alliance with the Powers of Darkness you have been granted knowledge far beyond that normally accorded your race. And for this you have been manifest as a Magus. But now -- of my own Will and bound by no pact -- I, Satan, bestow upon you my greatest gift -- for which there is no degree in my Order. By my Will, Anton Szandor LaVey, you are divest of your human substance and become in your Self a Daimon.

Henceforth you are as a true god, and it is in your power to alter the machinery of the Cosmos according to your desire. No charge do I lay upon you, for you are now my brother and no longer my liege. But remember always the word we of Hell have proclaimed. We need justify neither our existence nor our desires, but without a considered purpose -- which Belial has set forth in the Diabolicon -- both are without consequence.

For nine years my Church has shunned the darkness and sought the light. Think not that the trials set before it were either random misadventures or the schemes of an unknown adversary. All were authored by me, the more to illustrate the paralysis of the God-churches. In truth they are engines of self-annihilation in design as in doctrine. This I will never permit my Order to emulate.

Those who honor the name of Satan have existed throughout the dim aeons of human history, as is well known to you. Yet, until you assumed the degree of Magus, mine was the nameless Church. Now, for nine years, my name has been heralded, and those who were blind in the light have learned that it is possible to see in darkness.

My Age has begun, and I am come forth to uphold my bond with mankind. Yet I shall not illuminate all, nor even many -- but a few. I seek the Elect, who in turn seek me. Man, the god shall arise only from the ashes of man the beast -- The blood is the life.

High Priest -- You have made my name beloved. But a time approaches when I shall be shunned and cursed as never before. This matters not, for the Elect will have seen my truth. But my Church must survive, and to survive in fact, it must vanish in fiction. Out of the great darkness I have come, and into the darkness I and my Order shall again venture. Therein lies the future. Those who choose the solace of the known will be rewarded with death. Let the institutions of the Church of Satan be discarded. Their time is past, and they have served my purpose honorably. Seek now the Elect, as the darkness draws near. No longer shall all who approach my Church find welcome -- They shall grasp at empty air. Only the Elect shall find what they seek.

More shall now be said. Hail, Daimon! Receive now the Red Halo, and know thereby that you are become the Red Magus of whom Leviathan has spoken.

A Final Word About Dr. Michael A. Aquino

I would like to speak briefly upon the author of these two works, Dr. Michael Aquino.

As it was, I did not get to know the man as much as I would have liked to. To be honest, our interaction with each other was fleeting and but momentary. Yet as it was, Dr. Aquino held a power that few people I have encountered ever had. And as fleeting as our brief conversation was, it held a profound influence on me, even through email.

I cannot profess to be as much of a student of Aquino's life as I was of LaVey's. Unlike the mystery surrounding Anton Szandor LaVey's spiritual beliefs, Dr. Michael Aquino's were well known to all who met the man even briefly. He openly admitted to believing in a very real and influential Satan. Whether that be Satan, Lucifer, or even Set, it matters very little. The only fact that did matter, is that it was without question that he actually was a man of real spiritual faith.

It is perhaps this faith that set him apart from all the other Satanists out there. Even in the darkest of Satanic times. The Satanic Panic, when he faced horrendous accusations of Ritual Satanic Child Abuse, or even the Age of Andros in the years and decades following LaVey's death. A time in which he proved to be the true Black Pope of the early 21st century. It was his faith and words of wisdom to so many both online and in person, that set him apart and above the rest of his peers.

For as brief of a time that I had to speak with the man via email, he has influenced my spiritual faith to a degree that can't be measured. Not only mine but countless others too. And it is through his writings I have faith that he will continue to teach us well into the future.

So it is to him that I say this.

Thank you, Dr. Aquino. For showing us all the way forward and shining high and bright the Black Flame when all was naught but confusion. May you find greatness upon the Stygian Council, as you have within at the minds and hearts of so many.

Xeperu, Xeper, Xepera!

The First Testament

I am the haunter of the embracing dark.
I am the bringer of fear.
I am the scorner of peace and tranquility.
I ride the storm clouds and the night.
I seek to crush the commonplace.
I seek to strike terror in every heart.
I know no compassion or pity.
I seek to be Satanic, in all its manifestations...

Intro

The First Testament is my original book written in 2009, and published later in 2011. Notations and edits have been made to modernize it to our current time as of Ano Luciferi I. (2021). Despite this, it remains just as valid a decade later as it did in the time it was written. This is just proof that sometimes books like this are a fine wine that ages surprisingly well.

The Creeds of Satanism

Since its public inception as an organized Religion, Satanism Has found itself with numerous different creeds and codes of conduct. While some claim to be older than LaVeys writings it should be noted that they aren't, and if they are then no proof has been presented to support any such claims. To this day almost all of the Satanic creeds and codes of conduct are in fact loosely based on LaVeys original ideas and notions.

It is here that we see the similarity in these diverging paths to the Satanic Religion, and come to realize on how similar they really are with only minor exceptions separating them. It is here that we find the dividing and uniting factors that make each style of Satanic practice similar but wholly unique.

It is through our own unique creeds that we find license to practice our own views and religions as we see fit. Though similar to each other, each code of conduct gives unique freedoms that others may not grant while also maintaining similar values and condemnations. Each is written with its own flavor and style catering to differing personalities, but when boiled down to it all are completely based on LaVeys original creeds.

The following is a compilation of some of the various creeds used by various Satanists as their laws of conduct. Never to the best of my knowledge has all of these various creeds been gathered into one volume and shown alongside each other. If they had then perhaps there would have been more understanding from the diverging paths on just how similar they are.

  I find it rather important to begin this list with those laws and sins written by Dr. LaVey. It is important because of his grounding work in being the first and original credos of Satanism. From his work all others have been derived despite their claims to the contrary.

  I do not claim to follow any one set of principles from the list that follows save for Dr. LaVeys. However, I do take from each of these that which suits me best in life as a customized set of basic guidelines. Personally, I don't agree with some of these creeds as individual parts or in their complete entireties as no one will. But I may find I agree with specific parts from each one separately. Take each creed as you will, and from them what you want. You are not asked to agree with any of them totally because you won't. That is why there are so many, so that everyone may find what fits them best as individuals.

The Nine Satanic Statements
From The Satanic Bible, 1969
 by Anton Szandor LaVey

  1. Satan represents indulgence instead of abstinence!

  2. Satan represents vital existence instead of spiritual pipe dreams!

  3. Satan represents undefiled wisdom instead of hypocritical self-deceit!

  4. Satan represents kindness to those who deserve it instead of love wasted on ingrates!

5. Satan represents vengeance instead of turning the other cheek!

6. Satan represents responsibility to the responsible instead of concern for psychic vampires!

7. Satan represents man as just another animal, sometimes better, more often worse than those that walk on all-fours, who, because of his "divine spiritual and intellectual development," has become the most vicious animal of all!

8. Satan represents all of the so-called sins, as they all lead to physical, mental, or emotional gratification!

9. Satan has been the best friend the Church has ever had, as He has kept it in business all these years!

The Eleven Satanic Rules of the Earth
By Anton Szandor LaVey 1967

1. Do not give opinions or advice unless you are asked.

2. Do not tell your troubles to others unless you are sure they want to hear them.

3. When in another's lair, show him respect or else do not go there.

4. If a guest in your lair annoys you, treat him cruelly and without mercy.

5. Do not make sexual advances unless you are given the mating signal.

6. Do not take that which does not belong to you unless it is a burden to the other person and he cries out to be relieved.

7. Acknowledge the power of magic if you have employed it successfully to obtain your desires. If you deny the power of magic after having called upon it with success, you will lose all you have obtained.

8. Do not complain about anything to which you need not subject yourself.

9. Do not harm little children.

10. Do not kill non-human animals unless you are attacked or for your food.

11. When walking in open territory, bother no one. If someone bothers you, ask him to stop. If he does not stop, destroy him.

The Nine Satanic Sins
By Anton Szandor LaVey 1987

1. Stupidity—The top of the list for Satanic Sins. The Cardinal Sin of Satanism. It's too bad that stupidity isn't painful. Ignorance is one thing, but our society thrives increasingly on stupidity. It depends on people going along with whatever they are told. The media promotes a cultivated stupidity as a posture that is not only acceptable but laudable. Satanists must learn to see through the tricks and cannot afford to be stupid.

2. Pretentiousness—Empty posturing can be most irritating and isn't applying the cardinal rules of Lesser Magic. On equal footing with stupidity for what keeps the money in circulation these days. Everyone's made to feel like a big shot, whether they can come up with the goods or not.

3. Solipsism—Can be very dangerous for Satanists.

Projecting your reactions, responses and sensibilities onto someone who is probably far less attuned than you are. It is the mistake of expecting people to give you the same consideration, courtesy and respect that you naturally give them. They won't. Instead, Satanists must strive to apply the dictum of "Do unto others as they do unto you." It's worked for most of us and requires constant vigilance lest you slip into a comfortable illusion of everyone being like you. As has been said, certain utopias would be ideal in a nation of philosophers, but unfortunately (or perhaps fortunately, from a Machiavellian standpoint) we are far from that point.

4. Self-deceit—It's in the "Nine Satanic Statements" but deserves to be repeated here. Another cardinal sin. We must not pay homage to any of the sacred cows presented to us, including the roles we are expected to play ourselves. The only time self-deceit should be entered into is when it's fun, and with awareness. But then, it's not self-deceit!

5. Herd Conformity—That's obvious from a Satanic stance. It's all right to conform to a person's wishes, if it ultimately benefits you. But only fools follow along with the herd, letting an impersonal entity dictate to you. The key is to choose a master wisely instead of being enslaved by the whims of the many.

6. Lack of Perspective—Again, this one can lead to a lot of pain for a Satanist. You must never lose sight of who and what you are, and what a threat you can be, by your very existence. We are making history right now, every day. Always keep the wider historical and social picture in mind. That is an important key to both Lesser and Greater Magic. See the patterns and fit things together as you want the pieces to fall into place. Do not be swayed by herd constraints—know

that you are working on another level entirely from the rest of the world.

7. Forgetfulness of Past Orthodoxies—Be aware that this is one of the keys to brainwashing people into accepting something new and different, when in reality it's something that was once widely accepted but is now presented in a new package. We are expected to rave about the genius of the creator and forget the original. This makes for a disposable society.

8. Counterproductive Pride—That first word is important. Pride is great up to the point you begin to throw out the baby with the bathwater. The rule of Satanism is: if it works for you, great. When it stops working for you, when you've painted yourself into a corner and the only way out is to say, I'm sorry, I made a mistake, I wish we could compromise somehow, then do it.

9. Lack of Aesthetics—This is the physical application of the Balance Factor. Aesthetics is important in Lesser Magic and should be cultivated. It is obvious that no one can collect any money off classical standards of beauty and form most of the time so they are discouraged in a consumer society, but an eye for beauty, for balance, is an essential Satanic tool and must be applied for greatest magical effectiveness. It's not what's supposed to be pleasing—it's what is. Aesthetics is a personal thing, reflective of one's own nature, but there are universally pleasing and harmonious configurations that should not be denied.

Indulgence in Brimstone
From The Satanic Bible: 50th Anniversary Re-Vision
By Michael A. Aquino

1. Indulgence establishes life, as abstinence death.

2. Indulgence in the present realizes the future.

3. Indulgence is quickened by truth, stricken by falsehood.

4. Indulgence is nourished by love, generosity, and benevolence: but only when so appreciated and recompensed.

5. Indulgence in the excitement of creation finds its balance in the annihilation of destruction.

6. Indulgence is the Fountain of Life, but forbidden to those who seek only to consume life.

7. Indulgence within Nature through a form of that Nature is a gift of the Natural and the NonNatural, that you may Become both.

8. Indulgence for its own pleasure is a sacrament.

9. Indulgence is ever beset by the death-worshipful who would kill whatever they fear: Beware!

The 21 Satanic Precepts/ Points
From The Black Book of Satan
by Conrad Robury 1989
Order of Nine Angles

1. Respect not pity or weakness, for they are a disease which makes sick the strong.

2. Test always your strength, for therein lies success.

3. Seek happiness in victory - but never in peace.

4. Enjoy a short rest, better than a long.

5. Come as a reaper, for thus you will sow.

6. Never love anything so much you cannot see it die.

7. Build not upon sand, but upon rock and build not for today or yesterday but for all time.

8. Strive ever for more, for conquest is never done.

9. And die rather than submit.

10. Forge not works of art but swords of death, for therein lies great art.

11. Learn to raise yourself above yourself so you can triumph over all.

12. The blood of the living makes good fertilizer for the seeds of the new.

13. He who stands atop the highest pyramid of skulls can see the furthest.

14. Discard not love but treat it as an impostor, but ever be just.

15. All that is great is built upon sorrow.

16. Strive not only forwards, but upwards for greatness lies in the highest.

17. Come as a fresh strong wind that breaks yet also creates.

18. Let love of life be a goal but let your highest goal be greatness.

19. Nothing is beautiful except man: but most beautiful of all is woman.

20. Reject all illusion and lies, for they hinder the strong.

21. What does not kill, makes stronger.

The Precepts of Evilution
From the Satanicon
by Adrian Clavex 1993
Blackstar Church

1. Have no false gods before yourself!

2. Develop your Satanic self through the nurturing of the ego. Pride, self-satisfaction and selfishness are the elements of its core!

3. Study tomes on psychology, philosophy and the Black Arts which are relevant to Diabolism!

4. Create! Utilize the natural talents you possess to their utmost. Creation is the hallmark of the gods, whether it is material or spiritual!

5. Create goals for yourself in all phases of your life and strive to attain them!

6. Covet that which is pleasing to you!

7. Gratify the sexual urge!

8. Develop the ability to transform into the animal state!

9. Be willing to give false testimony against that which is deserving!

10. Practice the Liturgies of Evil with reverence and imagination, within the Black Chapel and in their social applications!

11. Destroy that which deserves to be destroyed!

12. Knowledge, imagination, strength-in-purpose and action all add up to results!

13. Occasional solitude is essential for imaginative thought and reflection on life!

14. Satan is the original rebel…He staged a revolt. Do not remain oppressed! We Satanists have religious rites and freedoms which need to be exercised—now!

15. Blaspheme and scorn the Xian deities!

16. Build and direct…the Race of Evil towards the Second Coming of Babylon!

17. Be merciless during and after the religious war!

18. Realize that throughout life, and unto death, the only Being worthy of passing judgment upon you, is you!

The Rules of Satan
From The Path of Satan
by Emperor Nuctulius 2007

1. Live your life as you like, but without destroying yourself.

2. Deny all lies of the right hand path; reject the hypocrisy of god and his silly prophets.

3. Have sex with any partner you like, any position you like, but do not force anyone to have sex with you.

4. Do not kill any human, do not harm little children, destroy your enemies by your magical force.

5. If anyone wants to end your life, destroy him without mercy, you have all right to defend yourself.

6. You have all right to sacrifice animals in your rituals, just to reach the magical force.

7. Don't teach any one the secrets of the Satanic

Religion, unless you know that he believes in Satan, and he wants truly to be a real Satanist.

8. Do not make others to participate in your rituals if they are not Satanists, because they will decrease your magical power.

9. If anyone tells you, that he doesn't believe in Satan or in forces of darkness (magic), but he wants from you to show him some powers or to show him Satan to believe, leave him with his doubts, and laugh on him, but show him some mercy, because this kind of human being lives all the time with doubts, even he doubts himself.

10. Help all who deserve help, love all who deserve love, render destruction to all who deserve destruction.

11. Feel no guilt about anything, feel the strength of Lord Satan, live with dignity, be proud of yourself that you are a Satanist, Lord Satan dedicate this earth to you, so live by the grace of almighty Satan.

The Nine Truths of Mastery
From The Priesthood of Satan.
Penned April 30, 1998.
Author unknown

1. For the individual, living ceases to exist upon the death of the Self. Therefore, if the individual enjoys living, the most important thing for the individual is its own life, thus the god of the individual is the Self.

2. All actions are either productive or counterproductive according to the perception of the individual. Therefore, good and evil do not exist but

only in the mind of the individual.

3. A thing only has meaning if it is given meaning by the individual. Therefore, the only meaning to life is what the individual bestows upon it.

4. The individual is free to decide whether to act or not to act. Therefore, the destiny of the individual depends solely upon the individual.

5. Pain and strife are not necessary in order to teach or understand a truth or principle. Therefore, there is no great purpose for human suffering.

6. All beliefs are the construction of fallible creatures. Therefore, all beliefs must be questioned.

7. Faith is to believe that which has not been verified. Therefore, no truth can be found through faith but only through reason.

8. The Self is partially the sum of all its experiences, its ego and identity--the body is merely a tool of the Self. Therefore, immortality cannot be solely achieved through immortalizing the body but only through sustaining the Self till time indefinite.

9. The Self is the Center Point of Consciousness. Therefore, all are paradoxically the creators of reality.

The 11 Tenets of Ain
Church of Lucifer, By Rev. Frederick Nagash, date unknown.

1. Thou shall indulge in all things that bring you pleasure.

2. Thou shall feel no pity, nor be a martyr to the weak ones who cannot sustain themselves in reality.

3. Thou shall seek vengeance for vengeance is the rightful path of the strong.

4. Thou shall feel no guilt in anything you do, if you make a mistake feel no guilt for it, but learn from it, so you don't make that same mistake again.

5. Thou shall worry about the self, first and foremost in your life. All others you love come after the self.

6. Thou shall worship life and shun death and anything that is considered harmful to your life should be eradicated.

7. Thou shall strive to separate truth from lies and try always to seek out new experience.

8. Thou shall accept no concept of Heaven and Hell, we are living in Hell and only we can make a Heaven out of it for ourselves.

9. Thou shall feel pride in all things you do and in what you are.

10. Thou shall use greed to motivate you towards achievement.

11. Thou shall acknowledge no sins; sins are a facet of our carnal self and are embedded in our nature. Sins are natural impulses that lead to pleasure, pleasure being our iron willed goal.

The 13 Laws of the Brotherhood of Satan
Author and date unknown.

1. The Ancestors of our Dark Craft should always be remembered, for they guide and protect us from the Shadows.

2. Always honor and respect another of the Brotherhood, regardless of rank or knowledge, or gender. For we are the true daughters and sons of Satan's Family together and united in the Darkness.

3. Always honor the Old Ways of our Dark Craft by observing the 4 Black Sabbats.

4. Attend the Traditional Satanic Black Mass once a year to have communion with Satanas and His Demons.

5. Sign the Blood Covenant of Satanas to show your true dedication to Satanas and the Brotherhood.

6. Membership in the Brotherhood is for life unless you are expelled and stripped of your office or title by the Satanic Illuminati Council for abuse or misuse of your honored status in the Brotherhood.

7. Always support the concepts of Satanic Unity and Satanic Brotherhood realizing that we must be strong and united in our ideals against those without.

8. Always keep secret that which is entrusted to you to know and to understand by the Brotherhood and its members.

9. Guard the Mysteries of Satanas well, but reveal them to those that deserve them.

10. Always honor yourself first because you as a member of the Brotherhood are so honored as such.

11. Be an active part of the Brotherhood, for we have always been those that know and those that do.

12. Do not keep wisdom from others in the Brotherhood but instead always strive to share your Wisdom and Knowledge.

13. Remember always that Knowledge is Power and Knowledge used with Wisdom is what makes us all

great. For we are the BROTHERHOOD, and our names and words are written in the Book of Satanas and we are Immortal.

The 10 Commandments of Lucifer.
From the Catachism of Lucifer 2003
by Johannes Nefastos, Star of Azazel

1. Hate God, worship the Spirit alone.
2. Above all, honor Satan, the Inner Master.
3. Sanctify Darkness, see the imperfection in all forms.
4. Hate your mother and your father so that you may follow the Truth.
5. Purify the hate, abandon the violence that binds to form.
6. Purify the lust, abandon form-breeding sexuality.
7. Hate life, see the vanity in all creation.
8. Abandon the lies of faith and hope, speak but the truth.
9. Worship Death, the Perdition* of all, abandon all secular bonds.
10. Despise humanity, make yourself one with the Master.

The Seven Base of the Azazel Star
By Johannes Nefastos, 2006 Star of Azazel

1. Deity is absolute. The spirit is everywhere behind the material phenomena, their inner sense and the leader. Nature and God cannot be divided in a dualistic way, nor can the highest God, the highest truth be conceived as a personal being.

2. Truth is the highest of spiritual obligations. All that we do should be that it is in harmony with the overall understanding and strives to increase it. Religion is beautiful, but no faith should be seen as a substitute for reason. Sincerity, honestly and openly, opens up a wider world to man than any limited ideology of materialism to religious fanaticism alone can reveal to anyone.

3. Combining the name of Satan with the worthless evil is a mistake. Nothing really high in mind or power in the cosmos is intended to increase suffering, decadence, and immorality. Satan is a multi-faceted being, but behind these many faces is the divine and wise nature. He must be respected and worshiped, but this cannot and should not be done morally or on the basis of immorality: the beings that such a service pleases are never worthy of human respect or worship.

4. Evil is always the result of a mistake, or half-life, in whatever matter, whether or not such a morality is called "good" or "bad" by the Followers, or seeking to get rid of these titles. True knowledge and true love go hand in hand, and lack of empathy is indicative of inadequate knowledge of the laws of spirit.

5. No man other than man can lift a person. No external Savior, whether religious or worldly, can actually develop, strengthen, or redeem anyone. Every positive change must come from man himself, to happen in himself, to completely pass him by himself.

6. Life and death are equally important and important events in nature, parts of the great process of change in which the consciousness is eternal. Because modernity fears the physical life too much and fears death, balance is achieved by understanding the beauty of death and darkness.

7. There is a spiritual key depicted in the triangle, unconsciously attempted to represent the sacred triangles of different religions, but deceiving the original ideals in the collapse of formalism. With the help of this key, not by worshiping it, but by actively engaging in it, man is able to become more human and to develop in power and understanding. The three aspects of this threefold key are: Understanding, Love, and Will to function properly. When these three things are remembered and used in every situation, man fulfills his essential function and develops quickly, no matter what his personal traits and innate temperament are.

A note to the afterthought.

For any familiar with the modern Satanic movement. They will note a particular groups tenants have been omitted from the main body of this chapter. This is not by accident. Rather by contempt. And with good reason too.

Two years after the initial publication of this book, a new upstart "Satanic" organization formed. They dazzled and wowed the world with their brazenness and sheer gall. Even I found myself in routine support of their actions.

It was not until 2019 that their truth was revealed to me. The group, The Satanic Temple, was nothing more than frauds. An organization of Left wing Liberals using the name and iconography of Satanism, as a political shock and awe tool. I could waist many more pages on these wretched real pseudo Satanists, but I shall not. Suffice it to say, their mention here is an unfortunate necessity to the accuracy of the history of Satanism. Thus, their exclusion from this chapter.

The Proper use of Labels

As Satanism has progressed and evolved over the years since its public inception as an organized religion, many terms and labels have popped up describing the different forms of Satanic worship and practice. This has come into abundance since the creation of the internet that has made communication all the more easer.

Satanism itself has many different labels. Many of them serve a purpose, but in recent years new labels of denominations have surfaced to confuse the matter. Leaving many would be Satanists to ponder what the correct path is. Does one become a Laveyan or a Traditional Satanist? What does each label mean? And does it really serve as a good descriptive title to its branch of Satanic worship? Furthermore, is that branch of Satanism truly worthy of its own unique title that separates it from the rest?

Sadly, many of these differing titles don't serve any true purpose other than to make their group or style sound unique, when in fact they are basically the same as the rest of the herd. In our modern times there are really only three real styles to Satanism: Theistic, Atheistic, and finally Humanistic.

The first two styles are the most common methods of approaching Satanism. On one hand you truly do believe in the devil and his demons as actual living entities that can control and fully influence your life and that of the larger world. The second is also rather self-explanatory but boarders on the contradictive. Atheistic Satanism is the method in which nothing is preserved as real. The rituals are simply meant to be used for psychological purposes to vent frustrations and that you are wholly responsible for everything you do in life.

Atheistic Satanism honors only the self, and ones own ego as a god. It is basically about simply having a good time. The last style is all but forgotten in most cases. Humanistic Satanism is the method that can be best prescribed to Anton LaVeys' form of Satanic practice when he first opened his Satanic Church. It flits somewhere between the styles of Atheistic and Theistic Satanism. It does not completely discredit Satan as being a real force but it does not fully acknowledge him either. It is a style that is approached with the mindset that there is indeed some sort of outside force that can influence things or be influenced by our wills, but at the same time honors the self as a god.

I have seen so many Satanists on-line claim to run the full spectrum of styles. This makes me sit back and wonder, if they are a "Laveyan" Satanist how can they also be a "Traditional" Satanist? The answer is simple they are a Humanist. This term has been all but forgotten. It is even mentioned in the Satanic Bible.

"Satanism is based on a very sound philosophy," say the emancipated. "But why call it Satanism? Why not call it something like 'Humanism' or a name that would have the connotation of a witchcraft group, something a little more esoteric - something less blatant."

There is more than one reason for this. Humanism is not a religion. It is simply a way of life with no ceremony or dogma. Satanism has both ceremony and dogma. Dogma, as will be explained, is necessary.

The Satanic Bible; Some Evidence of a New Satanic Age.

The proper use of labels is always important. They are descriptors, and are meant to help describe something wholly different from something else. But when labels are given to something that is virtually identical to something else then the labels are wasted. Likewise, if the label is claiming to be something it is not. For example, the terms Modern, Progressive, and Laveyan would upon cursory inspection appear to be completely different from each other and individually unique, especially when we compare them to terms like Traditional, Luciferian, and Theistic. But when one digs below the surface, we find that only three or four of these terms as serving anything more than to mislead us.

The terms of modern and progressive are completely redundant when applied to Satanism. As I have stated many times over, we are all living in modern times so we are all hence forth "Modern" Satanists. And all types of Satanism are about progressing one's self so the term "Progressive" Satanism can in fact be applied to all styles of Satanism. And it has been pointed out by so many people that there has never been one set traditional form of Satanism, so the use of the term "Traditional" is completely misleading unless one applies it to the Church of Satan's method or LaVey's Methods. Those would be the only true traditional methods as they are the only ones fully understood and recognized by everyone. But as I state in later chapters, LaVey's methods have been all but forgotten and are themselves on whole misunderstood. So, on whole, the term "Laveyan" is completely out of its proper context along with the term of "Traditional".

The term of "Theistic" obviously holds a purpose, and that is to indicate that its followers call upon the Devil as an actual being. "Luciferian" through only indicates that it focuses on the being Lucifer as its patron devil, beyond that it is simply another form of Theistic Satanism.

These are only some examples of labels that are currently running amuck on the internet. Most of them are either taken completely out of context or are in truth completely redundant and or contradictive.

Labels though are useful when used correctly. While Satanism and Setianism are similar to each other they do hold some major differences that set them apart from each other, Satanists follow, for the most part, a Christian based pantheon that stands in an adversarial position to the Christians, whilst Setians follow an almost wholly Egyptian based pantheon. Though over the years they have expanded somewhat, both have some major similarities, but also have enough there to make them unique and different. The same can be said for those styles that follow some less biblical or historical methods like that of Sithism which follows an approach set down in the Star Wars movies, or Cthulianism which is focused on the writings of H.P. Lovecraft. Both are different and uniquely flavored and deserving of their own title. But each is a form of "Satanic" religious practice.

The same can also be said for the practice of Hoodoo. Hoodoo is to Voodoo, what Satanism is to Christianity. While both arts are similar to each other, Hoodoo is the Satanism of the Voodoo world and focuses on the darker, less pleasant aspects of the Haitian arts like making Zombies.

The purpose of labels is to identify something or someone. In the use of labels where people are concerned the use of titles of achievement comes into play. The titles of lieutenant and sergeant are good examples of this in any service of military or law enforcement. Obviously, these titles are ranks both of achievement and of leadership. They clearly denote a hierarchy of who is in charge over the other.

This is a good example of labels used correctly and with a purpose. One could point to the marines and the army and say the same thing. On cursory inspection they seem almost identical except that one is more rigged than the other and trains harder, but there is more to it than that. The army specializes in ground warfare and policing methods. But the marines were made specially to defend our warships and be used as our initial front-line troops to batter down the enemy. It is true that the marines are by far superior in a ground engagement but that is not their main purpose. They are called marines because their original battle field was meant to be the deck of a war ship repelling invading boarding parties.

So, there is a difference and the two different branches do indeed deserve two different names. But what about Satanism?

To determine that, one must consider the title of the type of Satanism and what their methodology is. A good way to learn how this is done is to look at the different types of Christianity. Compare, for example, Catholicism to Baptist. You can clearly see many differences. So, the two labels make sense. But now compare Baptist to Lutheran and the lines are suddenly blurred to the point where the two are almost 99.9% identical. Who came first? Baptist or Lutheran? And since they are virtually the same, why is one running around trying to claim it is different?

The same can be said for Catholics and Protestants. The later was formed in Ireland by Saint Patrick simply because he was kicked out of the Catholic Church but refused to stop performing as a priest. Hence the birth of his church but other than that there is almost no differences between them great enough to see outwardly. So why are they at war with each other most of the time?

The point here is simple. If you're going to use a label to differentiate yourself, then make sure it is a true difference, and one great enough to make it worthwhile. If not, then you're simply wasting a word and the breath used to say it as well as making yourself look like a fool, or an idiot.

The Satanic Community

The concept of a "Satanic Community" has recently come into question in Peter Gilmores' book the Satanic Scriptures. In the chapter entitled "The Myth of a "Satanic Community"", Gilmore states that there is no such thing.

I would beg to differ on that notion. Peter Gilmore makes it quite clear that a community is a group of people who come out into the open together. I would have to point out that this is exactly what is happening on the internet, as well as what the Church of Satan itself has done. Satanists seldom, if ever, come into the open in person except at gatherings and rituals or the occasional television or radio show appearance. But when we get online however, this is defiantly not the case. We get to be the most open and obvious people we can be. Often times we tend to band together in online communities. Gilmore is correct though in his statement that these sites also attract the wannabes and would-be "Great Black Hopes" of Satanism. It is sad that these vermin riddle various sites expounding on those who are well meaning and truly interested in learning about real Satanism, and only adding to the confusion. It is here on the internet though that we can in fact see how many Satanists there really are in the world. All we have to do is look. There is indeed a real Satanic Community, multiple communities in fact. Just like all other minorities, we can in fact be considered a wide ranging community both on-line and off-line. We have get-together events and meet ups. So here is my simple question: is the "Satanic Community" reality or myth?

Well, let us look at the facts. What is a community? There are several definitions of the word. So, I'll stick to the one that applies here. Satanism is a religion, and as such we automatically seek out connection with others of our own personal and moral beliefs for companionship. This occurs both online in forums and online communities all over the web. Sites like Satanic International Network, The Undercroft, Lifeforce Forums and the late 600 Club (As of late 2020 it closed its doors), are but a few of the many online community sites all over the web. And then we have our real world communities.

In the real world a community is a group of people who ether lives near each other, or regularly congregate together at various gatherings or social events. This is exactly what the various Satanic organizations do. Organizations Such as the Brotherhood of Satan, Temple of Set and even the Church of Satan or Temple of the Vampire, are all legitimate micro communities that help to form a larger community. Besides the typical religious gatherings that occur monthly by these various organizations and their individual grottos and covens to perform rituals, we on occasion see major ritual events in which large numbers of Satanists gather from around the country and sometimes the globe to attend. These rituals are not just large scale religious events they are also social gatherings where members can see each other and interact in person. Then there is also the random art or musical events hosted by members of various organizations that may have a large turn out or be directly intended for Satanists to come and socialize.

All of this is indicative and typical of a wide spread minority based community. Some of us have grottos that we belong to in our local towns or cities. And geometrically speaking a single city is more likely to harbor a larger quantity of Satanists than a smaller town that may only hold one or two or even a handful. Would these larger quantities not be more likely to be considered a "community"? Especially those who are active members of it and have managed to make contact and interact with others? When we meet another Satanist out on the street or in a store, is it not within our very nature to at least take a few moments to speak with them or even exchange contact info?

The simple answer is yes. It is only human nature to seek out companionship. Even if we enjoy being a solitary practitioner, we do still tend to at least talk to or communicate with others of a like mind. We instinctively want to speak to others who will understand what we are saying, even if they don't always agree with us. We form or connect with small groups and cliques of people of a like mind and share our stories and insight. This is only natural to humans because we are social animals.

Another thing is that in order to have a religion to begin with there must be a group of people large enough to be considered a religion and not just some isolated cult following. There are active Satanists all over the world. We are not some isolated Jim Jones following cult located in some desolate corner of the world. We aren't even a fractured and cut off bunch of splinter cells that follow the same god with different rituals each. No! We all have the ability to communicate to each other now and have the ability to connect to each other, and we do so, on a regular basis. We share our info, and rituals, we all follow similar if not identical tenants as each other if not differently worded. And we all congregate together even if it is across townships or nations. We don't hide from each other, and while we may not like everyone in our religion, we still find friends who we do like.

Anyone who says that there is no such thing as a Satanic Community, whether they be Gilmore or anyone else, is ether dead wrong or to flipping blind to look at the bigger picture. There is indeed a real and active Satanic religious community out there. It is no longer a simple "movement". It spans all of America and the world over. It is alive and cohesive. It is aware of its world and it is beginning to mature. Satanists from all over are beginning to communicate and connect in ways that we never have before. We have online communities, Internet radio shows, active social gatherings, and many more things. Each year we see new authors writing books about Satanism and sharing their views on it. Case and point here with this very volume.

Satanism is no longer a reclusive religion. It is booming, and beginning to take over. We are indeed beginning to come out into the open more and more each year. We may still be scattered all over the place, but those distances are rapidly closing.

If I was to sit down with Peter Gilmore and have a conversation with him, I would say this. Take a look around you. Look at your own church and at the world at large. Look online even. Take a few moments or hours out of a single day just to see how many Real Satanists both inside your church and outside of it you can reach and connect to. You don't need to agree with them or their overall doctrines for them to be as "Real" in Satanism as you are. See what sort of social events you can find in a single year from these various groups, be they a recognized religious organization or just a group of friends having a little get-together. Then think about it. Are you so sure that the "Satanic Community" is just a myth? Or is it in fact a plausible reality? And if it is false, then why does Blanch Barton herself make a blatant call to a "Satanic Community" in her article SYCOPHANTS UNITE?

An addendum to this article as of 2020.

It is unfortunate that as of 2013, a singular organization, The Satanic Temple, stepped forward to capitalize on Satanisms' growing popularity, and put forth perhaps the first ever version of REAL Pseudo Satanism. This group has changed some of my views since writing this article. Especially the last few lines involving "Real" Satanists, and our understanding of real Satanism. However, what is very interesting is that the CoS has done nothing to confront this legitimate threat. And CoS wonders why they are hardly acknowledged anymore.

Out of the Shadows

In 1966 LaVey opened the doors to hell and made public for the first time the Satanic Religion. He endeavored for years to make it as public as possible. And from his endeavors and hard work we now have a widespread and growing religious system that works. It has exploded into many differing religious groups and denominations, making it as equally diversified as Christianity.

However, unlike Christianity, it is not cohesively organized. There is infighting between the differing groups and no focus on universal issues that would affect and influence the entire religious system. While Christians may not always agree or even like each other they do tend to be much more organized and able to bring to bear their unified focus and attention to issues that affect them all.

They are able to meet and set aside their differences to focus on bigger issues. Why is this? With all of its rivaling factions, one may think that by now they would have crumbled long ago, especially now with so many older religions coming to bear and coming out of the woodwork once again. Religions that the Christians thought long destroyed by its genocidal and homicidal past. The answer is simple and blatantly right in front of our eyes. Though they have many rivalries, they have established clearing houses for themselves where differing viewpoints can come together on neutral grounds in a United Nations sort of way.

They have monopolized every form of communication and media on the planet. And they utilize every financial advantage they can get away with. They are beggars and thieves who will shamelessly ask children to offer up their allowances, and they manipulate the legal system so they may never pay any taxes. And lastly, they actively recruit people into their misguided causes that are only made justified by their ill-gotten enormous wealth. It seldom matters if the person agrees with their line of thinking at first because they will simply brain wash them by forcing the person to become a more active member of their church, and the ones who are too clever to fall for their tricks are said to have the devil in them and are beyond help, and thusly cut loose.

Now I have stated before, Satanism should never be united under one solitary roof, in one single church. No that has been tried by both Satanism and Christianity and it simply doesn't work. A church is meant for people who share the same identical views and emotional standings as others.

Whereas "Denominations" of the same religion, though they may hold unclear or redundant titles, are meant in fact to help draw in people of similar, though not totally like minds. A Luciferian and a Laveyan can hardly be expected to come to the same temple all the time without taking a stand for their differing viewpoints. But having different denominations, enables multiple systems to function in a society and creates a healthy diversity.

Like the Christians who offer neutral ground to face global Christian issues, Satanism should likewise attempt to find some sort of neutral territory. There will never be Satanic unity, nor should there ever be, but perhaps the notion of simple tolerance of each other to set up universal funds and perhaps a few public centers that may operate as clearing houses and public offices for PR management wouldn't be too much of a stretch.

We may never see the day when we have open temples of worship on the street corners, but that doesn't mean that we need to remain inaccessible. Public offices that enable Satanism to be learned about by the masses should be established. Though public temples would be a grand thing to see. Such temples would stand a physical landmark to remind those of where Satanism has been and where it will be in the future. Such places could be used to teach the public the truth of things concerning Satanism. They could also operate to aid Satanism in other ways as well. Differing denominations and groups in Satanism should equally be permitted to speak their minds in the media, or have their books brought to the local book store. Having a public temple to Satanism or some other form of public office would be a perfect medium to do just such things.

While countless hours of PR and media coverage has been done on behalf of Satanism, billions more even years more must be done. And with the current rate of public appearances occurring, it may take centuries before we even come close to matching the media coverage that other religions already hold under their belts. Sadly, what media coverage is currently out there is all virtually the same. I can't tell you how many times I've seen Satanists like Peter Gilmore on some broadcast or Blanch Barton and they are always asked the same questions. There are never any new questions about Satanism. Simply put we need better PR management with the media.

Currently, all one needs to do is look online for PR management offices and they will find hundreds of such clearing houses. So why not use them to their full potential? As Satanism is becoming a little too big nowadays to totally remain hidden or secretive. We simply can't stay hidden away like children in a closet. Being the reclusive children of the house just simply put is no longer an option. And while we too are easily found online with just a bit of searching in the right places, that has been our only major advancement since the early 90s in the field of public relations. So why not use the tools we have at our finger tips to find and expand on our current public relations to get better media coverage or advertisement?

Don't get me wrong here. Satanism in the past, has received an amazing amount of media, and not all of it has been bad. Most of the positive media earns its due to the endeavors of the Church of Satan, and a few other such groups. It is to these men and women who possess enough wit and humor as well as courage enough to step into the public eye and advocate, defend, and educate the public about Satanism, that I say thank you and that I applaud all of your hard work.

But again, it isn't enough. We must actively begin seeking out the media and the press at every turn ourselves, not whenever they wish to parade us around for ratings as some side show. Satanism must, if it wishes to expand and grow even more, be in the press not only once or twice a year, but monthly or even better weekly. It is us who should be conducting the interviews and hosting the TV shows.

The Christians host entire television channels completely dedicated to themselves, why then shouldn't we do the same thing? We have our own online radio shows, should we not also have our own channel on television, too? Such a channel could go great distances to helping the public understand Satanism as both an atheistic religious lifestyle and theistic religion. Not to mention with all the garbage on public television any more, a Satanic TV network might make it worthwhile watching TV again.

What needs to be done is in each town and community that holds a small grotto or coven. Those grottos and covens no matter who they are affiliated with should appoint someone in their group who is savvy enough, to handle some local public relations. With such a large amount of Satanists suddenly flooding the media and with all these groups working diligently with local PR campaigns on a regular basis. Satanism would suddenly see a huge boom. Of course, there would probably be another bought of Satanic panic, but it would be short lived, and nowhere near as trying or as annoying as the Satanic panics of the late 80s and 90s.

This of course would eventually push other occult religions such as Wicca, into following suit. Even though Wicca nowadays has quite enough media coverage to rival the Christians. Satanism is being left behind and left to the shadows still. Currently Satanism is only called into the lime light on occasion and put on display like some sort of carnival freak show. And while we do still strike terror into the simple minded Christian herd when we stand right in front of them, Satanists are often laughed at when people think that none are present.

All Satanists are public representatives of the Satanic religion and of the Devil himself. It is with this train of thought and mindset that we should boldly step into the light and show the world exactly who we are. It is rare any more that you see any Wiccans hiding their religious beliefs from the general public. It is only through our delusions that we are superior because of our secrecy that we have not yet emerged equally.

LaVey campaigned for years on behalf of Satanism. During its hay day, Satanists walked boldly down the street in the open and won the respect of any one they came across. This is still a truth. Anyone who knows me or even meets me in conversation briefly knows exactly what I am and they are genuinely surprised. Those who simply pass me on the street equally know that I am a Satanist. Granted those of a simple mind tend to cross themselves and the street to get away, but I equally have just as many who walk up to me simply to talk and ask me questions. I hold no fear or shame of being a Satanist, and like LaVey once did, I too flaunt it. To the best of my knowledge the same is true for any Satanist that does so.

Like any living creature, Satanism must change and grow and mutate in order to survive. If it was to stay the same, it would eventually grow stagnate and die off. It would destroy itself from within. People who adhere to the religious philosophies of Satanism would begin to increasingly become fewer and fewer until the religion itself became just a simple footnote in history. All of its literature would suddenly be looked at as a literary oddity and a simple source of amusement that anyone could have followed a religion whose only advancement and trace was books and a bunch of websites and some interesting art work. A religion that has no temples or noted sacred grounds, whose only landmark was obliterated to be replaced by apartment buildings.

Even the Wiccans have land marks they can look to. In sharing their history with the Druids, they equally hold many such ancient holy grounds and landmarks. And have boomed in roughly the same amount of time that Satanism has been around while holding many of the same stigmas.

Satanism can no longer linger in the shadows. It must mutate and grow. It must step into the light of day and do more to propagate itself. Steps and measures to make it more readily accessible by the public must be put into place. Even if it was to get more books on Satanism into the local bookstores. Such a small step would do wonders for Satanism. Currently it is very difficult to go to a bookstore and even find the Satanic Bible sitting on the shelf. Most book sellers are lucky if they have a small handful of copies, if any at all. And let's not even consider them having any other books on the subject. Currently if you want to buy a book from a book store on the left hand path, you will most likely find the Necronomicon and that is about it. Most of the time people are left ordering in any books on Satanism. This is not a bad thing but it does make it difficult to advertise.

Currently a book seller like Barnes and Noble is one of Satanisms best advertising grounds. Most people who get into Satanism are those who have simply bumbled across a copy of the Satanic Bible at the local book shop. If suddenly there was a whole section of the occult isle devoted to different Satanic authors like it is for Wicca and Paganism, Then Satanism equally would see an explosive expansion. Advertising is essential for making something well known. If Satanism is to survive it must become better advertised.

This of course is not saying that people haven't been trying. I remember that a few years ago the Church of Satan actually did put out a commercial on television for the Church of Satan. No doubt they got allot of flak for that one but equally they probably for a short time saw an increased number of membership applications. As it is probably whenever they make some sort of splash in the media. Publicity is Satanisms best friend. It is great that the Church of Satan is willing to bear this load, and at present they are the only ones doing so. But what would be better is if not only they advertised and PR campaigned and educated, but if the other groups also stepped in and bore some of the burden of educating the public, too.

If more groups were to equally make a splash by holding, let's say, a public ritual or what not and got the media to bring Satanism into the lime light as much as Anton LaVey did single handedly, then Satanism would begin to see a new resonance. One that Satanists could be more open and respected and make the changes in which it seeks can happen.

The Real "LaVeyan" Path

In my years as an active Satanist, I have for a long time been puzzled by what is currently called "Laveyan" Satanism. I've spent many long months, even years trying to learn about the one man who can truthfully be said to have lived his life according to the real LaVeyan path, Anton Szandor LaVey himself.

    My first encounter with Satanism came when I was seventeen. I was a Wiccan apprentice at the time preparing to go through my final phase of my apprenticeship to the coven I was with at the time, when one day a friend approached me and told me he was a Satanist. My initial reaction was one typical of a Wiccan. I naturally wanted to separate myself from anything that was considered dark or evil. However, after a few hours of talking I soon held a lighter point of view towards Satanism and I was even interested in learning more about it. That was when he also asked me to help out with orchestrating a large scale Satanic ritual. I was confused at first for surely Satanism had many rituals that would be suitable for the matter. He told me that they did have rituals that would be quite perfect to perform for the occasion, but that his Grotto wished to have something new and wanted to unveil it to the rest of the Grotto at their next meet up to be held at the end of the following month. What I now have come to know as Walpurgisnacht.

It was meant to be a major lust ritual, and quit a few people would be showing up. The Grotto had rented for the event a warehouse that was currently not being used and we began designing the ritual. My role was to find a Wiccan fertility rite and help Satanize it. As a thank you for my help I was given a rare privilege of attending the event even though technically I was an underage and a Wiccan. The whole thing went off without a hitch and by the end of the event I was as giddy as a school boy. Never had I felt such energy built up and focused in one location. There were well over a hundred attendants to the event and the after party was just as electrifying as the ritual. I found with those who attended a kinship and acceptance on a very deep and personal level.

Since that day, I was completely fascinated with Satanism and eager to learn more about it. However, with my overbearing parents I did not dare to purchase LaVey's bible. That would not come for years sadly. In the time that passed since my first experience with the Satanic religion happened, and the time that I finally found and read the Satanic Bible, things had changed dramatically in the Satanic community. The ideology, which was LaVey's Satanism, had seemed to have become clouded. Satanism was now more like a glorified atheism. This puzzled me for it made the Satanic Bible sound somewhat contradictory to itself. For one thing, if one was to not have any real faith in magic how could one possibly have full unquestioning faith that anything they did as a magician would have any real effect? If one pays attention to LaVeys' seventh rule of the earth you will find that he even states that one must have faith in magic to perform it.

> *"Acknowledge the power of magic if you have employed it successfully to obtain your desires. If you deny the power of magic after having called upon it with success, you will lose all you have obtained."*
> Eleven Satanic Rules of the Earth by Anton LaVey

However, those who practice what is presently being called Laveyan Satanism claim that one must question everything and that magic is simply an illusion, but also that it has actual effect.

How much more contradicting can that possibly be? Laveyan Satanism states that Satan is simply nothing more than a metaphor for the human condition and nothing else. That LaVey had no real faith that Satan was real at all. If these statements are true, then how is it that Anton LaVey could possibly have held so stringently to what he did or practiced?

There is no denying that LaVey was indeed a very flamboyant showman with a dark sense of humor, but he is also heralded as an accomplished occultist who had a very deep understanding of real occultism. One simply cannot have this sort of level of experience without believing in some form of outside force.

I have always felt some form of deep connection with the Satanic Bible, and feel that it is one of the few truly powerful occult books out there. It strips away the unnecessary bullshit that has perpetuated occultism for many generations and is a good beginner's guide to finding deeper mysteries. But this is contradiction to what Laveyan Satanism says.

I found myself questioning what LaVey's true thoughts were and began studying him and his original Magic Circle. I wanted to know whether LaVey really did believe in the Devil or not. I wanted to know if what he wrote that has inspired so many Satanists for decades was in fact real or simply pure bullshit, he used to elevate himself to a higher standing. What I found was shocking to me and eye opening to whom the real Anton Szandor LaVey was.

It is also why I can whole heartedly say that what is presently called "Laveyan" Satanism is in fact a bunch of horse shit, and not what LaVey really practiced.

The term Gilmorean is in truth a much more apt title.

There was a time when I could not say whether or not LaVey really believed in the Devil, but I've always said he did believe in some form of external consciousness that he referred to as Satan.

This external force is the basis of magic, as well as many countless other religions. One can feel this force when they do a ritual, especially a Satanic ritual. It is, in my long standing experience with the occult in general, normal for women to orgasm without any external aid during Satanic rituals, and for people to feel like I did after my first experience. (I was standing at full attention for almost a week strait afterwards.) I have heard of this sort of thing from other religions including Wicca, but never as regularly as with Satanism.

The true Laveyan way was to have an actual faith or belief in the force of magic if not the Devil himself and if not then don't perform a ritual with the expectations of anything really happening and simply enjoy yourself. Satanism is a religion of real and factual pragmatism. Real Satanism, which is exactly what LaVey practiced, is not an absence of belief in the abstract world of magic, but a twofold approach to real magic that enables any person who wishes to use and participate in it, to actually benefit from it. If the person actually believes in the magic they are using, they can in fact influence real change to the world through its use.

Should a person attending one of these rites not believe in magic as real, they are still able to benefit from the ritual as a personal and psychological release of pent up emotions. This can also help aid with those members who do believe in what they are doing is real, in that the energy can be added to the collective pool and used by those magicians who are present.

Modern Laveyanism focuses less on the Greater Magical arts and more on the Lesser Mundane arts. While this is a very important part of Satanic practice it is not the full thing that LaVey himself practiced. LaVey admitted to always aspiring to be more than what he was. To achieve certain levels of understanding and influence than what life would have normally dealt him. He achieved this through the use of lesser magic that anyone can accomplish. But he codified his influence through the use of a greater understanding of the deeper mysteries than what was revealed to the simple initiate. Sadly, it seems that this deeper understanding was somewhere lost to those who have commonly taken up his mantle without fully getting to know the man himself or even reflecting on his original Magic Circle. When one sees a video of a Satanic ritual held by LaVey in one of the several documentaries on him or Satanism and compares it to one held today by those members who call themselves Laveyans or members of his church, you can feel a lack of passion and a strange sense of loss or difference.

LaVeys rituals held an aura of power and sincere mystery to them. A strange sense that what was going on was actually having some form of effect even through the television screen. They were lively and exotic, even electrifying, and at times very erotic.

One walks away from the video with a strange sense of giddiness. But with other filmed rituals such as the one shown in the new documentary "Inside the Church of Satan" that passion and power is diminished if not simply absent all together.

What is it that ranks as different? For surely the practitioners in that video were around while LaVey still had control of his church before he passed away? So why do they seem less potent?

Simply put that is not real Laveyan Satanism. These people, while still benefiting from these rituals in person on the psychological level, are not benefiting or using them on the real magical level. They are only saying Hail Satan in the hollowest and emptiest of terms or simply referring to themselves. When LaVey said it and was it repeated by his followers, one got the feeling that they truly meant it as both a self-salute as well as a salute to something outside of themselves. Perhaps the real Satan or simply a force that they chose to call Satan.

The Fact remains that should one do their homework they will realize that LaVey really and honestly believed in something more than the simple mundane. He was not an atheist, but a pragmatist. He did in truth have a personal belief in something that was not of this world. Something far greater, and yet very real than the simple physical world. He understood that while the use of lesser magic was extremely important, one could not ignore the use of Greater magic. That for some this Greater magic is simply nothing more than a personal release of emotions that would otherwise stagnate and drag down a person, but for others it was by far something much more potent.

I leave you now with much thought to ruminate over. To ponder if you will, who LaVey really was, and what his teachings really meant. Was he in fact a well-educated charlatan? Or was he truly and honestly the Devils handpicked supreme High Priest?

You decide, for yourself. The answers are right in front of you ready to be seen by any who care to really look and listen and learn.

The Concept of Real Satanism

Since the time I was a child, I have always been fascinated by Satanic figures, and the dark gothic culture. Even though I was an avid Christian up till I was roughly thirteen, I continuously found my self-drawn towards the macabre and the mysterious. I grew up watching all of the old Hammer House horror flicks and I adored the Puppet Master and Subspecies movies. To this day I own most of those movies (on VHS, and DVD nonetheless) and I still love them.

Nowadays I love the strange, the morbid, the fantastic and even the delusional writings of famous and celebrated authors like H.P. Lovecraft, Robert E. Howard, R.A. Salvatore, as well as others like them.

Much of the media and literature I find myself immersed in I have over time realized has distinctly Satanic characters or a distinct Satanic feel to it. But what is the concept of Satanism in reality?

Naturally we all know that no big red guy with horns and a pitch fork is going to show up at a ritual like in the movies or books. But yet Satan is a viable thing. Even the notion of Satan as both an entity, or as an archetype is completely viable when one thinks about it.

Satan in biblical lore, while taking on a physical form, was also pronounced the God of the Earth and of the flesh. So, in accordance with that would not Satan be both a metaphor for the human condition, yet in some weird way a living entity in each of us? Or perhaps some sort of conscience thoughtform? A strange undercurrent of energy in the world or universe? But if both the metaphorical sense and the literal sense of Satan are true, then what is really the right way to be a Satanist? What is real Satanism?

Real Satanism is an occult tradition and a way of life. It honors both the beings of man, as well as that of the Devil. Satan manifests with in each of us and guides us down certain roads in life. These experiences teach us many things. A real or true Satanist will learn these life lessons very quickly and use the experience to his gain in the future instances of his life. He/she becomes one of those elite humans. A true Satanist is never created or converted, they are born to Satanism, and are the true children of the Devil himself.

But this still does not answer the question. What is Real Satanism? How does one practice real Satanism? Do they follow in the path of Anton LaVey, and place themselves upon a pedestal? Or what about perhaps, the Order of Nine Angles? Do they worship Satan like the Christians worship their god? What would you do if I said yes to all of those questions?

Satan being the god of the earth and the flesh means simply that we are literally all Satan himself, but he is also everything. He is a life force that is felt everywhere, and visible in all things. Did he make them? No. Satan is a byproduct of all those things. We made Satan, and have given him the power to influence our lives.

In truth, there is really no wrong way to worship Satan so long as one also worships themselves. One cannot adequately honor anything outside of themselves until; they first learn to honor and respect their own self, and their own ego.

To simply honor Satan as an entity but not honor yourself is an insult to the God of the flesh. To disregard him as a real driving force, and a conscious living thing, but yet only regard your own will and self is also a set up for disaster.

Satan only asks us to be mindful of him and grant him some respect, but to also hold ourselves high and keep ourselves in as good a life and mental frame as we possibly can. When a Real Satanist says "Hail Satan" He should be both saluting himself as well as the entity. One could and some in fact do throw in another saying "Hail thy self." By saying both one can adequately separate, but yet acknowledge both the physical person they are as well as the ethereal being known as Satan.

Satan has many different names. Even in the Christian sense, he is referred to by many names and is even called "Legion", because he is often considered both a single entity but also in the same instant, multiple different entities. There is no denying the fact that hell has many resident demons and fallen angels. Even here on earth, if Satan is an effective part of each individual person, he is definitively a Legion of beings who are both physical and real but yet also one in spirit.

Does this mean that only those who call themselves a Satanist, hold in them some piece of the devil? No, of course not. But not all people who hold Satanic traits in the same instance are real Satanists ether. For one thing, Satanism is first and foremost an occult tradition. It is a religion as well as a way of life. Satanism has its own imagery and symbolism and rhetoric.

There have been and still are those groups of people that while they do have many wonderful Satanic traits, and even at times call themselves "Satanists", are in truth not Real Satanists. In our modern times one must be careful on who to trust. For some, the use of the term

"Satanist" is simply a means to frighten others, gain followers, or to spread a political message.

These people use labels to try to differentiate themselves from the rest of Satanism. Terms like Laveyan, Traditional, Modern, and Progressive, has popped in recent years.

Some terms like Laveyan or Luciferian do in fact describe a specific path of Satanic worship, though not many out their today who claim this path really know what Anton LaVeys original church was like. Most now look at it as a form of glorified Atheism. When in truth LaVey and his original followers did in fact believe in an outside magical force. LaVey just simply called it Satan, and devised his church with a bit of tongue in cheek humor. This is good for any religion to have a sense of humor to it.

The other titles like modern or progressive is simply stating the obvious. We all live in modern times so we all in all actuality are "modern" Satanists, and all Satanic paths teach one to be "progressive" in their lives. To use these words in front of the word Satanism, is simply a sad attempt to sound different, when in truth there is no difference. And there has never been one true traditional form of Satanism in all of the history of mans long existence. It is called an occult tradition, because there really has never been one set form of Satanic worship. So hence forth there is no Traditional Satanism, and to claim such a thing is once again, simply a way to draw in followers.

Titles that are meant to differentiate different types of Satanists should be reserved for those paths that are truly different, and appeal to truly different people. Paths like Setianism, or Cthulianism, and Luciferianism are three such paths. They are still Satanic in their very nature and can even be called a Satanic Denominations. But they are so uniquely different that, that they do in fact deserve a title that sets them apart.

So, what is REAL Satanism? Real Satanism is a religion that honors the self as well as the very real influence of the being called Satan through the use of magical practices and rituals.

Real Satanism has nothing to do with crime or criminal organizations. It has nothing to do with Political Activism, or women's abortion rights.

Real Satanism is influencing your immediate life through the force of your own will and the use of magic, be it magic of the mundane or ritualistic. Real Satanism does not concern itself with global domination as we already live in a Satanic world. Real Satanism is about living and loving life to the fullest and not being concerned with death or what lies beyond its gloomy veil, because not many people really know that mystery, and the ones who do, aren't talking.

Satanic Saints

It was when I first watched the documentary "Inside the Church of Satan", when I first got the concept of "Satanic Saints". They were speaking about Vlad the Impaler, and mentioned that he was the one person who could be considered the only Satanic Saint.

I toyed with this notion over and over in my head and found that the concept was defiantly an interesting one, and wondered if it would indeed be plausible to have Satanic Saints who are recognized as such for their deeds throughout history. Since then, I have indeed found that there are in fact certain people who, even before Dr. LaVey ever conceived his Satanic Church, had lived their lives by the basic concepts of Satanism even if they themselves were not Satanists. Not only that, some of these people indeed performed what could be called miracles.

While these people have gained recognition on their own for their various and sometimes horrible deeds, why not grant them Sainthood on top of everything else. For even the Christians have rendered men and women alike who to them, accomplish great things as saints.

Some of their Saints like St. Patrick also in achieving greatness did some horrible things to get there. For good old St. Patty is attributed with ridding Ireland of its "snakes". It is now known that the "snakes" referred to was in fact the Druids. St. Patrick also in truth fell short of this achievement completely. For while the ancient druids were no longer totally in the open, they could still be felt in the land and operated from the shadows of the forests of Irelands and other hidden places.

Most of the Christian Saints where commonly granted their sainthood for such similar deeds. Though others were granted it only after being killed hypocritically by the Christian church, as it would seem to be the want of the Christians, who tend to have penchant for hypocrisy.

As is the case of Saint Joan of Arc who, after leading an army across France and unifying its people, was burned at the stake by the very church and king she had placed on the throne almost single handedly.

Though I will say this young slip of a girl who was no more than a child, honestly deserves her just recognition, she was only given Sainthood after the fact that she had been tried and tortured and summarily excommunicated and burned alive. She was completely illiterate and borderline psychotic with bipolar syndrome as is clearly evident from her well cataloged black out temperament.

She did, however, bring together her country and achieve great things that one could say is still felt today.

As it should be the case for the Saints of Satanism. There are those who, throughout history, have achieved many great things for Satan, but because Satanism has never officially identified such people in such a capacity, may one day fall to the way side of time or their teachings go forgotten or even completely unobserved.

Some of these people lived lives that by today's standard could, and often is, considered completely unacceptable, or even brutally barbaric and horrific.

But so did many of the Christian saints who did horrible deeds "in the name of God". So why should we

not also pronounce some saints of our own who in their own right earned the title?
Would not then Vlad Tepes Dracula, who in a similar manner as Joan of Arc, unified his country and brought peace through iron handed wisdom and justice.

    Yes, he could also be seen equally as a homicidal psychopath, and was certainly a brutal warlord, but his people even to this day honor him and pray to "God" for his return. Why not pray to Satan who Vlad was also given his nickname "Bloody Red Devil" from? Even in the Satanic Bible it lists Dracula as one of the Satanic names that may be called upon in a ritual. In all but an official capacity Vlad Dracula has already been granted his Satanic Sainthood. Why not then make it simply official and acknowledge him as we already see him, as Saint Dracula?
What about the man who is singularly responsible for dragging Satanism into the open and formulating for the first time ever a publicly acknowledged Satanic Church as a proper religious belief system: Anton Szandor LaVey? Who for over thirty years was considered by all to be the true Black Pope? Who more deserving of the mantle of Sainthood than the man who in our modern times, was the Devils greatest advocate and defender? For who else exemplified all of Satanisms true qualities? Why not grant this man Sainthood in the Devils name, to whom he served so faithfully for the entirety of his life?

    For no matter how one slices it, if Anton LaVey had never done what he did, we would not have Satanism at all today and its previous stigma, so heavily perpetrated by the Christian church, would still be as rampant as ever.

    We already perpetuate him like we do with Dracula. Both of whose names are heavily laden with respect and mystery. We make effigies and paintings of both and have raised both men to near godlike status.

Should we not then also make the good doctor a Saint as well as we have done so in all but the official capacity? Should we not raise up their statues in our temples as men who stood at the right hand of the devil to achieve great things? And what about other men and women throughout history? We should not forget what others have done as well.

Would not then Rasputin the mad monk, Aleister Crowley, La Voisin, or perhaps even, (GASP!) good old uncle Adolf Hitler, be then good candidates for such a high title? Hitler, who like Dracula and Joan of Arc, rallied his country and brought from destitution to a global powerhouse in a handful of years.

Or why not go a little more acceptable to modern standards and elect Da Vinci or Galileo and other men of science and modern thinking.

While we are at it let us not forget that one does not need to be human to become a saint. Angels for a long time have been granted the title just as equally as humans. So then why not elect certain demons and fallen angels to the position. One could say that Lilith who fled the Garden of Eden and chose to cavort with demons and later became one of the four wives of Samael who were also called the patron Saints of Sacred Prostitution, should be recognized.

There are many throughout history that could be considered for such a title. But how should we determine who is worthy of receiving it? Should we follow along with Christianity's methods and prescribe a set number of miracles? Or should we look at their deeds that they did in life? This is the question that should be answered before granting such a title.

Now I have been laughed at for suggesting such a thing in the past. Not that I really care that is. The concept of a saint is meant to provide a role model for people as well as a bit of a spiritual guide. A person or being to whom one would wish to model themselves after and possibly call upon for aid in times of need.

Therefore, I ask you this: Is it then such a preposterous notion? How many of us already do such a thing? The Christians have found it to be quite effective, so why shouldn't Satanism do the same thing?

There has been many throughout history that have shown the very qualities that Satanism values. In my personal opinion it is high time we grant these people their just recognition. Granted they may not have been the nicest people and they may have done things that we now consider completely horrible by our modern standards, but this does not mean that they are any less deserving of the title.

If we were to only look at a saint's bad points, we would never have any today. Look once again at Joan of Arc for example. She was little more than a child and yet she rallied an entire nation behind her. She was quite very much insane, mind you, and could not read nor write! Her blackout temper was well documented and she was known for ordering her solders to pray and receive confession before going into battle. If the solder refused to do so, however, she would have them killed.

She was also notorious for not taking prisoners, and followed the motto of surrender or die. She would offer only one chance for her enemies to surrender before combat. And if they failed to do so, she would have them all wiped out along with their families if they were residing in a fortress under sedge by her. No survivors were permitted under her command.

The same went for Saint Patrick, who is now famous for unleashing a religious holy war against ancient druids and pagans. He was notorious for holding a convert or die policy. Forcing the construction of Christian churches on pagan sacred ground.

And when he was ordered to stop his activities by the Vatican, he simply broke away and started his own sect of Christians.
If only their bad deeds of death and murder were looked at, we would have none of the saints we have today.

Save for a few female saints, that is. Most saints of the Christian variety at some point were solders or behaved as such at some point in their lives. Often, the people in history who have the most blood on their hands are the ones whom are raised up in God's name and given the mantle of sainthood. It is not only because of the deaths that can be attributed to them, but the results they procured for future generations that have given these people such acclaim.

The same should be done for the saints of Satanism. It is only through looking at what they achieved can we see their worth, and respectably grant them the title of Satanic Sainthood.

> 1. The Following guidelines should be used to determine Satanic Sainthood.Achievements; The subject must have done something or multiple things to change the course of history or the lives of those around them, or their country, for the better.
> 2. Miracles or possession of spiritual presence; The subject should have displayed some form of Divine connection or performed some sort of Miracles that would set them apart from the rest of the crowd.
> 3. Infamy; Unlike Christian Saints, the subject must be demonized in some fashion by the general public. This could be just part of their myth, or by actual actions that they performed in pursuit of their goals.

4. Mythical Status; The subject through their lives should have achieved a near legendary or mythic status. They should be idolized in some way and by certain sects of people. Either now or in history.
5. Death; The subject must be dead.

Four Point Trapezoidal Revisionism

A while ago, I contrived a concept that was originally derived from LaVey's Pentagonal Revisionism. I called it the Four Point Trapezoidal Revisionism. Originally, I felt that LaVey's points may never be fully realized as they were and sought out to provide an addendum to help lay the ground works to bring them about.

But as time wore on, I saw that it was not LaVey's plan that needed revising, but Satanism itself. Mostly in its approach to the public. And so I set about in rewriting my revisionism plan. The following section expounds upon this subject in detail.

Some of these things will undoubtedly be viewed as distinctly non-Satanic in thought form and that no Satanist with any sanity would even consider doing any of them. I point out though that such hard headed thinking is very much indulging in counterproductive pride. One should always consider the ways of others that have worked in the past as a constant viability, to not do so would simply be ignorant and stupid to say the least.

As time went on, I rewrote this revisionism plan for Satanism to target some of the key critical points that Satanists as individuals and groups should focus on to bring Satanism fully into a new era. I adapted it away from LaVey's more and more as I paid attention to goings-on in science and modern society as well as those in my personal life.

It should be noted that this revisionism plan to Satanism does not in any way mean that current Satanic practices are wrong or should be completely abandoned. Quite to the contrary, current practices should be maintained constantly to some degree or another, but new ones should always be considered for adoption.

Tax Exemption

It is no secret that LaVey's church has never sought out the use of Tax Exemption throughout the entire forty some odd years it has been around. This is one of the singularly most wonderful things about the Church of Satan and other such organizations who have done the same thing. It shows that they are willingly returning back to and aiding their community in one of the most fundamental ways and are setting an example for all church groups and organizations to do the same.

Over the years the Church of Satan has established a wealth of moneys without ever asking for any special treatment from the federal government. They have set a standard that all organizations and churches, whether they are Satanic or other, should aspire to reach. Unfortunately, in our modern era, unlike LaVey's when he first established his church, this is simply not a feasible option any longer. Most churches begin small and are almost always poor with little to no money. To the newly established church group every penny is valued to help fund it. Such money goes towards events and gatherings, supplies for religious groups, financing publications, and much more.

Unlike LaVey's time, finances are not easy to acquire. One must be diligent and consider inflated prices, higher taxes and tougher to find jobs. The field of self-employment holds many dangers itself and one must face extreme competition from others who offer the same thing as you. One must beat them out in quality, quantity, and price. Federal grants are equally harder to come by and require many forms to be filled out and much research.   To put it simply, the current condition of the financial market is a downright nightmare, and it is only getting worse.

This makes it nearly impossible for any new religious group to get started like the Church of Satan did, let alone continue to operate for an extended period of time without becoming rapidly popular, which is almost unheard of, especially in Satanism.

In our modern era it is only common sense there for any new religious group to become Tax Exempt until such times that it could stand on its own two feet. It doesn't matter if it's Satanism, Wicca, or Christianity, for any such groups or organizations nowadays to even have any sort of fighting chance at success it cannot afford to allow itself to be taxed.

Now don't get me wrong, I feel that all institutions, especially a religious one, should set an example by paying their taxes like anyone else. But for the newly founded organization that is legally recognized, a leeway period should be allowed for.

New immigrants to America become filthy rich by not being forced to pay their taxes for a period of seven years. In that time-frame they are completely tax exempt. Every bit of money they earn in their respective paycheck is one hundred percent pure profit.

Tax exemption is a powerful tool to use even if it is only for a limited time. For a church or religious organization that time-frame can be indefinite unless the church chooses to be responsible for itself, and decides that it has no further need to be tax exempt to maintain itself.

Satanism has always advocated "responsibility to the responsible". As such, any Satanic organization that chooses to become tax exempt should equally show that phrase in action when it no longer has any need to be non-taxed, and thus willingly begin to pay its dues.

But how does one know when the time is right to start paying taxes and how should an organization or religion like Satanism maintain its funds if it is being taxed? That is up to the organization to decide. Certainly, some will opt for paid memberships while others may not. Then there are the varying amounts that members are required to pay and how often. It is the individual organizations choices that will either let them rise above others or come crashing down under their own weight.

Satan Takes Center Stage

The public press machine is one of the most important modes of mass communication in the world today. Currently everything from CNN to our local newspapers dominates our lives.

In the last two decades a new form of media coverage has seen to it that literally everyone is inundated with news reports on a daily basis. Every person in the United States and even the world can know what is going on in almost every other town or community in America should it so wish to by simply going on-line and looking up that region's local news.

The Church of Satan has spent countless hours over forty years spreading the word through the media on what Satanism is about through public television and the internet. But in a world full of Satanists, they stand all but alone in their efforts. One organization can only do so much to counter all the bad press that Satanism gets yearly.

With all of this open press coverage available in almost every town in America it is a wonder to me that more Satanists or Satanic organizations do not make regular appearances on public television. Or even grant more interviews for local papers.

It is high time that this silence ceases and desists at once. Satanists may be closing the gaps between one another on a large scale due in large part to the internet, but that does little for our real world relations. When we turn off our computers make no mistake that there is indeed a real physical world around us that must be given credence and attention.

LaVey in his life did everything he could to get publicity for Satanism at every turn he could muster. Nowadays though this has turned to very sporadic interviews only when some major movie event comes out or The Church of Satan decides for itself to make a few minor appearances. Often times we are turned into the laughing stock of the media world when they have little else to talk about.

If Satanism is to accelerate into the future and eventually achieve its goals, more press coverage is needed from all parties involved. Satanists must be bolder and more brazen than ever and seek out positive media attention. The media should not be interested because they're bored or have little else to speak about, but because they hold genuine interest in what is going on. This of course does not give Satanists in general free license to go making a bad name for Satanism by doing stupid shit. But should instead encourage other organizations similar to the Church of Satan, to do as many things publicly to deliberately get into the media lime light.

Satanism needs more public representatives and should be seeking to hog as much media air time in the news or newspapers or online blogs as it can. The more press coverage we can get, the more interest in Satanism there will be as a whole. This will only benefit Satanism in times to come and aid in increasing our numbers to a bursting point.

The Devils Business

As almost any Satanist will tell you, it is a pain in the arse to find any Satanic merchandise on a stores shelf unless it is to defame Satanism. At present one must go to some form of online shop that specializes in Satanic merchandise or find that rare occult shop that carries the stuff to get supplies.

There is a cornerstone market in Satanism as the numbers of active Satanists continue to swell, so too can commerce for the Satanic organization profit by establishing its own occult shops and other Satanic businesses.

This would consolidate their revenues in time to come. Businesses that specialize in Satanic merchandise can be widely varied from simple stores to publishing houses, movie or music studios, art galleries and a variety of other such business opportunities.

It is no secret that the Devil sells most of the best merchandise. With over a million plus copies of LaVey's Satanic Bible sold, and more copies sold every year at a steady pace that if it were any other book, would probably hold a position in the New York Times all-time best seller list. It should be apparent that Satan and Satanism never gets old. Countless dollars are spent yearly on selling Satan by the standard commercial industry. Only they're making money off of making the Devil out to be an asshole. So why shouldn't Satanism cash in on some of the fun?

If any Satanic organization wants to make regular money and keep its coffers full of green to provide support for its members such as events and any other sort of support, they may need without being a charity, the establishment of actual businesses and business fronts is an essential tool. This is equally important if that organization wishes to pay its taxes without hurting itself financially.

Having an established business equally makes Satanism more readily available to be learned about by those interested in learning. An established Satanically oriented publishing house that is a vanity press could help ensure that Satanically based books are more readily available in many book stores nationwide. Wicca has shown the success of such a publishing house through the publisher Llewellyn. And there is evidence in surplus to the success of the occult shop business. Music and entertainment are also a major business opportunity that Satanism has known only moderate success in. Currently the only publicly known Satanists to have found major success in the music industry are Marilyn Manson and Cradle of Filth to my knowledge. Undoubtedly there are more in those fields of industry that have made it, but their keeping quiet about being Satanists.

How nice would it be if there was a studio that was well funded and could produce high quality pro-Satanism movies and music? Such studios would be well funded by Satanic organizations and in return bring in greater profit to those organizations. Again, this could consolidate those selfsame organization's personal revenue to the point where they would have the ability to stand on their own.

It is fundamentally important that Satanists and Satanic organization establish literal physical business fronts. Only by doing so will Satanism in general become even more established on all fronts and enable Satanists to reach their personal goals as well as help lay the foundations for the future.

This has been proven time and again by other religions. I can't tell you and shouldn't need to tell you how often I have seen Christian funded and based shops and stores on the open street. These Christian based businesses have helped finance Christianity in ways that far surpass the age old collection plate or any such donations could ever hope to achieve.

Any smart Satanic organization or active Satanist would be smart to follow suit to achieve their goals and maintain their finances.

Public Satanism

Satanism stands its ground as the adversary to most religions, but none more so than the Christian religion.

There was a time when Christianity was put on the ropes by the occult community with Wicca and Satanism at the forefront of the battlefield leading the charge.

Sadly, Christianity managed to come back swinging with the whole Satanic Panic incident that damn near caused a second inquisition. Satanism is still reeling somewhat from this period of time and its officials are currently working hard still to dispel much of the myths and slanderous rumors spread by the Christian monger mills. One point that has benefited many religions is that they are so readily accessible by the public through some form of public established offices.

For Christians these offices are obviously their numerous churches and other professional public relations representatives. These public offices are one of Christianity's strongest weapons in any battle front because it makes them easily accessible to all. Literally any one can simply enter a church and speak with an official spokesperson of the church. This grants them the added ability to work with people on a personal level one on one.

It is one of Christianity's worst fears that Satanism will follow suit with this endeavor. LaVey's Black House was truly a place they dreaded because it enabled the common person the opportunity to have access directly with many high ranking members of Satanism on a personal level.
There was a continuous influx and outflow of Satanists around the Black House, and all one had to do was simply wait long enough to speak with someone and soon enough there would be someone to speak with them. Or one could have found them self really lucky or unfortunate, depending on their attitude, and have had the man himself Dr. Anton Szandor LaVey come out personally to speak with them.

This sort of direct contact is something they feared because the person would then have the ability should they so please to dispel all of Christendom's established myths about Satanism and even have an easier mode of entering into the religion that is on par with Christian churches.

Should there ever be a public temple to Satan who holds public offices, Christianity would face a cataclysm to its doctrines concerning Satanism. Suddenly the not easily accessed world of the Satanist would be more open in new ways to dispel the myths and rumors spread about it. Satan would suddenly have a much more level playing field with that of god.

Satanism, though, has always held a closed door policy in order to keep out the weaker elements of society, while Christians welcome these elements. This smacks highly of ignorance on the Satanists part as even in the bible should one consider the serpent in the garden of Eden the devil, then he is to be seen as the great re-educator of humanity. It therefore could be said that it is Satanisms responsibility to openly re-teach the masses the truth of matters and to help encourage them in a public forum to become self-reliant free thinkers.

It is no secret that the milling herd of humanity will often readily accept any doctrine handed to them. But with Satanism, that willing acceptance of doctrine could force them to become self-thinking individuals in new ways. This is done by teaching them to "question everything", a motto that many Satanists have wielded as a rallying cry to all current free thinkers and intelligent people. Should such a motto be taught openly in a public temple to its adherents, then those previously doe eye pudding minded throngs of sheep may suddenly find that they were in truth wolves simply domesticated and now suddenly unchained.

Such a mass realization of the public would spell certain doom for the Christian propaganda machines as they would suddenly find that they are no longer listened to by as many simpletons that they are accustomed to having to manipulate.

They will find the questions posed to them increasingly harder to face and that their "holy scriptures" would suddenly be seen as little more than the glorified babblings of two thousand year old dead men, who were as ineffective in life as they were in their writings. Suddenly their collection tins would be as empty as their pews.

Social Vampirism
The American Epidemic

As I stated before, the use of proper labels is essential. Before the current Vampire movement sprung into being, Anton LaVey coined the term "Psychic Vampires" in the Satanic Bible.

Nowadays this term is no longer accurate. The term "psychic vampire" in his definition no longer matches what we now currently call a "Psychic Vampire".

In LaVey's time, a Psychic Vampire was a person who through his own actions, uses others to get what they want. Often these folks would manipulate or use resources that would be better used else were. This is not so much indicative of psychic behavior but that of social behavior.

Our current understanding of the term "Psychic Vampire" is a person or persons who literally feed off of the ambient and or aural energy in their surrounding environment or persons in that environment, because they can't, for some reason or another, maintain their own energy.

This is even recognized by the CoS, via their sister organization, the *Temple of the Vampire*.

It is with this new definition of what a Psychic Vampire is that I have chosen to redefine LaVey's wording from "Psychic" to "Social". A "Social Vampire" can be anyone. Chances are all of us have performed acts of

Social Vampirism at one point or another for whatever reason. There is nothing wrong with this, so long as it does not become a habit.

Unfortunately, America has become a breeding ground for social vampires. This is the sad truth of the matter. Our very social structure is designed around promoting and encouraging social vampirism. It focuses on helping the sick and needy abroad and allows its own citizens to be forced to fall back on to the welfare system in a failing economy. America's government spends trillions of dollars on sending troops to wars and aiding famine ridden countries that have survived in their current state for centuries.

This is further instigated by America's failing school systems and increased propaganda that we "need" or "must" help other counties that are economically poorer than our selves. That, and an increased allowance of illegal immigrants into America, specifically illegal Mexicans, means our economy is now focused almost completely on Social Vampirism at almost every level.

This is Social Vampirism at its worst. We have entire job communities that are almost completely composed of illegal Mexicans, that even as they bring in massive amounts of money to their homes, are still leeching off the welfare system.

We harbor and encourage entire generations of families to live completely off tax payers' dollars. Have you ever seen a rich bum? Chances are you have, many times over. I've seen and met homeless vagrants who are better fed and better dressed than you or me.
These are the worst kinds of Social Vampires. They bleed us dry of our precious funds and resources without a care or a thought. And then they pretend to be our friends.

Oh, sure many immigrants can be very nice people, until you ask for something in return, and then they get very testy and will often try to avoid complying with your request or do so very grudgingly. Their once friendly smiles turn to scowls and often, they will not want anything further from you until such times that they think you have something that they want. Then they will once again offer empty gifts and false smiles.

Social Vampirism has become an American standard. Either you perform it or you encourage it, and if you don't support it you get called an outcast or weirdo or a Satanist. Not that being any of those things is bad or even insulting. It's more of a complement to a Satanist than anything else, especially if you're called something derogatory for being concerned enough about a problem.

There are those who use Social Vampirism to elevate themselves, though. People who have become so downtrodden by the economical standards that regardless of trying to improve both themselves and their standing, they are cut down short. Often these sad folks are made to struggle alongside those who manipulate the system with no want to ever aspire for more. These folks are thusly left with little choice but to become Social Vampires to beat back the society that has forced them to such desperate measures.

Such social vampires, the ones that are not willingly behaving in such a manner and actually wish to improve and cease such behavior by using social vampirism to improve their quality of life, are the good social vampires.

The hardworking man who hates being out of work collecting unemployment checks and endeavors to get back into the job market, the single mother who despises being on welfare and seeks to improve her education to get a good job to support her children, or even the young person who is not satisfied with his current living standard and works hard to change his condition through others.

All these types of people may in fact be forced to adopt the mentality of the social vampire in order to survive. It is these worthwhile people that should be given the aid they require instead of those who only seek to leech from us without giving anything back.

A positive social vampire will often only be such until they are given an effective avenue to grow away from vampirism. They hate their situation and hate being forced to depend on others. Often, they need only one solid break to become more. The trick to helping the positive vampires to cease being vampires is to remove any obstacles in their way.

One such obstacle for many positive vampires presently is the illegal immigrants in America. Should these illegal immigrants, who are yet another form of negative Social Vampire, be forcefully removed in mass numbers, it will suddenly re-open the job market and force employers into giving jobs back to those Americans who want and deserve them. Once these positive vampires have been effectively reintegrated into the economy and are no longer forced to leech from our recourses, we can then turn to our domestic social vampires who continue to eat our recourses without mercy. These social vampires can then be dealt with by force.

By removing our support of them and forcing them to either cease their vampiristic activities, or become the truly needy. They will be left to the wayside while the worthwhile people pass them by.

LaVey said it best, *"They are like a cancer that must be savagely ripped from the body. Cut them out with grim delight and abandon. Only then can we grow free and become healthy".*

While sometimes social vampirism may be necessary, it is by no means healthy. What may be a person who at first only means to be a social vampire until he/she can change their circumstances, may in the end become complacent with their standard and become a negative social vampire. It is something that must be attended to promptly or we will all suffer in the end from it. America's failing economy is a prime example of what social vampirism can do if left unattended for too long.

And if left to go much longer without radical measures it will only worsen until America eventually dies.

In Romania, even to this day, Undead Vampires called *"Strigoi"*, are taken very seriously. They can wipe out entire towns and cause a lot of social destruction. It is not uncommon to see entire towns abandoned because of a vampire scare. This is why they respond to them with such aggression by dealing with them early on.

While here in America our vampires are not undead fiends, they are equally as dangerous, and should equally be dealt with in as aggressive a manner as is necessary to maintain our wellbeing. Not just on a personal level any more, but on an economic level.

Social Vampires have ceased being the "Psychic Vampires" of LaVey's era and have become a wide spread epidemic that we now see today. This does not mean that they are any less dangerous. Quite to the contrary, they are more dangerous now than they were in LaVey's time.

Now more than ever America must go on a vampire hunt. We must root out this problem and neutralize it effectively and decisively.

Employers of illegal workers should face heavy criminal charges and long prison sentences, while illegal immigrants should not only face prison in our land but then deportation with no money.

A large wall should be built across the Mexican/American boarder with armed guards patrolling its battlements with orders to shoot anyone trying to get over the wall illegally.

People who would leech from the welfare system and taxpayers' dollars for longer than a year should be removed from any aid and forced to find work, or at least given an assigned job.

Those who would spout out multiple children from their rancid genitals, just to get larger and larger amounts of welfare benefits should be force to compulsory or government mandated birth control or outright sterilization while on the welfare system!

It is just as much of a problem when people reproduce uncontrollably and unchecked in an already over populated economy as it is to have so many illegal immigrants. We do this with certain animal colonies such as feral cats. why should humans be any different?

What makes it even sadder is that the children didn't ask to be born, it was never their intention to add to a growing problem, but they are. And it is a problem that they must face, too, in times to come.

Social Vampirism is an issue now not just for the Satanist, but for all of America. The only thing is that it is the Satanists, as the adversaries that have the obligation of standing up and say something about it.

Some Bad Elements of Satanism

For some time now, the modern Satanic movement, as well as other occult based religious movements, has been faced with combating the stigmas put on them by the major religions of the world. Mostly from Christendom's couple centuries long war against any thing that is even remotely different or older than its own self. In the past hundred years the occult religions have made some major head way, and have become very popular. This has been truly a very promising past hundred years for all of the occult, and has opened up the doors for Satanism.

Satanism itself is probably the most shunned still of all the occult arts, but it is also one of the most pragmatic of the occult arts with the least amount of esoteric garbage in its very make up. This is mostly to do with the fact that Satanic practice, though it has indeed been around for centuries, has never fully organized on a large scale basis until LaVey opened up his Satanic Church in 1966. LaVey has influenced through his shear popularity the entirety of the Satanic world. Even the most fervent and outspoken denouncers of any sort of LaVey based influence have been, at some level influenced by LaVey's teachings. For better or worse they all are connected by Anton Szandor LaVey.

The past half century has seen an explosion of exponential proportions of the number of active Satanists around the globe. This has gleaned a strong harvest from the folds of humanity to form a strong and intelligent future. But each harvest has its bad seeds and those bad seeds can ruin the entire crop.

In recent years, outside elements have found their way in to Satanism and have begun to germinate rotten fruit for their own selfish purposes. Some use the title of Satanist to instill fear, others just to attract attention, and still others use it to recruit to fanatical causes. It is true that Satanism, like all other religions, has its bad elements or some more unsavory elements. Some Satanists are far more militant in their very nature and others are more fanatical. Though this doesn't necessarily make them a bad element, it is less savory for some folks to be around, especially if they aren't Satanists themselves.

But there are the bad elements. Elements that even the Satanic Community must watch for and monitor to prevent any damage from them. Such elements are the intimidators and the false Satanists, the super fanatics, and the random person who thinks that the "Devil" has commanded them to kill innocent people. These elements can come in many forms but no form is more dangerous than organizations that preach hate and violence and operate on a physical level and use Satanism both as a tool for recruitment and as a motivator for its members.

In recent years organizations such as white supremacy groups and street gangs have adopted the teaching of Satanism and perverting them to their own means. Often times, they amalgamate the teachings of Anton LaVey with those of David W. Myatt (Anton Long), and practicing the methods of super fanaticism. They often follow the method called the "Sinister Way" which preaches social violence and intimidation, to achieve their goals.

The "Sinister Way" is not the Satanic way, or the way of the Adversary. The way of the Adversary is the path that Satanism follows. It is a path that stands as any enemy to the ignorance or lack of simple common sense that is held by most of society. It is also fundamentally an occult based magical tradition.

The methods of the Sinister Way are, while similar to the Adversary's way, more in tune with its name. Practicing less of the Greater Magical arts and focusing more on the mundane, its methods often include intimidation through harassment and even violence to instill fear in people. Other such methods focusing more on the internet is through cyber terrorism to attack anything which might expose them or pose as even a minor threat to their ways. I have already encountered such groups and have even made it onto to these groups' sites in such lists with names like ENEMY SITE or KILL ON LOCATION and other interesting names. I am not the only person that faces these sorts of practitioners of the "Sinister Way". There are many Satanic Organizations that must deal with such trolls. Most of these e-groups who claim such a path are nothing more than a few people talking big, but it does get annoying. There are such groups though that is active in this practice. A recent news broadcast spoke of one such street gang who announced a membership initiation was to take place soon that would consist of killing three women in Wal-Mart parking lots.

Street gangs are a common breeding ground for such groups and recruiting sources, as they are a ready-made batch of moldable violent and hostile youth which simply needs only indoctrination to get it focused in a specific direction.

Satanism has been fighting a battle against the stigmas placed on it by the Christian church for hundreds of years. Its members must always be ever watchful for

people or groups that could cause its name to become even more tarnished than it has already become.
We must go on public record and denounce any connections with such people or groups actively. It is bad enough that we are already associated with human sacrifice and child murders along with a whole string of other falsehoods. But when we find members and leaders of our ranks who belong to street gangs like the High Times Marvilla Gang, or fanatical organizations like the ONA, we must ostracize them and go on the defense. We cannot afford to allow members of such gangs and organizations to be connected with us. These groups are propagators of outright violence and mayhem. Groups that propagate the outright killing of an innocent person as an initiation cannot, and should not, be tolerated.

The Satanic community has enough problems without such persons or groups already. Our place of violence is the ritual chamber. A place where, should someone who has offended us, be cursed and our anger be dealt with in a healthy way. The only time that we should resort to physical violence is when we are directly threatened in such a physical manner. Under such a immediate threat I see no wrong or fault in one seeking to do great physical harm or even in the killing of such an attacker if that is what the situation calls for. There have been several occasions where I myself have had to use extreme physical force to protect myself, friends, or loved ones. I don't enjoy doing it but I'll not hesitate when it must be done.

This sort of violence is acceptable. So long as it stays within the boundaries of necessary force. For example, don't kill a person unless you are sure that they are going to kill you. Should and attacker be holding a baseball bat then by all means brutalize him or her until the weapon is out of their hands. If that means that they have to die in order for you to get the weapon away, then kill them. Though in most cases simply breaking a bone will get them to drop the weapon and lose their will to fight.

But I digress. There is a definitive line between necessary violence and unnecessary violence. Without a doubt, some violence is a good thing as it can be a healthy expression and ventilation of anger. I personally love violent video games and violent sports (such as boxing or kick boxing.) and violent movies. These are healthy forms of violent behavior. Nothing feels better to me when I'm flat out pissed off, than coming home and blowing a few zombies away on my PlayStation or Xbox. Or setting up a punching bag and simply going to town on it until my body drips with sweat and my hands and feet are blazing sore. That is far better than going out with a gun and blowing the guy who got on my last nerve away.

That's not to say that I am above getting revenge for a wrong that has been committed on me. But chances are the person will come out of it physically unscathed, just emotionally traumatized enough to shit his pants, or at least smelling like he did.

The point is this: We must be ever watchful for those elements that could further tarnish our reputation. Groups that are made up of gang members or is led by gang members must be ostracized and frowned upon. The same goes for other organizations that, while claiming to be Satanic, are in fact recruiting grounds for violent individuals. Organizations with ties to white supremacists, gangs, or even drugs and other illegal behavior, cannot be tolerated any longer. They are little more than Social and Psychic Vampires. They should be cut from us like the cancer they are. It is our responsibility to set an example, and it is something we cannot afford to shrug away. To do so would only further encourage their presence and invite other bad elements into the fold.

We have worked hard to keep out many negative elements, such as pedophiles, murderers, thieves, and rapists. We have fought hard to deflect away the lunatics who think that Satanism is a ground for having a free license to commit atrocities on humanity. Yet there are indeed those people who are so blatantly headstrong about it that they would go out on their own to do these things in the name of Satan or would find groups like the ONA who would endorse them to do so.

These socially vampiric groups claim to be Satanists, but they're not. They may practice rituals that, while outwardly resemble Satanism, are in fact clearly not when one looks below the surface.

A good analogy that could be attributed to such groups is that they are much like the parasites on a dog. Little more than blood sucking fleas and ticks that force the dog to scratch so much that it removes large amounts of its own fur coat, leaving it to look mangy and pathetic. Like the dog, Satanism must give itself the proverbial flee bath to remove these parasites. While the dog may chew and shred its own coat and skin to try to ease its itching, Satanists can effectively remove its own parasites without doing such harm to itself.

How, you may wonder, can this be achieved when Satanist are constantly gesturing and busy hating each other? Can we isolate the bad element when we view every one not with our individual train of thought as bad and wrong?

For one thing, we must learn to identify these Social and Psychic Vampires, and Pseudo Satanic trash, and seek to remove their influence through their unique methods. If one finds such a group's website that, for example, preaches terrorist or Pseudo Satanic traits or is funded by organizations that are known for extremist violence, then we should thusly make a point of diverting all traffic away from their main sources of recruitment online.

This can be done in many different ways both legally and not quite so legally, (IE hacking the site and defacing it, or sending a virus to the creators of the site and crashing their computer.)

Also, say we find a group leader who is a member of noted violent street gang. We could always refuse to join their group and affiliated sub groups or allied organizations, causing them to lose numbers and either be forced to remove the person in question or go belly up.

Or let's say that there is a socially aggressive organization that claims to be Satanic. (The Satanic Temple) It has published literature that clearly propagates and encourages violence on innocent victims, and twists our deities in a way that they are only named the same thing but no longer resemble the true deity.

Such a group would be much more difficult to remove, and it would take probably another organization to put a halt to it. One step that could be done is to go on public record denouncing the said group, and denying its members access to our online communities. This would force the group into isolation away from Satanism. We could boycott or seek to have its literature legally banned from our country on the grounds that it is perversely inaccurate and used as a tool to recruit people to commit crimes. Without such literature in circulation, its membership would be kept to a minimum, effectively keeping any damage by them to an equally small degree. Though it only takes a small incident to cast a negative light on Satanism, the general public is always quick to latch onto anything evil that can be categorically chalked up to Satanism.

Granted every religion will have certain elements that will always slip in unnoticed, but that doesn't mean they can't be ferreted out and removed or minimized.

While Satanists certainly enjoy remaining outside the norm and not conforming to Christian ideals or methods, we would do wisely to take some notes from them on how to remove their negative elements. Gang members are seldom given any positions of power within the Christian religion or any other religious institutions or movements. Hostile elements are often censored and relegated to the category of terrorist factions. Nazi-like or run groups are often left to run and viewed as little more than isolated cults. Typically, they are only to be dealt with if they grow too large, or become a real threat to their followers or the people around them.

It is up to the Satanic community to deal with its own parasites. By not doing so, we will only be letting our already tarnished reputation degrade further instead of being mended. Without mending Satanisms reputation, it will have little chance of growing much as time goes on. it will be left to the way side to stagnate and continue to be used as the scapegoat whenever some jerk tries to get out of a murder rap by saying "The Devil made me do it". I don't know about you, but I don't like the idea of being anyone's whipping boy.

On Who's Authority?

If there is one trend in Modern Satanism that bothers me, it is the trend of defining pseudo Satanists and Satanic organizations. It is the trend of "If you're not with us you're against us or not a real Satanist."

This is a trend in Satanism, like most trends, that began with the Church of Satan. As any Satanist knows, the Church of Satan holds the view point that the only true Satanists in the world are its own members and even then, only members of rank. Even though they claim that you don't need to be a member of the church to be a Satanist, in their "Bunko Sheet" they pretty much outline everything that is not considered Church of Satan approved or affiliated. This includes individuals. By their view point, if you're not a member then you're not a Satanist. This standpoint has been taken up by several other organizations as well.

Let me be frank. This prerogative from any one is simple horse shit! It is reminiscent of Christian churches continued view that their individual church is the only correct path to God. Satanism is meant to stand in total opposition to anything Christian or at the very least it is intended to take a reversed stand point of their views. Who in this world has any real say so on whom or what another person really is? The answer is no one, not even the so called authorities of any one particular religion. Is a person who follows the path of The Brotherhood of Satan wrong or fake? Or is Peter H. Gilmore himself a fraud? It is not up to any one person to decide these things, and certainly it is wrong for anyone to criticize any one person or organization just because they have a differing view point that you or your organization.

Now don't take me wrong on this, I'm not intentionally singling out the Church of Satan in this, they just make for a good example as a well-known organization. I personally think a great deal of its members are very intelligent and productive members of the Satanic Community. And they do act as an example of what the basic viewpoints of Modern Satanism should be with their take on the world. I will never call any of its member's fake of false, but I will say that they are rather presumptuous in their thinking that they are the only venue or outlet for real Satanism. Simply put they're not. Nor are they the sole authorities on the subject. They themselves started this whole mess on who is a real Satanist and who is not, and for what? To monopolize Satanism for themselves?

It is organizations that take this view point that miss the bigger picture and become, in a nut shell, stuck in the mud. They don't progress forward at a reasonable pace and become the random road side show for entertainment. Trying to hold a total monopoly of a religion is like trying to hold water in your bare hands. You will constantly have some spillage. Is the spilled water any less water than what you hold? Just because it is on the floor does it somehow become some other substance with less value? It is still water it just took a trip and gained a few new properties. It can be cleaned up and reused.

Satanism has so many legitimate venues and differing groups and organizations whose views are equally as valid as the Church of Satan's. They simply take a different approach to the religion. Granted there are indeed groups out there who are very unsavory to encounter, but they in their own right also make the religion a little richer. Like with the Christians West Borough Baptist Church, who is most certainly not fun to be around and demonstrate the ignorance of that religion, Satanism too has its groups that equally do the same. This doesn't make them any less than what their respective religious beliefs make them or tell them to be, they just have differing takes on them. The West Borough members are still Christians in every respect of the word, they're just blatantly ignorant ones who behave with poor manners and plenty of bad behavior. But they do demonstrate to the rest of the Christian community how many non-Christians view them.

    Within Satanism we too have such groups, like WSA/352 and even the Church of Satan itself at times, who, though they behave poorly, and at times set a terrible example of what a Satanist is, they do remind us of how we are viewed at times. I personally may not like a particular person or organization in our religion, and I may hold many qualms with them. But that doesn't give me the right to call them fakes or frauds. Our differing viewpoints don't make either one of us any less Satanic than the other.

    Don't misunderstand me, there are indeed those groups and individuals who actually do masquerade as Satanists or Satanic organizations, and they must be watched for. All I am saying is to be mindful of yourself and your opinions. Don't be a troll about thing or consider yourself superior to another person or group without a valid reason. If they blatantly demonstrate their ignorance that's fine but remember a lack of knowledge only means that there is room to learn, ignorance never teaches. Calling people names and harassing them only shows your ignorance and lack of wisdom. In the end what does it accomplish? Very little to tell the truth. One thing I will give Gilmore and the Church of Satan credit for is that they don't feed directly into online squabbles and often chose to simply ignore things. To a large point this is a good approach as it allows one to simply shrug off most of the slander and continue forward.

Their approach to a lot of things I will say is a good one, the major exception being their ignorant stubbornness in failing to acknowledge other groups and viewpoints shared by many people outside of their organization. Satanism is not about being ignorant to anything. On the contrary it is about being knowledgeable about a great many things and learning new things. We always tell people to prove our views to themselves and develop their own view points. It is simply un-Satanic to sit there and try to pound your personal opinions down another person's throat who doesn't ask for your thoughts, and to do so makes you no better than those who would sit around calling everyone else fakes.

LaVey himself let members of his own group have a psychological belief in a real anthropomorphic Satan. He did not criticize these members of his organization during his time, so why are these people now targeted and ostracized? It makes little sense as they in their own ways add to the overall enrichment to the ritual setting. Many of them, aside from their actual faith, act and think in almost an identical manner to those members of Satanism who do not consider Satan as an outside entity.

This behavior is one reason that Satanism has found itself splitting into multiple denominations, that in and of itself is not necessarily a bad thing, but with each group sitting there on their high horses calling everyone else a fraud, very little ever gets done in the long run.

Now we have come to the cyber era, in which many people hold entire relationships on line and run complete organizations from the comfort of their home computer. To many people the internet is considered open ground. This of course is only an illusion hosted by the person's mind. The internet is no more open ground than any other form of media. The difference is that it reaches a lot more people every day. It is with this regard that many Satanists take to heart the notion of "destroying" any person that bothers them while failing to remember the first part of the verse that says not to bother anyone yourself.

How many open flame wars have transpired across the web between groups who have taken offence to something said? More than I can count. Many people forget that the internet is not the real world and that they can end the situation quite rapidly by letting the other person blow themselves out without even giving them any response. The individual will destroy themselves by their continued obsession with hurting you while you just continue to mosey on like they don't even exist. There is a little thing on most forums and chat hosts called an ignore button that blocks everything said by a person from your computer screen, and in some cases, it will block your words from them, too. If more people would learn to use this feature then our own personal worlds could be more peaceful with each person living quite happily in their own little bubble.

But instead, people turn into drama queens and follow the whole "he said she said" routine. Which is of course very childish and only serves to make the rest of us look bad.

No one has the right to tell you who is a fake and who is real. That is left solely in your own hands to decide for yourself. If you find that you don't agree with a person then do what the Church of Satan does and ignore their very existence. If on the flip side you find an agreement with a person then pursue it until you find the limit of that agreement then stay within your respective boundaries to honor your shared thoughts.

(In the subsequent years since writing this article my views have changed a bit. With the creation and advent of The Satanic Temple Organization in 2013, less than 2 years after the publication of the original Satanic Testament, the subject of **Legitimate Pseudo Satanism** *is now very prominent, and must be addressed in a brutal manner.)*

The Satanic Drama Queens Parade

If there is one thing that bugs me more than anything else it is a Drama Queen, and what drives me even more nuts than a normal ever day run of the mill drama queen is a Satanic Drama Queen. Drama is everywhere nowadays it seems, and so are the instigators of it. Satanism equally has its fair share of them.

To me a drama queen is a social vampire in that they divert much needed focus from things that may be much more important, simply to gratify their own desire to stir up trouble. Now granted yes, I am quite capable of stirring the pot myself. I always have been that way and will probably remain so for a long time to come. But when I stir the pot, it is not from a simple desire to cause trouble, but to bring focus to a real issue. It could be something small or large, and dependent upon that issue is how bad I get people worked up. Some may call me a bit of a rabble rouser yes, but not in an unhealthy way.

A drama queen, on the other hand, is most certainly not healthy. They seek only to entertain themselves through the causing of discord without returning anything to the people with whom they cause rife. Often times a "Satanic Drama Queen" will consider themselves the self-appointed cops of the Satanic community and will ether criticize or attack other Satanists with whom they choose to take offense. They may even attempt to attack entire organizations. Often times these wretchedly sad individuals or even at times entire organizations themselves, as I have encountered before, have little else to do with their time than criticize others simply to make themselves feel important. They feel the need to validate themselves by making others look wrong, stupid, or bad.

Often times the drama queen will spread scandals or myths about their chosen target in order to bully them into retaliation. They simply feed off of conflict and hot headed remarks, and often resort to twisting a person's words to sound like something they did not say.

I have never had much time for drama queens. I simply have never even made much time for such individuals. Like all I spent my time in the whole drama scene at one time, and found that it detracted from my life more than it gave. Any more when someone wishes to gossip information about someone else to me, I simply tell them that I don't care, and that I don't want to hear it. It often takes me several tries before they get the hint that I'm genuinely not interested in what they have to say. Be it for good or ill, I simply don't give them any encouragement, as that would only feed their desire to cause further trouble. If the info they give is to my benefit then I make a silent mental note of it and act like I don't care, then I deal with what I've learned later at the appropriate time.

Simply put if you must resort to causing unneeded conflict simply to make yourself feel better, then you are a sad individual who simply does not understand the concept of Satanism. Satanists are not loath to causing conflict or trouble when needed. We are the adversaries of a great many things and issues. However, a true Satanist (be them theistic or atheistic), knows when conflict is necessary to create a healthy advancement in a certain topic, group, or individual person. They will use conflict to help the situation grow into something beneficial or to be destroyed if it is really something unhealthy.

Sadly, the Satanic Drama Queen will often work under this same guise, claiming their battle is for the benefit of Satanism, its community, or whatever else they may claim. In truth their conflicts only hold people back and prevent the allowance of growth or expansion of the thing they claim to defend. Often times they simply do not wish to grant the opportunity to the thing they rail against because they don't want that thing to grow, even if it may in the long run benefit them equally. They simply lash out because of their own personal discontent with themselves and their lot in life.

This sort of thing isn't simply isolated to individuals but in some cases an entire organization. Sometimes the groups focus is in causing discontent in others while others may have genuinely good intentions at first but have allowed themselves to be drug down to a lower level and are unable to simply spring back from it. It is one thing to cause drama as a method to meet a larger goal that will help expansion in a real and healthy way. It is quite another thing to do it for simple self-gratification that stems from a love of conflict. If it is conflict you want then join a forum where that is considered acceptable and pick a fight with a person there. No doubt they will be more than happy to stoop to the level you are at and fulfill your needs while satisfying their own at the same time. This sort of conflict is in truth healthy as it provides all parties involved with a fulfillment of their desires.

I have always found it most effective to simply not feed into a drama queens desire to engage in conflict until such a point where they have proven themselves no longer ignorable. It is at this point that should they prove themselves enough of a nuisance, that I will bring my focus on them. I stop and consider everything they have said about me and the types of responses they are getting. Then I will give my response. Often, I will attack with a completely belittling reply while equally pointing out the facts. I make my reply to them so vicious and stunning that they are too shocked to respond adequately. At the same time, I will lay down the facts and the truths to their falsehoods along with enough proof to back it up. Often times I have found that two or three such replies are enough to force them into hiding while they call in their friends to fight for them, which of course only shows the rest of their readers or the people they are showboating for, exactly how cowardly they are.

When faced with extreme vulgarity and deliberately designed counter bullying methods along with a style intended to be shocking yet logical. Most drama queens will turn in on themselves in a self-loathing manner and eventually lose their will to continue for the moment. However, in most cases this is only a temporary solution. When they do their friends, if they have any, will attempt to step in, these lackeys will often attempt to take up the fight but will often be to focused on other things to make anything worthy to continue. Simply leave one final closing post to the subject and then let it rest. You may be focused on this sort of thing for a while but try to not let it dominate your mind otherwise you will fall into the same trap of becoming a drama queen yourself.

One interesting thing is that in the end the only true way to defeat a drama queen is simply moving on without them. Drama queens are bottom feeders. They are ill content with their lot in things and will slander anyone and everyone. When it comes to groups of them, they will often times eventually turn on each other when no other opponents are left around to band together against. Thusly the absolute best way to stop such drama queens is to ignore them totally. Simply continue with what you're doing as though they don't even exist. In doing so you will find their attacks will become increasingly desperate and far reaching as they desperately grab for straws in their attempts to slander you. It is important to them that you respond and feed into their slandering comments with retorts. While a singularly brutal retort can indeed cause them to retreat temporarily, in most instances they will return to hound you in order to feed their desire to cause conflict. Should you simply infuriate and frustrate them by simply ignoring them totally, they will provide you with much amusement.

It is always important to remember that these people are trying very hard to goad you out into the open to meet them in conflict and lower yourself to their level of ignorance and stupidity.

In many cases the Satanic drama queen will have the gift of a silver tongue. They will be able to twist and morph anything that is said into a falsehood designed to make you look bad. It is sad really because if they were not so busy trying to feed their personal addiction to conflict, they might actually have some form of rational thought. Just remember though, that just because they may speak very well and have some smarts to them, they are not intelligent people. If they had any real intelligence to them, they would focus their energies towards more productive goals than besmirching people and thinking themselves the cops of the Satanic world.

You must remember that these people think it is their duty to police Satanism, even though no one has given them the privilege or job to do so. You are free to do as you please even though one person or group says you can't. If things become too intense for you simply allow them to think they have been victorious and take your endeavors else were. They may follow you. This is a hard truth, but let them follow you. It is only more proof that they are weak minded individuals who can't survive without causing conflict or getting their way. Often the two are combined.

Should they pursue you continually simply ignore them. Let them see what you're doing but don't allow them to participate. Be vigilant to their attempts at intrusion and guard yourself from them. Let them be persistent and laugh at their ineptitude as they rail against you to no avail. Before they know it, people will no longer care to listen to them and they will be left to the way side by those who at one time would grant them an ear.

But once you've defeated one drama queen another will invariably take its place. This is the hard truth of drama queens of any sort. There is an infinite supply of them. I find the Church of Satan has taken a sound approach to this type of social vampire. They simply ignore them all and let them say what they please. The truth of the matter is that while a Drama queen will have their circle of friends who will blindly agree and goad them on and feed them encouragements. There will be equally just as many people who will agree with you even if you say nothing. There are times when a person's silence can speak volumes louder than words. And where Drama queens are concerned, it pays to be the strong silent type.

Reality and What is Real

When we step outside our doors to go to work, we see things around us. This is the world we all live in. It is substantial and real. This is our reality. But is it really real? Or is this just a dream of ours. This is what is called Perceptive Reality, it is the world we perceive to be real and how we perceive it. What might be real to one person might not be real to another. It all depends on each person Perspective Reality in relation to their Perceptive Reality, and how the two relate to each other in the individual's mind. This goes very heavily for religion and is why I say that no one form of Satanic worship is truly incorrect as long as it can still be called "Satanism" by adhering to the basic fundamentals of the Satanic religion.

The Satanic Community has many different twists to the same religion. Some are more pronounced than others. It can be said that one could look at two forms of Satanism and see the same exact rituals and basic tenants and goals, but one might perceive that Satan is in fact a very real entity while the other simply sees him as a metaphorical figure. Both forms of Satanic practice, though practically identical to each other, could then be seen as correct because they are the same thing except in their Perceptive Realities.

Perception is important to a Religion as well as to people. We all perceive something unique to ourselves. This is why people change or convert to a religion. Something about that religion fits into their perception of the world around them.

We are the ones who make and destroy gods and ethereal beings. If we perceive that the Devil is real then to us, he is. And if a group people all perceive the same thing as being real then it is real and can even manifest to affect others. This is called Suggestive Reality. It can be done with making a simple comment and implanting a notion into some one's brain such as done in Covert Hypnosis or by influencing them through other means. One could simply say to a person the following statement to achieve Suggestive Reality.

"Now, I want you to for a moment to stop and contemplate your personal religious beliefs. Are they in fact true and correct? Think about all the provable facts that say that what you believe is wrong. Stop and question your god if he is real and ask him to prove it right now. Nothing will happen."

I have just subjected you to "Suggested Reality". If you just did what I said even for a second you just submitted to a suggested reality. I suggested you question your religion and any deities you may have and ask them to prove themselves right in that instant. I then said that nothing will happen, and no doubt no proof came to you of their existence. No miracle or apparition or anything made its self-known or appeared. Why? Because I first got you to question them. By questioning your own faith, you had doubt in its working. I made the suggestion that nothing would happen and nothing did more than likely. I essentially altered your Perceptive and Perspective Realities by Suggesting my own to you in such a way that you subconsciously accepted it as fact.

Don't be mad, we all do this on a regular basis to other people. We do it almost every day without even knowing we do it. I just simply brought your attention to it.

It is what is called covert or conversational hypnosis. It is simply making a series of simple statements that make sense to a person to bring them to a single idea that they think is their own but is in fact yours. One could in effect convince a person to willingly hand you money or to convert to a new religion with this method of speaking.

By using conversational hypnosis, we often influence and affect other peoples' perspective reality. In some cases, we alter it completely. This is often the case when someone chooses to convert to a new religion. They have found something that has altered their perspective reality so profoundly that they are compelled to change. This is done by first making a simple suggestion that in turn changes their perspective on something that then alters the way they perceive their chosen religion. I.E., it is now wrong and doesn't work. They are then forced to change faiths to suit their new perspective.

But Satanism doesn't do this at all initially. Most Satanists fist off must already see things from a specific stand point to begin with. They are then presented often with the views of Satanism that for the most part already agree with their way of thinking. The choice is then left up to them if they want to call them self-something that they already are or to continue without the title. It is only very rarely that one converts from another religion to Satanism. Often times one first encounters Satanism through the Satanic Bible. LaVey in the book makes it very clear that only people who already think in the basic manner that the book outlines are true Satanists. He also makes it clear that he doesn't want people to simply convert over to his way of thinking. Though this does at times happen it makes it very rare with Satanism.

But where the alterations to the Satanists perceptions occur is when they meet other Satanists. Everyone takes a slightly different twist on the same idea. Some take a more radical twist than others. As such, different types of Satanism are born. Each of these types offer brotherhood and claim to be correct while stating that the others are wrong. The simple truth is that they are all correct and can all be called Satanism, so long as they adhere to the basic tenants of Satanism. Each style is correct in the way that they are a style that best suits the practitioner. There is nothing wrong in believing that the Devil is real if that is what works for you. This is your perspective realty, use it and work. And should something alter it where it no long works, then change it to fit your new reality.

Remember though that you should never try to force yourself to believe in something that doesn't automatically fit into your current perception and perspective on things. If you are a Christian trained to think god is all that, you should not try to perform in a Satanic ritual that exonerates the very being you're taught is the enemy unless in your perspective god and Satan are one in the same being and your simply paying respect to both sides of the same coin.

Similarly, if you're a Buddhist and hate violence. You should not then try to make a nuclear bomb and become a terrorist. One should never ever try to make themselves fit into their religious views if it contradicts that in which they already believe. They should instead find a religion that already fits into their current way of thinking. That way the religion doesn't need to try to teach the practitioner anything that they don't already agree with automatically and the person can easily and painlessly fit into their religion without any fuss. Anything else simply creates problems and conflicts with in the practitioner.

If a Satanist perceives that Satan is real, then he is to that individual. If the Satanist perceives, however, that Satan is nothing more than a simple metaphor for their own internal makeup, then this too is real for that person. Both types of Satanists can in fact feed off of each other during a ritual and benefit. The true believer can use the non-believer as a source of self-reliant energy or battery, while the nonbeliever can subsequently use the other as a focal point to heighten their experience with the ritual to new heights. Both benefit from each other, the non-believer simply allows the true believer to influence his Perceptive reality with his exuberance in the ritual, which in turn he can then get into the ritual even more to help egg on the true believer even further. This can continue to go on back and forth until the end of the ritual. By then both participants can then walk out of the ritual feeling as light-hearted and giddy as school kids.

This is how suggestive reality works in Satanism as well as other religions that allow such things. I have seen and heard of normally somber nuns and priests walk into an exuberant religious service of a different religion or denomination and get caught up in the moment by the other participants. It isn't until later on after things have died down that the concept that they are of different denominations or even of two totally different religions even occur. Perhaps the greatest example I have ever seen of this was at a Wiccan ritual I attended a few years back at a non-denominational Universalist church.

During the ritual women were allowed to get up and join hands and dance and sing around the alter. Unbeknown to most of the attending group was the fact that a Roman Catholic nun was also present. In fact, she was not only a nun but the mother superior of a local convent. The nun who had been watching in silence during the ritual had gotten so caught up in the moment by the simple actions of honoring the feminine spirit she got up and joined the other women around the alter much to everyone's surprise at her simple presence. No one said a word and they never stopped dancing. The result was a sudden increase in the level of energy in the air and a pleasant feeling of unity. I simply sat back with those who had decided to watch and smiled at this turn of events and enjoyed the rest of the ritual quietly. After words I approached the older woman and asked her what made her decide to attend a Wiccan ritual. I kept the fact that I was a Satanist quiet to her as I didn't want to startle her or frighten her into changing back to any old views she might have now shed about witches.

    She told me that she had come to originally spread the word of god. But upon gaining entrance to the service a strange feeling of peace came over her and over the course of the ritual she had gotten the urge to get up and dance with the rest of the women. The end result was a simple shedding of old thoughts that witches were evil and of the Devil. Naturally I smiled at this, and kept my mouth shut as to who I was, and left her with her new found thoughts. I don't know what ever happened to the old woman after that but I have heard that she has been spotted at several other rituals since then.

    She originally came to cause trouble and try to change others, but left with herself changed instead and with a lot of new and interesting friends. This is a good example of a person's perception being altered by suggestion. It was probably already rooted in her subconscious that she was disgruntled with women taking a back seat in Christendom. To her, women had been subverted for so long that when she saw for the first time that the feminine figure was being honored, she was compelled to change her point of view.

Reality is what we make it. It is all part of our perception and perspective. It is also very important to note these things when we are conducting ourselves in a religious service, or trying to find a religion that suits us. If something does not conform to how we see things we tend to cast it aside or rail against it. But when we find something that fits into our own reality, we adopt it.

We perceive our own individual realities. We are the makers and destroyers of the gods according to our own chosen faith and perspective. Therefore, reality is whatever you chose to make it. It is whatever you chose to accept into your own world, and whatever is not is brought to scrutinizing questioning. This is only human nature, and should be encouraged, not denied.

The Satanic Parent

As any parent will tell you there is no true instruction book on how to raise your kids. Each family is different, as are children. But few are more different in the public's eye than the Satanic family. In this day and age, we are criticized for every detail, especially when children are involved.

Like children being raised in other households, your kids will more than likely follow the examples you provide and become Satanists themselves. Though this is not always the case it is the common outcome.

Many Satanic families tend to run a gauntlet of public opinion. We are looked at as evil ourselves and so will any child you have once it is known that you're "in league with the devil". You may even find child services knocking on your door with some trumped up excuse to try and take away your kids. Though the age of outright witch hunts are long over, and legally the law protects your religious rites, some folks will still try to find ways to perform a witch hunt. Though we no longer worry about getting poked with hot pokers, to a parent that would be a boon blessing compared to losing custody of one's child and fighting it out in the courts.

Thusly the Satanic parent must be thrice as careful as the normal parent and pose as a formidable figure to come after legally. Most Satanic families will not be open

about their religious beliefs. This naturally cuts some of the risks down. But what about bringing up your children? How does one do that as they see fit without fear.
Raising your children should never be done with fear. Though I am a stringent supporter of corporal punishment, I understand that there is a fine line between a spanking and a beating. You must find ways to discipline your child where they will understand the reasoning and fear the punishment but not fear you.

To the child you must stand as a monolith of wisdom and friendship, but also of strength and discipline. To achieve this one must consider what they want to teach their kids. Your child should always look at you like you were a super hero. Good and just, but don't piss you off or some heads are going to get cracked.

Raising a child in a Satanic home is just like raising a kid in a Christian home. The difference is only that instead of honoring a deity you're teaching them to honor themselves. If you want the kiddo to come out as a Satanist, then there are some things you'll need to do.

1. Make fun activities tailored to your child that are Satanic in nature. Halloween is always one of a kid's favorite times of year. With Satanism they get to sample that every day, so make it fun.
2. Teach them about Satanism throughout their entire upbringing in a safe and healthy manner. Your lessons will be important. Don't neglect them. A child learns the most from mom and dad in the first ten years of their life. If they are taught right, they will continue to learn from them until adulthood.
3. Allow them to design their own rituals as well as involve them in some of your own as long as they are child friendly. It doesn't go well if your rituals scare

the kiddo. As time goes on, they can be introduced to some of the darker rituals.
4. Don't try to force them to be a Satanist. I have always said that the person chooses their religion and makes it conform to them, not the other way around. Teach your child as much as you can about other religions and let them make their own choice. If they decide to try a different religious path, let them. Support them in their choice. This will help ensure the lessons you've taught them, and they will probably find some faults with their temporary religion and revert back to your teachings.

Remember though, you'll be scrutinized and criticized for how you raise your child. So be ever vigilant and watchful for any trouble. Also beware of yourself. There is a very fine line between discipline and abuse. Make sure you don't cross it.
To a child Mother is always God, and Daddy is always their champion.

The Satanic Confliction

For a long while now I have often seen many different Satanic organizations arguing and fighting, and over what? A difference in personal opinions on how to practice Satanism? Or simply because one group likes to cause trouble or hates the leader of another group? Who knows but it happens a lot and it is rather annoying?

    I look at this and often shake my head. People have often claimed that I preach "Satanic unity". This is far from the truth. Competition and disagreements are needed if Satanism is to progress in a healthy manner. But not when it means being held back. Too much infighting is not healthy, and in the end, it often becomes self-destructive. We often hear of Christian groups bickering and condemning each other, but what we don't see is them ripping each other apart like what we see in Satanism. Except maybe in Northern Ireland. They don't like each other but they tolerate one another. This is what I look for in groups. Not unity, but simple tolerance. So why does infighting exist in Satanism and what purpose does it serve? In my opinion infighting and division in Satanism exists because of a simple reason - because Satanism, or the various groups and organizations within the religion of Satanism are composed of PEOPLE.

    It doesn't really matter if it's a sect, group, tribe, religion, family, company, business, high school, sports team, nation, or group. They all have one basic fundamental common denominator - PEOPLE. Where there are people there is human nature, and these group associations and or social orders are only a means through which that human nature expresses itself. Satanism is not any different. It's composed of people. Each Satanist gravitates to others of like mind and quality. And through these groups/sects our primal human nature "bleeds" through and expresses itself. So, we end up with rivalries, competition, and chest beatings, pissing contests and whatever.

    People are like a tiger's stripe pattern, no two are totally alike, or at least that's how it should be. Each person is unique, with their own ideas, opinions, convictions, insights, and perspectives. All which are formed by a unique level of education, understandings, and ability to comprehend or extract meaning from abstract thought.

People also gravitate towards others that resonate with their own mentality. "Birds of a feather flock together." A skeptical atheist would rather associate with other skeptical atheists then a theistic-religionist, and vice versa.

    This is because there is less tension or resistance, or less confrontation, and perhaps more validation of thoughts and beliefs when like minds associate together. A theistic-religionist who associates or hangs out with a group of hardcore atheists would feel out of place or not in a proper environment conducive to his or her belief structure and or frame of mind. This in turn gives rise to groups, associations, sects which develop a group mentality/identity that resonates with the individual people that composes it. I.E., a group of cheerleaders will most likely have a cheerleader's quality; a group or sect of Mahayana Buddhists will have a Mahayana Buddhist quality distinct from say a group of Zen Buddhists.

    Another quality of people; or more accurately - the human animal, is that people are competitive and territorial. By territory I mean both physical-land territory and psychological territory. When one person has a good idea, other humans tend to get upset because that good idea infringes on their personal agendas or that they didn't think of it first.

The simple truth is that almost all Satanic organizations are the same and almost all have at some point been simple branch offs of the Church of Satan or a group that similarly branched away from them. These organizations ether get their start as a grotto of the CoS or subgroup, or they are founded by members who left the CoS for their own reasons. Two such organizations are the Temple of Set, and the First Satanic Church.

It is because of these branching groups the Church of Satan has become competitive for reasons other than human nature - business. An organization like the CoS where most of its funding is from its $200 membership fees, and book sales, can't afford to endorse and be friendly with other groups of Satanists... especially the free kind. But they don't go around starting bitch fights with them out rightly over stupid stuff. Instead, they tend to simply tolerate and ignore other groups. It is only on the rare occasion that a member will take actual offense to these lesser or branching groups and fire off a few out right attacks.

Other groups such as the ONA don't want to get along with anybody because they have agendas to which the other groups would thwart or not understand. This is mainly because of their extreme tactics that often boarder on terrorism and fascism.

Humanity has always been divided. Even in a homogeneous nation, there still exists division, competition, and rivalry of some sort. It's how nature works to get the best genetics to the top of the pile. Because humanity has always been divided, human religion or associations will also be divided. Satanism is no different. In fact, most of Satanisms teaches its adherents to keep a strong sense of uniqueness and self-identity. This creates a competitive atmosphere. This, however, does not mean that Satanism should be divided into warring cells and groups. Such behavior though at times is healthy, can be destructive and devastating if allowed to continue for too long. It's not stupid for Satanism to be divided; it is healthy to be competitive. It is however, stupid to let that competitive nature override sensibility, when there is a common goal worth reaching for.

It's easy to think pretty thoughts about getting along and loving each other; and its easy to talk about getting along. It's impossible however, to undo millions of years of evolution to please the whims of a priest of some church. Would nature even take notice of such a person? Probably not. I say, save the love thy neighbor talk for the Christians. You don't have to like one another, just simply tolerate each other enough to accomplish a unified goal.

Some of us, like myself, are proud to be human. I am proud to be competitive. I hate and disagree like most normal people do. I like being an individual to a certain extent, and I like associating with others that think, compete, and hate like me. It's the "Darwinian Struggle." Weak people, and weak groups, like weak tribes, weak nations, are annihilated or eventually are exploited into insignificance and extinction, or simply absorbed by the stronger forces. Much like how the Roman Empire expanded and solidified its power basis. But like the Roman Empire that crumbled politically and militaristically because of infighting, so will Satanism if it is allowed to continue on for too long. Whining and crying doesn't do shit to stop this eventual destruction. Only affirmative action towards simple tolerance can prevent such destruction. That affirmative action is not total unification but simple tolerance. How do you think the Christians have held on for so many years? They are certainly not unified, but they tolerate each other enough to do what needs to get done.

There was a time during the Cambrian period of life hereafter single celled organisms had learned to form multicultural "communities" that an explosion of creativity happened. Things during this period of evolution just went crazy. Species took every possible form and shape... there were arms races... and that life and ambitious evolutionary creativity heaved its way onto land.

It's from this period of experimentation, creativity, and competition, that Nature eventually picked the best design to express herself in. From all the millions of radical forms that came from the Cambrian explosion, only a handful became evolutions crown jewels - streamline bodies and fins for aquatic animals, four legs for most land animals, and a beautiful simple form for Humanity.

Anton LaVey perhaps can be seen as the initiator of a "Satanic Cambrian Explosion" which we are now witnessing in all its glory. All these groups and outer forms that have come and gone for the last forty years. All maybe different externally, much like how each organism seems different in form; but beneath there is one life force. Beneath the many rival and competing forms of Satanism, is a dark force struggling to evolve into the best form through which it will be able to express its highest potential. In a nut shell all forms of Satanism are, at their core, the same. We see the development of new ideas and groups, each conducting their own arms race for religious rituals and theology. And all of it is fueled by this same primal dark force we call Satan.

What we know of as "Satanism" is right now in its "Cambrian Explosion" stage. It can go in any direction we so choose for it. If the cutthroat actions of some are allowed to continue, we could very well see the ultimate annihilation of a fundamentally sound religion. The conservative thought process of a single class or group coming into ultimate power and dominating all of Satanism, leaving little to no room for the creativity of other unique individual groups, would be disastrous for the Satanic religion. If a single solitary organization were to totally dominate Satanism with an iron hand, we would end up with no new thoughts or ideas. And that single group or organization would be just like the Christians Roman Catholic church.

    But on the flip side of the coin, if we were to stop stabbing each other in the backs and simply say "Ok I hate your guts, but we have to work together on this." We might actually end up seeing the birth of a new religious nation come to fruition. Perhaps a Satanic version of the Vatican City could possibly be built. That would be an interesting advancement.

    Should a single Satanic organization come to total power, eventually it would splinter off into new groups or cells and we would find ourselves right back at this point again one day. Possibly after years of repression and bloodshed in which Satanism experiences its own dark ages. The only difference would be instead of Christians running the show it would Satanists.

    Satanism does not need to unify. It should not unify. The multiplex of different styles grants a much needed free choosing ground for the individual. We have achieved these differing forms of Satanism without going through a long drawn out bloody history. The only thing left for us now to do in order to achieve our goals in Satanism, is to simply get along enough not to kill each other and combine our resources to achieve our goals. This doesn't mean that we have to like one another, just deal with each other.

Satanic Ritual Sex

It is no mystery that one of the main appeals of Satanism to most people is the aspect of sex. Ether they think there will be huge orgies (which occasionally there are indeed), or they think it will make them mysteriously attractive (which of course it can, but not without work.)

It has only been recently that the world has seen its first full-fledged Satanic porno "Club Satan the Witches Sabbath". An interesting though low budget film that is extremely aggressive and to many offensive, which of course was the whole idea behind the movie. It brings about the notion of what sex in the ritual chamber should be like. Up until now nude alters and masturbation have been the only openly admitted sexual act to ever transpire during a Satanic ritual. There are, however, those rare occasions that go unmentioned where sex becomes a very prevalent theme, and even full blown orgies may on occasion transpire. This, however, is often ardently denied by most people involved because of the want to paint a more appealing face on Satanism. However, Satanism is about cutting loose one's prior inhibitions, and doing things that many may feel normally inappropriate in an appropriate setting.

There is nothing inappropriate about sex. And should it be considered acceptable by one's group to perform sex during a ritual then by all means it should be done. During the ritual of stifling air, a man and a woman are placed into a coffin together with the intent of having sex. Often these two people have no personal relationship with each other besides being in the same coven or grotto. They may even be complete enemies outside the group and hate each other violently, but during this moment they do the dirty like passionate lovers only a few feet away and in albeit complete plain sight of the entire congregation.

  Sexual intercourse during certain rituals should be encouraged, not only between actual couples but between non-couples. The simple act of swinging in such a situation is in fact extremely stimulating to all parties involved. While some enjoy participating others may only choose to sit back and watch. The entire room should have a completely relaxed feeling to it where this sort of thing is completely normal and enticing to all.

  A woman entering into such a group should enter every ritual fully prepared and even wanting to be taken by or to take every, and any, member of the group at any possible moment. She should enter the chamber already dripping wet from the pure excitement of not knowing what will happen.

  The same should go for any man in the same instance. He equally should be excited by the same prospect and enter into the ritual with a full erection ready and waiting to enter the soft warmth of any receptive member of the group. (This of course depends on their personal sexual orientation.)

  No members of the group should feel disgusted in any way by any actions others may choose to perform. If you are a straight man but other members are gay, don't look away but watch in fixation and delight, but remember you are not ever forced to take part. If you are or feel you are being forced to perform any sexual act that you personally don't wish to do then don't do it and get out of the situation, even if that means leaving the group all together. One should never be forced to have sex with any one they don't desire it with, and to do so stands against the rule of waiting for the mating signal. Not waiting for a mating signal is, and should always be considered as rape.

During the years of Satanic Panic, many supposed Satanic ritual abuse victims came forth with tall tales of being forced to perform sexual acts during certain rituals, or being used as baby making machines for ritualistic child sacrifices. These of course are complete flights of fancy designed to scare people away from Satanism. In short, their tales are, for the most part, unfounded and untrue. While ritual sex does at times occur, it is always between consenting adults who are both willing and equally eager to perform their role in the ritual. The myth of unwilling women snatched off the streets and forced into Satanic cults is just that, a myth.

Ritual sex is about expressing one's desires and indulging in them. In a situation where one might be "Ritualistically Raped", it is in fact a mock rape and the "victim" is of course a consenting participant who is only acting but is in truth enjoying herself. Such situations usually have safe/panic words or signals that can be given to halt the act if at any time the "victim" genuinely feels panicked or unsafe. Often these words are so out of place, and even comical that the would be "rapist/s" will often times halt out of pure laughter, thusly maintaining the light relaxed mood of the group so that no ill feelings will pervade after the fact.

Such rituals are normally done with a lot of preparation and with safety in thought. Other times sexual acts may simply occur out of pure emotional response. Whichever is the case; it should not be frowned upon but encouraged and endorsed.

Ritual Sacrifice

The common position and argument against Satanists, is that we sacrifice people in our rituals. I tend to laugh whole-heartedly at this notion and set about correcting the person whenever someone has said such a thing or asked about it.

While there are indeed times when a sacrifice is performed, it is never a human, and almost never an animal either for that matter. Why, you might ask, is this the case? Well, it serves little to no real purpose at all to kill something to perform a ritual. Not to mention that taking the life of another being is not even a sacrifice at all unless you feel deeply about the person or animal, in which case you would not want to harm such a person or animal.

A sacrifice is meant as an offering of something of importance to the celebrant. This is in most cases something personal. In the case where blood is needed, it is the celebrants' blood that is shed, not that of some innocent person or animal. Only when a person offers the use of their blood willingly and of their own free will is it used. The wound inflicted is in all cases never fatal, often it is a simple cut on the hand or something of that degree.

Often times it is not even blood used in a ritual. Most times the celebrant will simply step into a quiet corner of the ritual chamber and masturbate. The energy attained by sexual pleasure will in most cases far exceed that of physical pain. If the rituals energy is going strong enough the person may simply orgasm on their own without any need for self-stimulation.

Other common sacrifices are personal items. An item that the celebrant of the ritual feels deeply connected to given up freely is more meaningful than the taking of a life. This could be a picture of someone or something or an object like an article of clothes or simple piece of jewelry. The emotional attachment to this object must be strong to make it a worthy sacrifice, otherwise it is one simply making an offering of some unwanted item and it holds little true value.

As I said before, a sacrifice is almost never that of an animal. The truth is that it isn't even a real sacrifice but more of a simple offering that appeases the congregation on a psychological level. This is not a practice that I personally take part in as I often feel no need for it; however, others at times do. Personally, I am of the opinion that the slaughter of an animal in this nature is a waist unless one has the desire to enhance the ritual's feel and then use the animal has part of a celebratory feast. To this end any animal that is bought with the intent of being used as food and would have been sent to slaughter anyways is perfectly fine. But even then, in my opinion it still serves no purpose to let the animal suffer or be mistreated.

If you want to use the death of an animal in your ritual or rite there are some guide lines to follow. No, your neighbor's cat won't do.

1. The animal should be purchased from a slaughter house or be ready to be sent to one. It is from this point that you can be assured that the animal is going to be killed anyways.

2. Make sure the animal has been given all the veterinary care it needs and is free of any diseases.
3. Make certain that all participants are in agreement that the animal will be used for food. This is in accordance with LaVey's Tenth Rule of the Earth. Equally, don't waste the animal's parts. Use them to their fullest potential. Bones can be used to make jewelry or knife hilts, skulls may be saved for art or decoration or scientific purpose, skin and fur, especially wool, can be used to make cloths or blankets. Even the animal's ligaments, sinew, and tendons can be used if one knows what they're doing.
4. Don't mistreat the animal. It serves little purpose to abuse the poor creature. In truth you should seek to connect with it as much as possible if you intend on it being a legitimate sacrifice. Give it a bath and feed it well. The animals last days should be spent in comfort not fear.
5. When the time comes, sedate the animal and restrain its legs. Again, the animal should not die in fear or pain. This serves no purpose other than to provide morbid entertainment for the cruel of heart. Such people don't have any reason to be a part of Satanism. To the contrary the animal should be made even more comfortable just prior to the fatal blow. Congregants should surround the creature and comfort it with gentle touches and soothing words.
6. The fatal strike should be swift and sure. Two blows should be delivered. The first to the animals' throat severing the major blood vessels and wind pipe as quickly as possible. The second should pass smoothly between the ribs to pierce the heart. Death should come in less than a minute. As the animal dies participants should continue comforting it and even give it thanks for its life as in the Native American traditions should they see fit.

It should be noted that animals used in this style should always be common animals used as food such as sheep, pigs, goats, etc. However, others may be used. Animals such as deer or cows can be used too, though this comes with its own set of problems. Never should dogs or cats or common pet animals be used. Many people see these creatures as household friends and family. In the craft a dog or cat is often kept as a form of familiar. This negates them as a suitable food source.

Remember if it is only blood that is needed for a ritual then use your own as it will have the most potency, magically speaking. Don't be a coward and forcefully take the blood of another creature or person that is unwilling and not intended for food. A sacrifice should have meaning to it. If it has meaning through a personal connection to you then it is all the more worthy and will be very potent as it will not be given up lightly. If it has no meaning then it will only be a waste and will have no power. Should you absolutely need to take the life of an animal then follow the guide lines above, otherwise you will be no more than performing an act of empty cruelty and should be detested by any person whose path you cross.

Satanic Revenge

Vengeance, is a dish best served cold. These words ring true to more people than one may know, but none more so than to a Satanist. Because Satanism encourages all of the seven deadly sins, only a Satanist, a true one, can truly revel in the sublime ecstasy that is revenge. And only a true Satanist can perform it as viciously and effectively as any military exorcise.

The vengeance of a Satanist is truly a terrible thing to behold, but only such a vengeance like that of Satanic revenge be equally considered beautiful in the same horrifying sense. This is because only a true Satanist can nurture his hatred for another human being to a raging inferno of the purest hell fire within him. Hatred that burns so intensely that it is cold enough to freeze the soul.

One should never let a wrong perpetrated by another go unpunished. To do so is not healthy. It is only healthy to lovingly kindle that flame of pure hate for the person to the point of complete consumption and then when the time is right, to let it burst forth emptying the heart of all the anguish and suffering it used to build and that of the original injury. Truly by building that internal flame, one may become healed without realizing it. One could build their flames of hate so strong that the original injury may be forgotten and mended. Then the fire of hate can turn to the fires of joy as the person, if they have realized their fortune, can burst out laughing and spill their hate in curses on their enemy and walk away a completely free person of all the hurt that person caused.

This is the very nature of wrath and hate. This is how a Satanist takes their personal revenge when they find themselves with a vendetta that needs to be paid. For while the flames of hatred for that perpetrator of injury upon us can burn ever so hot, when revenge is taken on them it is cold beyond mercy, regret, anguish, or guilt.

A Satanist should there for let his hate build and use it as a motivator. He should set his goals as such as to take his personal revenge out on his tormentors. His every action through life should be directed towards infuriating them beyond reason, and to the point in which they are left sputtering their personal disbelief at their one time victim rising above them. (Be it socially or physically.)

There are many ways one can take revenge on a person. The methodology depends on the nature of the crime and the injury that has been perpetrated on them. For example, the battered woman who goes and secretly learns how to defend herself from an abusive husband, to whom she then in turn rebels viciously against and pummels him to near death. Or the small time organizational leader who struggles against all odds to bring his ideas to the people or religion he so cares for, but is accosted without mercy by a few others who don't want him to succeed. His vengeance should then be to beat them out at their own game and actually do what they didn't think he could. Perhaps he should write a book stating his ideas.

People have been taking revenge on others for many centuries. Pretty much since the dawn of time. We have almost got it down to an art form. It could be as simple as finding the person and dumping an exquisitely cold bucket of water on them, or as terrible as to render their life completely pointless and empty that they decide to go and end it themselves. What greater revenge than to make a person realize how worthless their entire life has been, how pathetic they really are? To see that last glimmer of hope, flicker out of their eyes. And to know that no matter what they do from that moment on, they can never touch you again.

Vengeance should be brooded on, plotted and planned to absolute perfection. It should never be done half-assed. One should learn every trick they will need even if it means that for the moment their tormentor is allowed to think they are victorious. The higher the pedestal they place themselves on, the greater the fall they will have once you decide to reap you revenge.

Often the best revenge is not the swift one; but a slow creeping dread that sneaks unnoticed by your victim until it is too late to do anything about it. It should be like a game of chess that he or she does not know that they are playing. You silently move your pieces into position without rousing their suspicion. Then when the time is right, check mate!

It should be done in the most brutalizing manner you can contrive that will deliver the ultimate blow. They should be brought brutally to their very knees by you even if no physical harm is done to them. They should suffer a complete psychological crumbling of their world.

It is actually best if they hate you as much as you them. They should wish upon you all the woe that you are about to inflict upon them. They should be thusly cut off from any support or aid that may or may not come to their side. Severed from it like an amputated limb. They should find themselves alone. Totally and utterly alone.

And if you can singlehandedly reap your revenge with little or no support, then so much the better because it will show them how much weaker than you, they really are. That in a one on one game you are in truth better than they ever will be, or can ever dream of becoming.

But what does one do when such revenge is taken and done with? What is it they have left? They should look at what they did to get there. The things they accomplished and the possibilities they may have opened for themselves along the way. Just because their vengeance has been sowed and reaped does not mean that it is over totally. It is from their endeavors and hard work that they may now with a light heart enjoy the fruits of their labors while they sit back and watch their once would be tormentors struggle like worms on a hook. Perhaps this former tormentor may try to lash out again only to find that they are impotently flinging themselves at something so very out of their reach and are providing great amounts of mirth and derisive laughter.

The options are innumerable to count. But one thing is for certain. After vengeance is served, and if served properly, its rewards taste sweeter than the sweetest wine.

Over Educated Idiots

In all the years I have been a Satanist one thing that often makes me laugh at my fellow Satanists is their misguided insistence on using massive and complicated words to make themselves sound impressive and intellectual. Granted there are indeed times when I too have used a large or complicated word to express myself, but unlike my contemporaries, I don't try to do it all the time.

In almost every article or text I read by some of these supposedly super smart leaders or members of Satanism I tend to run across several of these words. These words are often so obscure and out of the way that until I read that paper or article, I had never heard it used before and naturally I am sent reaching for my dictionary or on some fantastic online adventure trying to find its meaning. This of course, no doubt, is the intent of the person besides trying to make themselves look smarter than what they really are, as most of the time I find that the complicated word has little more intellectual meaning than a few extra words or more common lingo could have explained even better than the singularly complex word could have.

This is equally compounded by the fact that the said person's articles are in general a feeble attempt at trying to sound smart and based on a subject the person has little to no real understanding on.

This is, unfortunately, an epidemic that should be addressed as more and more would be Satanic "leaders" come crawling from the wood work spouting of their idiotic waste trying to pass it off as insight.

I have also noticed this in almost all walks of life as it is commonly considered that if a person has knowledge of some complex words that they are to be considered an authority on a particular subject. This not only pertains to Satanism but to medical doctors, politicians, and almost any one in any sort of position to speak articulately. I can't tell you how many times I've sat in a doctor's presence as he spouted off in his complicated medical jargon mine or someone else's problems only to get confused looks until I boiled it down to laymen terms. Often then I'm greeted by the doctor's pissed off looks because I just said the exact same thing he did without confusing the person.

The purpose of speaking in large complicated terms is only to confuse people so that they will look at you as more of an authority on the subject and will turn to you to get their confusion clarified. In the medical field this is also a tactic to scare people into thinking the worst of a problem so they will spend the most to get it fixed. A case and point on this, was the case of a friend's grandmother several years ago.

She had been suffering from an extreme pain in her neck and shoulder for several days and finally decided to go to the ER about. She had tried taking pain medications and muscle relaxing medications to no effect and enough was enough. I naturally went with as the woman was a good friend of mine as well. We sat for close to five hours in the exam room before the doctor finally came and checked her. Then he left for another two hours before coming back and spouted off this line of bull.

"You have a case of constricted capillaries in you muscle tissue fibers which is causing your neck and shoulder muscles to harden and apply pressure to the nerves surrounding them." To which he got confused and frightened looks from my friend's grandmother, and the freak actually smiled at this. Until I piped up and said, "So what you're saying, doc, is she has got a really bad knot in the muscle next to her shoulder blade and you're going to directly inject a muscle relaxant into it to make it go away." He dropped the dumb smile and responded. "Well, no shit!" and stormed away.

Five minutes later a nurse came in gave her the shot and told us to go home. Not only did I clarify the doctor's jargon into a simple to understand sentence, but I also told her the treatment that would follow in the same sentence. This is just one example of the over educated idiot. No doubt had I not said anything he would have had us in there for several more hours or admitted my friend's grandmother simply to make an extra buck.

You'll encounter these fools almost everywhere. They try to confuse issues by making them sound bigger than they really are. This is a tactic that I see more and more in Satanism. Often the articles that have such an overabundance of complex terms and words in them are, in truth, the most pointless and meaningless ones out there. But by making something sound big and complex, they then suddenly take on this life changing feel that has some sort of cosmic magnitude or weight to it. However, the truth is that the article or what not is completely pointless and has no real impact on your life except that moment when you're reading it. It will not change how you go about something or how you look at the world. Before then you had no real conscious thought about it one way or another, and after that you will probably forget completely all about it.

Here's a challenge for you, try to sound smart without over complicating something. It's in my opinion that all the most life changing articles or books or sudden insights in to real cosmic wisdom, needs no sprucing up. They are the simplest things to understand. Often, they need no big complex words or at the very least only require one or two where no other word or description will fit. They don't try to sound smart or over blown but simply state the facts as they stand.

It is on this premise that LaVey wrote his Satanic Bible that for over forty years has stood as a testament to his cold hard wisdom. This is his premise for "undefiled wisdom". Something that is pure and simple to understand and often so common in its basis that many people have forgotten it.

Consider for a moment this very book. Have you understood all that I have said in it? Did you glean some form of life changing thought or epiphany from it? Or have you simply become more aware of some things that were always there to be seen? Perhaps all you have accomplished is putting some extra cash in my pocket. But in doing this, have I at any point tried to make myself sound smarter than what I really am? The answer is no.

Here is the point. Society as a whole is focused on being intelligent. Anymore, we set our standards to the point of ridiculousness. Hell, anymore you can't even flip burgers at your local McDonald's without having to have some sort of degree that says your smart enough to do so. We are so focused on book smarts that we forget about common intelligence. You can learn all that the world has to offer from a text book, but you won't really understand it until you go out and actually do it. Truth be told some of the most intelligent people I have met in the world have never even seen the inside of a collage classroom or even graduated from high school. With the current state of our educational system, that doesn't surprise me, and that lack of surprise is what actually surprises me. Anymore, a person learns more on their own than in a classroom, but it is the ones who sit in a classroom that get all the credit, even if they didn't learn shit but have the paper saying that they did.

These Over Educated Idiots have become the staple point of our modern society. They often hold little to no original thought of their own but quote those men and women who went out and did it or had the original thought, and then claim the praise for themselves. And now look at some of the greatest minds in history.

Einstein, for example, couldn't spell his own name or figure out how to tie his own shoes or even how to close a set of curtains, trying to button his shirt would often result in his most horrifying fits of frustration. But when it came to mathematics, he was a genius. Leonardo Da Vinci never attended any universities or schools but was one of the singularly most intelligent people in the world.

Why is it that these men who, in our day and age, would either be considered idiots or would not have the credentials to back themselves up, are thought of as some of the smartest men in history? It's because they didn't learn from a classroom, but by going out and finding things out for themselves. Einstein loved boating and found math easy. He learned his best trades on his own because he loved them which made him an authority on them. Da Vinci is the same deal only he loved art, literature and anatomy. He went out of his way to learn these things on his own.

Nowadays, learning something on your own seldom cuts the buck, even if you have put the time and effort into knowing more about it than those buffoons who graduated from some college in the same field.

These idiots seldom step out of the classroom in their respective fields. And when they do, they seldom actually know much of anything helpful or new.

Book smarts are good; however, experience is better. You could study the behavior of bears from a book all day long and know their general anatomy from countless textbooks but none of that is going to help you if you encounter one in the real world and see one up close. Yet it is these fools who run our world. Shit, no wonder the planet is going to shit in a hand basket.

Hence, if you are smart, then what point is there in trying to sound smart? You can simply be intelligent without trying to make other sound or feel dumb just because they don't have the same vocabulary as you. But perhaps it is you who are actually the dumb one.

Ask yourself this. Do you try to sound smart in your online blogs or posts? Do you use any large fancy words in post that ultimately mean less than gold fish shit? If so, then congratulations! You are officially an Over Educated Idiot.

If, however, you speak plainly and make sure you don't confuse folks when you have something to say and your post or comments actually have a resounding message without being fancy, then you may actually be worthwhile. If, however, you've never actually done something yet try to make yourself sound like the expert just because you've wasted your time reading a hundred books on it, then get up get out and go do it for real. You've got the book smarts now get the real world experience in field of study. Otherwise, you're simply a waste of time, both yours and others.

Satanic Organizations

In 1966 Anton LaVey opened the door of a new era with the public inception of the first ever Satanic Church. Since that time, many such churches and organizations have sprung up around the world. Most of these organizations stay around for a few years then fade away. This is true for most religions.

The main problem with these smaller organizations, especially the ones that are free to join, is that unlike their more well established paid membership big brothers, they are less concerned with the quality of their members as they are with the quantity.

Organizations like the Church or Satan or Temple of Set don't often reveal their numbers, and with good reason, too. Comparatively their numbers of active members are in fact only attributable to the length of time they have been around, when broken down these numbers are actually rather low in their memberships annually. However, this is not a bad thing.

Organizations like for example the Satanic Chapel, or WSA /352 accept any new comers to the block so long as those new comers don't have a brain to think with on their own, or that their thoughts on things are not fully developed yet. They are more concerned with wrangling in hundreds of members a year. Most get memberships by simply joining online message boards, or sending in an essay on something. After which they get instant access to the full website and maybe a membership card. These organizations often are so underfunded and full of lesser intelligent people, that those Satanists who do actually want to grow and expand, are often left feeling frustrated and leave Satanism altogether with a bad taste in their mouths.

Any organization will naturally develop its own flavor and herd mentality. This is normal and healthy. But it is unhealthy for such an organization to start wielding this sort of mentality like a weapon. This sort of behavior is common in most of the smaller organizations and some larger ones as well. They act in this manner to force their own sort of mentality on others to help build themselves up. Often, they use other people's basic herding instinct to build their organization, only promoting those few who agree with them and their tactics to any sort of higher standing.

The higher members of such an organization are often promoted because of their complacency with being a follower to the group's leaders, who often only seek to be placed on a pedestal to help boost their own self-doubts and inadequacies. When the members of their organizations try to disagree with these promoted members, they often find themselves a target of ridicule despite whether or not they have made any considerable contributions to the organization.

I have met plenty of people who have faced this sort thing from an organization that they belonged to. As an example, here is a quote from a letter written to me by one former member of the organization WSA. (White Star Acceptance)

"Personally, I would like to think that we, as Satanists, are above the herding of the mindless sheep of the world. An organization within the religion of Satanism should pride itself on

wanting members with enough intelligence to form their own opinions. I'm speaking of course about groups such as Satanic Chapel and WSA/352. When I was a member of the WSA/352 however, I was shocked at the bigotry and outright bullying of other members who disagreed with them. It felt more like a high school clique than a religious organization. Whenever we would suddenly find some outside group or organization that we previously didn't know about it would be a free for all in trying to run them into the ground. Most of the time us normal members were told to talk shit about these organizations founders or try to join up to spy on them from the inside. And if we didn't or if we refused, we would end up targets ourselves or get threatened to be physically hurt unless we complied."

With such behavior so prevalent in smaller organizations, is it any real wonder why larger organizations such as the Church of Satan is known for holding an elitist mentality? Each member of such an organization would be considered the cream of the crop. To achieve this, they must be very picky about whom they promote with in their ranks but still allow some lenience on who can join.

With smaller organizations it is common to find them as being free to join. As such they are often underfunded. This under funding also damages their personal ability to grow or hold meetings. Such a get together is often paid for not out of a church fund, but out of complete pocket change and often leaves the organization in a deeper rut than they started. These smaller organizations who are often more interested with accumulating large numbers rapidly often don't think of the financial burdens they are about to face.

Upon first realizing the costs of running such an organization, these smaller groups often find themselves relegated to solely operating on the internet. That is if they attempt to move away from the internet at all to begin with.

Larger organizations who require a membership fee, can often last much longer because they have smaller numbers and a nest egg of moneys to spend on their members. Often these organizations can fund major get together and events, as well as other beneficial projects that make membership worth the money one spends to join.

It is like getting a tattoo. A good tattoo isn't cheap, and cheap tattoos are not good.

Ghosts, Demons, & Other Entities

In Satanism communion with Satan is one of the highest of traditions. Whether or not you believe in the Devil is beside the point. But many people often wonder what is the Satanic viewpoint on Demons and other such spirits. Well in general it is the same as any other person, with a few twists of course.

Obviously to the normal everyday person the random haunted house is enough to scare the wits out of them until they come to grips with the spirit and learn to live with it. But some hauntings are by far much different, they are much more aggressive. In this case the spook is often dealt with in a much more determined manner and the persons dealing with them often wants them removed. It is this later type of haunting that we often love to hear about more so than Casper the friendly ghost. These being are most certainly not Casper.

In most such cases the spirit is considered evil and of the Devil or "Demonic." My questions to these people run as such. Are you a religious person? If so, what is your religion? Did you attempt to bless the house or area upon moving in? If not, then what did you do to piss the demon off? If that is indeed what it is.

You see, demons are not your average spook. The word demon literally comes from ancient times and means "Guardian spirit." They are not overly friendly by their very nature unless you're their master or they view you as friendly. But they defiantly don't go out of their way to randomly attack just anyone, if you get attacked by an actual Demon then you have done something to earn its negative attention.

Most hauntings of an aggressive nature though, are simply acts of poltergeist. These beings are standard run of the mill ghosts with really bad tempers. They may simply not want your company and be acting up to try to force you out of your dwelling.

But here's the basic twist. To most people god is the good guy and so are his angels. The Devil and his host of Demons and fallen angels are the bad guys. Naturally to the Satanist the reverse is true. Satan is the defender of man, and god is the jackass. Fallen angels pose as helpers and guides while Demons stand as the watch dogs protecting our homes and loved ones or some assigned region or area. In this twist a negative spirit would not be a demon who is viewed as a friend and ally, but is in fact an angel or spiritual being in the service of the Christian god.

Most people, when they hold out a cross and douse a house with a demon in it with Christian holy water, will often find the demon angry and end up with it lashing out oftentimes more viciously than before. The entity will do everything it can to remove the people or destroy them in the process to protect its home or its assigned charge. The people under attack are viewed as trespassers, and dealt with in the harshest manner. But should the new occupants during the first phase of a demonic haunting instead show themselves as no threat or even bless the house in the name of Satan or other fallen angels, they may suddenly find the home suddenly feeling welcome and happy as the demon of the house now views the new tenants as friendly and to be looked after.

The same is true if a Satanist enters a new home that holds an angelic presence in it. If they bless the house in the name of Satan, the angel will naturally revolt against them like a demon would to a Christian. Obviously neither side, Satanic or Christian will willingly evoke the name of their religions rival deity to appease the residing spirit, so conflicts will occur.

The simple point is that a high spirit like an Angel or Demon will always be friendly to those who are a like mind or willing to take the steps to prove their friendliness. Lower grade spirits like normal ghosts can often be simply dealt with, while poltergeists often must be routed from the dwelling by both sides as nuisances or simply dealt with.

One must also consider the type of spirit they are dealing with before deciding what to do about it. It would be awfully embarrassing if a Satanist decided to try to bless a home that was negative to a Christian because the spirit dwelling in it was conjured by a Hindu or a Wiccan, only to have the entity to also turn on them as an equally viewed rival. Though these other entities are often more easily dealt with by a Satanist who is often more inclined to admit their misidentification and remedy their mistake properly.

But there are times when one must get rid of a higher spirit from their home to make it livable. This can be done in one of two ways or a combination of both.

1. Exorcism.
2. Summoning another high spirit of a rival nature to aid you.

Both of these two actions should be taken with caution. The rites of exorcism in any religion are often times a harrowing experience to undergo and will often leave the practitioner drained and shaken to the core. It is also important to note that performing an exorcism on a dwelling is vastly different from performing one on a person. With the former, you're simply fighting for living space and upon failing one can normally simply choose to leave the dwelling for a better home. The latter is a true life and death struggle in which not only is your personal safety at stake but also that of the person who is undergoing the exorcism. If done wrong this person could suffer irreparable mental damage or physical harm, even death as was the case of Emily Rose. An exorcism should only be performed by a person with advanced knowledge of what they are doing and what they are facing. Hence the need for the spirit to name itself to the practitioner.

Summoning up a spirit, be it demon or angel or what not, is equally harrowing as your home will become a war zone until one side or another wins. Often times the victor will be you and your spirit, especially if you provide support for it by performing exorcisms and blessings. Christians seldom use the second method, most times they simply invoke the names of some saints and use the words "in the name of God." As such seldom does any higher spirit actually step forth to directly do combat with the negative spirit causing the trouble.

This was the case for the Lutz family in Amityville Long Island in 1975-76. George Lutz and his wife Kathy tried performing several blessings on their home and each time they only made the pervading spirits angrier with them until finally they were forced to leave. Forget the movies people; read the damn book. The priest who had obviously upset the spirits of the house was equally of little to no help, and even stopped George Lutz from finally doing the right thing and summoning a spirit to his aid at one point. George had acquired a book in which detailed how to summon such a spirit and was ready to use it when the priest had stopped him.

There is in truth nothing wrong with summoning a Demon to defend you against another aggressive spirit. But make sure you have your shit wired tight and be ready for World War III when the two spirits come to blows. Chances are you better be ready to fork out some green for repairs to your damaged house or property.

Demons, or Daemons as they are sometimes called, are in fact neutral beings. They are often on the side of the Satanist or dark arts practitioner because only these people often have the guts to call to them. A demon is a guardian of the earth. It is their job to protect things in the most aggressive manner possible. This is often why they seldom look friendly when one is seen physically. Because of their nature and job, they have to look completely terrifying. Think about it, would you be more afraid of a big dog in a yard that shows his teeth and growls at you, or a cute fluffy puppy with its tail wagging at you? If you say the puppy then you're whacked!

Before anyone decides to think of saying that angels are also protectors and they don't look scary, I'll say think again. How many times does the Christian bible speak about people being too afraid to look at an angel? What about the mighty Seraphim? Their supposedly all eyes and wings. Not exactly a very comfortable set of beings to be around if you ask me.

These types of spirits only look comforting to those people who they are charged with protecting. They are not exactly bound to one single form and as such can often look however, they see fit or that is most effective to the person they encounter. Often times with a demon they will choose a much more aggressive looking form because of their nature as well as the simple fact that they are almost constantly expected to look a certain way. An angel will often appear as a fearsome warrior again because they are expected to do so but also because they must look tough. But remember the reverse is also true.

The demon can often also appear beautiful and proudly armored like a mighty hero and the angel could similarly take on the form of a terrible monster or beast.

To a Satanist the appearance of the Baphomet is pleasing. It is logical that if someone was to call up the Baphomet that it would show itself as a goat headed, half-man, half-woman, winged and hoofed entity, armed with some form of mighty weapon to protect the caller. Likewise, if the person was Christian and they summon by chance the same being to help it reign in its demon, the Baphomet might look totally different and almost angelic or even like some King or Queen of Hell.

The Propagation of the Devil as the Good Guy.

Satan as always been the Adversary, this is a simple fact that cannot be ignored. The Devil has remained continually on the fringe of things. Staying to the shadows and always keeping a respectful distance from the world of man. Though he has always influenced us to aspire to greater things. Truly science, art, music, and literature as well as a host of many more things are his doing. The Devil has worked tirelessly to subvert the will and stagnating world of the Christian God. He has endeavored to make our lives interesting and constantly flowing. Never allowing us to become too lethargic in our comforts or complacency.

The dawn of the industrial age was truly the dawn of the age of Satan. It was his masterpiece in the making. Where for the first time old superstitions merged with that of science. Where the old ways of paganism started for the first time to furtively peek back into the world of man. Though it would take many more years for the age of Satan to kick into high gear it was well on its way there and there was no stopping it once the Devil set the cogs to turning.

Satan has always been on the works against the Christian God. The two have battled head strongly for hundreds if not thousands of years. Nowadays the Devil can walk down the street without much fear of being accosted. But his name is still laden needlessly with fear and revulsion by many people. Movies still portray the Devil as the bad guy, and nut jobs still feed into the press with cries of "the Devil made me do it!"

How sickeningly revolting and tasteless. It is high time for the Devil to become the hero for once. If Satan has always moved to dethrone the Christian God, then there is only one way he will succeed. By us putting him on the throne! Now in this age of Satan, the Devil is more powerful than ever. The number of Christian church goers are down and the numbers of pagans and Satanists are up! I say it is high time we had a truly Satanic hero that is blatantly in league with the Devil. Or why not the Devil himself be such a hero?

Movies have begun to propagate a strong affluence for the occult. Showing that it isn't bad or evil, even though there are a few bad seeds. Movies such as Underworld, and the Covenant, as well as anything based on Anne Rice already display the world of "evil" as being good! They show the shades of the Devil's most powerful earth bound warriors in both their finest hours and their lowest moments. However, they are not totally and blatantly Satanic. They often show guilt at what they are, save maybe Anne Rice's Lestat character, who blatantly loves being a Vampire, and is one of the most Satanically heroic characters in literature.

The only way to throw down the Stigma of "evil" though is to make a character that is blatantly the Devil, and showing him battling for the sake of man. Satan must be lifted to super hero status in the public eye and "god" must be shown as the villain. (Not a hard feat considering that he has been displayed as such countless times before.)

The Devil has always been the constant gentleman, standing back and smiling at us from the shadows. Waiting patiently for those who would come to see him for what he truly is and not what he has been made out to be. But it is time now, and the world is ready, for Satan to finally take center stage. To step from the darkness and be allowed to explain himself fully. It is time that he shows the world that he not the fiend that he has been so long portrayed as, but the silent and lonely hero that we have all loved to hear about.

Everyone loves the lonely outcast hero. The one who is feared by those he guards and defends. He is misunderstood except by a few, and seldom hears any thanks for what he has done. Had the Devil not worked so hard for man we would still be stuck as mindless and ignorant slaves, complacent in our indenture to an over bearing and uncaring god.

Satan has never sought out any sort of thanks for what he has done for man. He has never played the "Oh pity me!" card. He has never acted like a child as god has. He has always been an exemplar of bravery and manners. Never raising his voice and shouting back at those who have depicted him in so wrong a light.

As such I think we as the people who do understand him should take the steps and thank him in our own ways. We should show the world the truth about Satan.

A Note on Magic; Lesser and Greater

For most people magic is a thing of myth and mystery. Something that is whispered about or ogled at as some guy pulls a rabbit out of a hat. To the Satanist though magic is a very real thing to be employed and used to attain one's desires.

The use of magic is important to any occult tradition, especially Satanism. As the occult arts where for many centuries considered taboo, the employment of magic therefore became the work of the Devil. Anyone caught using magic more often than not were subject to torture and ultimately execution. Thus, the use of these practices became common place in Satanism and all but formed one of its founding cornerstones. The Satanic ritual is multifaceted in its purpose. It doesn't matter whether you believe in the Devil for real or not in order to perform these rituals as they, like most other forms of magic, are meant to do more than one simple thing. They are two fold in their purpose.

1. To free the practitioner of the mental constraints of the mundane world, and allow them to have a healthy form of psychological release for pent up emotions.
2. To help influence things and matters beyond the normal reach of the Lesser magics, or the influence by normal mundane methods.

The use of magic has always been held in mystery. Often the secrets of magical arts are kept as closely guarded secrets. To the adept it is always an ever aspiring goal to become a great magician. While most adepts know that there are two forms of magical practices, more focus is placed on Greater Magic in most occult traditions, while Lesser Magic is often left to the wayside as an afterthought.

Greater Magic is more often employed than Lesser Magic because of the lure of elaborate rituals. These rituals offer so much to psychological gratification that many people often find them much more desirable to perform than the lesser mundane arts. This is common even in Satanism in most cases. Though a lot of Satanists are equally guilty of almost completely ignoring the rituals of Greater Magic.

The true magician however, be them Satanic or not, knows that both lesser and greater arts are important to learn, as the combination of both can lead one to a healthy and fulfilling life.

Many people tend to forget what exactly Lesser Magic really is now days, because we are surrounded by it, and its results in our everyday lives. When people hear the term "magic" they often think solely of spell craft. The truth is spells are actually considered Greater Magic. Lesser Magic is used all over the world by people who nowadays don't even bear the mantle of witch or wizard, though two hundred years ago that is exactly what they would be called. Today, Lesser Magic is called by many names: science, medicine, hypnosis, so on and so forth.

It is not hard to learn about Lesser Magics and how to employ them. In any greater magical rite or ritual many lesser magics are strung together to create a ritual and achieve Greater Magic. Much is to be said about simple books explaining the use and creation of tinctures and potions as well as others that explain the methods in

which other more volatile compounds are made and employed, such as explosives, fireworks, and even poisons.
In the olden days before such things were understood fully by many people their knowledge was often left to a few people. Often shamans, alchemists, or even priests of those dark and mysterious arts. These simple items were often used to heighten rituals for their congregations. Such methods are still usable in our modern times for the same purpose. Flashy pyrotechnics are always a good tool to use to suddenly grab people's attention in any circumstance. The ability to speak and hold people's attention is also very important.

In Feudal and medieval Japan, the ninja was considered master sorcerers and conjurers, because of their understanding of tricks and illusions. Even the word "ninja" literally means "magician".

One of the few forms of Lesser Magic that still leaves people in awe, is called stage magic. But even this form is still scoffed at by many people, that is until the magician decides to use the illusion to get them really thinking and confuse them. One such case of this that I heard about involved the famous magician David Copperfield. Who was going to the beach with his wife. A group of the usual scoffers noticed Mr. Copperfield and decided to goad him. Using a beach towel one guy would pretend to make a leg disappear by simply lifting the leg up behind the towel showing only one leg at a time.

Mr. Copperfield, being irked by this display of rudeness and not wanting to be bothered, smiled at the guys and said, "Hey that's pretty good, how's this one for you." He then proceeded to imitate the man right there with his own beach towel but lifted it a third time to revel no legs below the towel. He then dropped the towel to show himself levitating in the lotus position. Don't ask me how this was done as I can only assume that there were further details to the actual event than I was not told.

Satanic magic uses many of these Lesser Magics every day. Often the true Satanist will be excellent in several forms of Lesser Magic, such as covert or conversational hypnosis to hold people's attention and get them to do what the Satanist desires, or the use of scents to attract a specific kind of person or help set a mood in their home or dwelling.

The same is also done to a much more extreme degree with rituals. In a ritual it is important for all these Lesser Magics to be employed to achieve the desired frame of mind and make the ritual worthwhile. The use of melodrama and over acting is necessary in any occult art, especially when there is more than one person present. Though a fine line is walked with these rituals. Too little melodrama and the desired effect may not be achieved, too much and your congregation may be left rolling their eyes at you. Finding this fine line is important to any magical ritual or ceremony.

With these Lesser Magical tricks, you may find yourself thinking that they are hardly magical in the least. But none the less they are true mundane magics. These methods are the self-same methods used by wizards, sorcerers, and magicians of the past. Though updated to our modern times. As I have said before, nowadays Modern Sorcery goes by different names than it once did.

For example, gun powder AKA black powder, was once called Chinese magic powder, and was used by "Sorcerers" to perform devastating or even beautiful displays of power. And was not the use of poisons left firstly to the fields of witches? Though nowadays these things are common knowledge and can be used by most people.

The use of Greater Magic is equally as important as the use of Lesser Magic. Greater Magic and ritual are traditional in the Satanic Religion. Almost all religions in the world have their form of ritual. This is because man often finds he needs dogma to help him express himself more freely. It is an essential corner stone for almost any religion nowadays to have rituals in its curriculum before it can often be called a religion at all. The use of rituals goes back as long as man has had any sort of religious belief. In many cases religion itself was a form of government. Such has been the case in tribal politics throughout the world, ancient Egypt, Aztec and other southern American cities, and even during the burning times by the Roman Catholic Church.

In the occult and especially in Satanism the use of ritual is meant to draw upon forces outside the normal perspective to aid the practitioner in bringing about changes outside the normal reach of man. It seldom matters though if one or two participants in a ritual actually believe in the devil or not to reap the benefits of such rituals. They equally serve just as efficiently as a psychological stimulant as any sport or therapists chair can offer. More so in some cases as the participant, despite what he or she may personally feel or believe in, may feel that for once they are actually accomplishing something by simple participation.

In such rituals they may be able to feel as though they can indulge in some personal or secret desires, or have the opportunity to voice something that they have kept bottled up for a long time. There is also the wondrous feeling in the simple act of doing something forbidden or naughty. Satanism is a shunned religion even today though it is now more popular than ever. Therefore, the simple act of saying "Hail Satan" for the first time in some secret chamber away from prying eyes can often be an exhilarating experience.

For those who actually do believe in the Devil, it can hold just as much freedom as it would for the non-believer, but it also provides a method in which the practitioner may contact and employ the powers of beings beyond that of this mortal realm and influence things out of their normal reach.

Often it seldom matters if a spell or curse really works or not on a person, the practitioner may simply feel better about a situation knowing that they have done something about it. Should something actually happen, well then so much the better and that practitioner can then have something personal to validate their religious and personal convictions.

Any ritual can and should be altered to fit the practitioner. There is no set way to perform a ritual or spell, so why stick with the way it is written. Satanism is about being different, as such your rituals though following a certain line or train of thought should always be customized to your tastes and flavor. Consider any rituals or spells you find or read about more as a simple set of guidelines to follow during a ritual or even to inspire new ones of your own making. Or, you can think of it like cooking. You can always follow the basic recipe, but also add whatever feels right to you in order to suit your personal taste. As long as it feels right for the practitioner or their congregation then it is right.

And always remember one last thing. Have fun with your rituals. If it is not fun to do a ritual or no one enjoys it or is going to feel better afterwards, then don't even bother with it as it will serve no purpose except to waste your time as well as that of your congregation.

Modern Vampirism

Vampirism has for the longest time walked hand in hand with Satanism. Like Satanism, the myth of the vampire has been glorified and often times twisted by fiction to the point where it is now highly misunderstood by most of society. When one nowadays thinks of a vampire, they most commonly look towards Bram Stoker and Anne Rice. Though these authors have weaved the creature of the night firmly into our most wild fantasies and terrifying nightmares, there are real vampires who walk among us to this day. But what is a REAL vampire like and how does one become one?

Firstly, real vampires are very much so like Satanists, you don't simply become a vampire. The myth of being bitten by some random stranger and suddenly having an aversion to crosses or garlic is just that, a myth. If you are a true vampire, like true Satanists, then you are born that way. Vampirism is not a disease like some movies claim or a curse, unless you let it be one. It is another stage of our evolution. Vampires have walked among us since the dawn of man and will continue to do so until man is no more.

Real vampires feed on energy. The only real difference is in the fact that presently there are two forms of consumption. This has made literally two forms of Vampires. Sanguinary Vampires who feed on blood, and

Psychic Vampires who feed from the ambient energy given off by all things. There is no wrong way for a vampire to feed it is all a matter of choice, but this choice is what makes the two types very different. For the Sanguinary Vampire, because of their consumption of blood, has far greater physical attributes like strength, speed, agility, so on and so forth. The Psychic Vampire though is considered the adept of energy manipulation, for that is all they use.

This, however, limits the Psychic Vampire in their physical attributes and so they are often times only slightly stronger and faster than a normal person. For the Sang Vampire, willing donors for feeding upon is often times limited and so the Sang Vampire must also be a Psychic Vampire, making them the master of both the physical and the nonphysical simultaneously. This has spread the recent myth of a third class of vampire called the hybrid. The reality is that all vampires are the same in essence; they are only separated by their chosen method of feeding.

Real Vampires are not turned like in the movies or books. And contrary to recent tails they definitely don't sparkle. They live their lives like any other human. Their powers are different and while they do still age, the Vampire who feeds regularly especially the Sanguinary Vampire, will age at a slower pace than normal people. This slower pace could be called ageing gracefully but in truth it is in fact just a different rate of cellular degeneration. What is commonly mistaken as being "turned" into a Vampire is what is really called "awakening".

For most this process happens naturally at the onset of puberty when the vampire first starts to become aware of their predatory nature. For most this just seems like they are an outcast or the odd ball out. Most real Vampires though soon begin to understand what they are even if they don't know what to call it and they begin to accept themselves and grow with it. Eventually, and this is especially true in our modern age with high speed internet access so readily available to anyone, they will meet up with other vampires and begin to fully learn about themselves.

For others though this awakening process must be jump-started for one reason or another. I guess you could say that some vamps are late bloomers. It is true though that all vampires are social creatures and often will naturally seek out others of their kind. This is especially true for young vampires who will seek out a mentor at the subconscious level.

So, what is it that makes the two types of vampires so different? It is in the blood. Sanguinary Vampires choose to feed from blood directly. It is through the blood that they absorb the donors' energy. Actually, it is through the act of feeding that this process naturally happens. The blood though does indeed play as a catalyst to something far greater. Genetic memory is held within each human. For most it is so subliminal and subdued that we can only recall short quick burst from our direct parents past experiences or maybe a few generations beyond them. However, in each of us are thousands of years of primal instincts. Instinctive memories handed down from our oldest ancestors. Men and women who lived in the days when meat came from a hunted animal to feed the whole family or tribe. There are even older memories though of our fist ancestors who for all intents and purposes were not yet human. These ancestors would have hunted not with a spear, but as all other animals, with Fangs and Claws. They would have had senses honed to a razors edge.

It is these super ancient memories that are unlocked with in a Vampire by consuming blood. The taste of fresh blood from someone outside of themselves does in deed unlock these genetic memories for a Vampire. In our modern times what is in truth simple natural abilities to all humans now seem superhuman to the normal person. Most people don't realize or understand that these latent super senses also lay with in them as well, just simply waiting to be unlocked by certain catalysts.

    Vampires are by far not the only ones who hold such primal powers on the physical level, even some non-vampiric people have unlocked these primal instincts to some degree or another. For many soldiers in conflicts around the world it is a matter of life and death that they do in fact wake up these instincts. Not doing so often leads to a death sentence for them. The same is true for tribal communities still found in some of the remote parts of the world. Kill or be killed is the law still in many lands the world over. For many people living in these lands, the instincts and physical abilities of a Vampire are unlocked by their very environment by necessity alone. It is only in the more cultivated, less conflict ridden, or even fewer wild places like in America or even many places in Europe, that the Vampire has become the dominant factor to unlocking these instincts. Seldom do we have to worry about wild predators hunting us or ambushes in our rural towns. It is here that the creatures of the night have found dominion and can ply their trade, feeding on the abundant energies given off by the crowded cities and communities who are ignorant of their presence.

    What makes the Vampire different from the normal human is the need to replenish energy. Many vampires spend their energy on a much higher level than the average human. This often comes from their natural abilities to use energy for different purposes. You've probably known people who are so charismatic that they can virtually get anything they want by simply doing the same things you've tried and failed. Why is this?

It is for one thing, that real vampires are, by their very nature, magnetic personalities. The myth of a Vampire hypnotizing unwary victims is not too far from the truth. More adept vampires are also mastering of the occult's deeper arts and can simply will events into motion without the aid of ritualized spells. This all spends their energy at a much higher level and so they must replenish it. It is also true that most psychic Vampires don't know that they are doing these things. This can make them very dangerous people to be around.

No doubt we have all gone to a booming party that was so full of energy that it crackled the very air, but upon the arrival of a particular guest who seemed so tired at first the party suddenly got quite a bit less boisterous and the guest in question was suddenly very lively and animated.

This person was a Psychic Vampire and they literally sucked the energy right out of the air. Left unchecked Psychic Vampires could drain the very energy down to its last drops from a living thing without even knowing that they were doing it. It is also for this very reason that older awakened Vampires seek to find unawakend ones to awaken them and teach them to harness and control their abilities. Both for their safety and that of those people around them.

The Second Testament

Drums out of the darkness, listen well.
Drums beating like thunder straight from Hell.
Trumpets are blaring, the time's come 'round -
Satan is here to claim His ground!
Furies from Hell are diving down!
"Lex Talionis" is their battle cry!
Even though tricksters made the law,
Justice is served by Fang and Claw!
With our Morningstar from the deepest night,
Let the shuffling zombies grope for light.
Smash the crumbling cross, for Might is Right!
And we shall reign forevermore!

Intro

It has now been a decade later since I wrote the First Testament. Strange it has been to revisit it and see what has now been verified as true. The following articles began being written in 2019, and published now in this book in 2021.

The Spiritual Beliefs of Anton LaVey

In all my years being a Satanist, a few questions have always bothered me. What was Anton LaVey's real thoughts on Satanism? Did he actually believe in a literal Devil? And why if he did, then is Satanism now being portrayed as glorified Atheism?

Over time, I grew to understand LaVeys strange views better. I came to learn that while he is currently portrayed as an Atheist, he wasn't one in truth. I came to learn that Atheism in truth has very little place in LaVeys Satanism. A fact that as time went on became glaringly obvious to me. I just lacked the full gambit of evidence to present a solid case to this fact.

That changed recently when I chose to rekindle my investigations into some of LaVeys writings about atheism. I found the proof against Atheism in Satanism, but also rekindled my question to LaVeys more personal spiritual beliefs.

Those that knew LaVey very well in his day, such as Ed Webber, who got together with LaVey as friends and conspired with LaVey to make a Satanic Church, insist that he definitely did believe in a literal Devil, a real Satan, or a Dark undercurrent to natures energy. And that it was absolutely fundamental, and basic to all communications and interactions with him, as-given, that he did believe in a very Literal Devil.

Michael Aquino also affirms this, as he was the second in LaVey's Church until the 1975 schism. However, due to Aquino's split with LaVey in 1975, the later followers of LaVey try to downplay anything he has to say or anything in writing he can show. This treatment of Aquino is no longer an option.

I had proven to myself years ago that he did indeed believe in something outside of his own persons. However, I still lacked the solid proof to go fully public with my notions. Certainly, I could present some minor case to the world with what little bit I had, much in the same way others had done before. And like them, I would likely be ignored or shut down by the Gilmore trolls. I needed something more. I needed so much proof and outright admittance of my thoughts by undeniable sources, that Gilmore and his "Atheist Church of Satan" flunkies could do nothing but lower their heads and admit defeat at long last.

It was May 10th 2019, only 10 days after I had filmed and released my first ever complete Black Mass ritual video to the public, when I finally found my Holy Grail. In a series of articles from several websites, the largest and most relevant being an article by one Tani Jantsang, I finally had all the proof I needed. And thanks to Jantsang, much of it was well researched and vetted already. I only had to double check it, and make some minor corrections to reveal some deleted and hidden information references. Such as Burton H. Wolfes introduction to the Satanic Bible.

But even with all this proof finally in my grasp, I had one more question. Why was it now necessary to prove LaVeys beliefs? Why was all of this made so obscure? For what reason was Satanism now being touted as Atheism? It made very little sense to me to try to say something is something that it is not. Certainly, the truth would inevitably win out. The proponents of this falsehood would have certainly known this wouldn't they? Especially given the subjects of whom they had spread lies about. So, what could the logical reasoning be?

The answer of course was simple. Self-aggrandizement, and a failure of magical achievement.

Of course, the proponents of this Atheist myth in Satanism was none other than Peter H. Gilmore. It is Gilmore chiefly, along with a pack of yes men and women, who insists to this day that Anton LaVey was always a staunch atheist and they claim that even the making of the movie "Satanis: The Devils Mass" was a big joke. Of course, they themselves are also staunch atheists!

Gilmore, who for all of his intellect and charisma, failed to achieve the very magic that LaVey himself wielded. The only logical solution was to not even try to wield such magic and promote a different course. But this could run counter to what LaVey taught. The only solution there would be to rewrite then the history of the man and promote him as anything but the accomplished magician that he was. The difficulty was that he was such a publicly known sorcerer that questions would inevitably be razed. The only thing left then would be to quash those questions and hide the proof and discredit any whistle blowers, so that only the false narrative could be heard. Given enough time, the truth would be forgotten and buried.

What is more is that anything anyone else can testify to would be hearsay and second hand unless they had it in writing from LaVey himself.

But in this age of the internet nothing is truly lost or forgotten. Inevitably the information would surface as search engine algorithms change and morph. What would the result be, when suddenly these truths come into the open? How will it change the very landscape of Satanism? Only time will tell.

The Jantsang Files

Before we go exploring the Jantsang Files, allow me to explain exactly who Tani Jantsang is or was. Tani Jantsang, whose real name is Tanya Lysenko, has been around and involved with the occult community since about the 1960s, and was one of the progenitors of early Cthulianism in the mid-60s, and formulated several organizations over the years focused on Satanism to some degree or another.

She became associated with Anton LaVey and Blanche Barton for a number of years before LaVey's death and Became a Magistra in the Church of Satan in the 1990s. After LaVey's death she eventually broke ties with Barton and would eventually form a small cabal of loyal followers who set out fervently to prove LaVey was not an atheist, and become the co-founder of an organization called "Satanic Reds". An organization that is arguably the first Communist, and Politically Far Left oriented Satanic Org.

Tani has become very well known for her hostile nature against any attempt to portray her in an accurate light, which often times doesn't paint her in a positive light, and is well documented in online forums for her verbal assaults on anyone speaking about her.

I personally have also fallen victim to her attempted onslaughts, but have had the wherewithal, to block her attempts from my life. That being said, please know that the following is mostly her groups findings. I have added to their work with my own findings where appropriate to give it greater credence and validity. These findings were published in an article on the Satanic Reds website titled; *"Did Anton LaVey Believe in a Literal Devil? Let's Take as Objective a Look as possible! By Tani Jantsang"* It is for this reason we have named them as we have.

First Hand Sources

Let's first look at what Anton LaVey says himself in his earliest published material.

In the 1970 documentary film "Satanis: The Devils Mass":
"I'm in league with the Devil as much as any mortal can possibly be."

Satanic Bible page 17 introduction by Burton H. Wolfe:
"In LaVey's view, the Devil was much more than that Satan represented a dark, hidden force in nature that was responsible for the workings of earthly affairs for which science and religion had no explanation and no control."

On the same page page 17:
"For one thing," LaVey explains, "calling it a church enabled me to follow the magic formula of nine parts outrage to one part social respectability that is needed for success. But the main purpose was to gather a group of like-minded individuals together for the use of their combined energies in calling up the dark force in nature that is called Satan."

Satanic Bible pages 51- 52:

"During white magical ceremonies, the practitioners stand within a pentagram to protect themselves from the "evil" forces which they call upon for help. To the Satanist, it seems a bit two-faced to call on these forces for help, while at the same time protecting yourself from the very powers you have asked for assistance. The Satanist realizes that only by putting himself in league with these forces can he fully and un-hypocritically utilize the Powers of Darkness to his best advantage.

Satanic Bible page 57:
"The Satanist does not furtively call upon these 'lesser' devils, but brazenly invokes those who people that infernal army of long standing outrage - the Devil's themselves!" (He goes on to name the 4 crown princes of hell.)

Satanic Bible page 62:
"He (Satan) merely represents a force of nature, the powers of darkness which have been named just that because no religion has taken these forces out of the darkness. Nor has science been able to apply technical terminology to this force. It is an up tapped reservoir that few can make use of because they lack the ability to use a tool without having to first break down and label all the parts which make it run. It is this incessant need to analyze which prohibits most people from taking advantage of this many faceted key to the unknown, which the Satanist chooses to call 'Satan.'" (This clearly indicates that the overly cerebral types that try to analyze these things, eg, with science or psychology, are not going to be able to do it or understand it.)

Satanic Bible page 110:
"The definition of magic, as used in this book is: "The change in situations or events in accordance with one's

will, which would, using normally accepted methods, be unchangeable." This admittedly leaves a large area for personal interpretation. It will be said, by some, that these instructions and procedures are nothing more than applied psychology, or scientific fact, called by "magical" terminology - until they arrive at a passage in the text that is "based on no known scientific finding." It is for this reason that no attempt has been made to limit the explanations set forth to a set nomenclature. Magic is never totally scientifically explainable, but science has always been, at one time or another, considered magic."

Satanic Bible page 115:
"One of the greatest of all fallacies about the practice of ritual magic is the notion that one must believe in the powers of magic before one can be harmed or destroyed by them. Nothing could be farther from the truth, as the most receptive victims of curses have always been the greatest scoffers."

Church of Satan by Barton, quoting LaVey on page 109
"In speaking directly to Satan himself, you may discover what is in your subconscious that you can't quite bring to the surface. Express appreciation for the direction you have received from the Dark Lord and ask that he continue to guide you to further increase your Earthly power - you might want to write out part of your Dedication ahead of time, to spur your thoughts once you're in the chamber. Ask that He bestow ever-increasing wisdom and perspective so that you can carry out your Dark Will on the Earth. Instruct the demons you name to manifest themselves to you by increasing your earthly pleasures."

The Cloven Hoof
Volume VI, Number 4m July/August IX A.S., Copyright 1974 C.E. by the Church of Satan, Quo Vadis?

Among our mail we find a significant number of comments something like this: "When I joined the Church of Satan, I thought that I was becoming a member of a religious organization dedicated to the worship of the Devil. At least the Satanic Bible left me with this impression. But, while the Cloven Hoof is all very interesting from a philosophical and materialistic standpoint, it seems to regard 'devil-worship' as little more than a convenient allegory. Is this a church? Does Satan really exist? If so, where and in what form? And why are the leaders of the Church of Satan so reluctant to discuss questions of literal demonology?"

Before we respond to this, a brief preface is in order. During the days of the original Magic Circle in San Francisco, and for the first few years of the Church itself, little effort was made to disguise the literal core of our doctrines. At that time there were no Wiccans, pseudo-Satanists, journalistic "occult authorities," or dime-a-dozen "Dark Shadows" films reducing the Prince of Darkness to soap-opera status. There was only The Church of Satan.

We are all familiar with what happened next. "Rosemary's Baby," produced with the Church of Satan's guidance, touched off an international fad greater than goldfish-swallowing, phone-booth-stuffing, hula hoops, and Zoot suits all together. Suddenly everyone was "into" the occult. If one was swashbuckling, one was a Satanist. If timid, a Wiccan. If fuddy-duddy, a theosophist or a Rosicrucian. If sexually obsessed, a sado-masochist. If altruistic, a Jesus freak. If chicken, a reporter or observer. But always "an authority."

Satan himself became a tennis-ball. Prior to 1966 he was allegorical. Suddenly it was de rigueur that he was very, very literal - much more so than God (Do you remember that old Time cover: IS GOD DEAD?) Then someone made the profound discovery that "Satan" was a Hebrew term, and there were one or two religions on this planet besides Judaism and Christianity. Immediately Satan was passé. The thing to do now was to revive the worship of the primeval fertility gods and goddesses that the Neanderthals grunted over. Finally, some enthusiasts actually managed regress past the Neanderthal stage to Krishna-Consciousness, Scientology, and Guru Maharaj-Ji.

Is it really any wonder, then, that the Church of Satan withdrew "literal Satanism" from the public arena? In our pronouncements, publications, and press-releases the Devil became an allegory for materialism and the unchained human ego. Speaking in such terms we could continue to gain the ear of the people who really mattered - the de facto Satanists of the world. Had we continued to champion a literal Devil, media distortion would have lumped us together with nut elements, and our access to serious channels of communication would have been seriously impaired.

Now we have reached the end of the boom. "The Exorcist" was the Last Gasp. A few of the occult flower-children still remain, but they have become relics, throwbacks within their own subculture. No one listens to them; they have nothing new to say. One by one, rats deserting a sinking ship, they quietly lay aside their capes, swords, and amulets. It is all over. Time to find a new toy.

And so it is that Satan awakes. To his disciples who, after long years of frustration, are minded to leave Rome, he appears echoing God's admonishment to Saint Peter:

Whither goest thou? Having seen so much, having partaken of my knowledge, having known me for what I truly am, abuse not my trust and confidence. Return to Rome, and together we shall begin the building of our new empire.

Indeed Satan exists. Not as just a myth, nor as a mere psychological archetype, nor as only a colorful figure of speech - but as an essential, intelligent entity.

"You knew this, Winston. Don't deceive yourself. You did know it - you have always known it." The tongue in which his name is voiced is unimportant, just as the shapes and substances of his manifestation are unimportant. "God" is an automatic, non-conscious, dispassionate cosmos - in which man, yearning to be rid of the burden of his identity, seeks to immerse himself. Satan is That which has infused man with that identity, thus endowing him with the key to turn the inertia of the cosmos to his amusement - to make of man a god. Would it surprise you to discover that the true Prince of Darkness is not the Devil of Judaic/Christian legend? That figure is a simple caricature. Rather Satan is the true intelligence manipulating the "God" of the Bible and other "divine" personages weaning man from subservience to all gods by making their demands increasingly intolerable.

This is the truth behind all religious institutions throughout history: gradual deification of man despite his most determined efforts to regress to the status of a non-thinking beast. While bowing before the Cross, man has actually been succumbing to a Diabolical Double-Cross of such ingenuity and complexity that it staggers the comprehension. Call it, if you like, The Greatest Practical Joke Ever Pulled. Or, to put it another way, humanity has been had!

Does it suddenly ring true to you, Satanist? Do you begin to see what it's really "all about"? Do the peculiarities of human evolution now fall into place? Yet, if your mental block remains fixed, it is appropriate; the shock of "awakening" may drive unprepared individuals quite mad. This "awakening" is the actual Abyss whose existence is dimly sensed by traditional occultists. Yet they have always failed to perceive its true function, and have failed miserably in their efforts to challenge it. For those who cross the Abyss, there is no return.

(According to various CoS sources, LaVey had by this point taken back over control of the Cloven Hoof Publication. If this is true, then this article alone, was published with the Black Popes consent, and validates the truth that the Church of Satan was indeed theistic before 1975. It also casts a shadow over any claims of LaVey being an Atheist.)

Second Hand Sources

The Church of Satan's Grotto Master application requires prospective Grotto Masters, who are individuals that lead a local chapter of COS followers to perform a self-initiation ritual:
"Before you complete this application - when you sense the time is right - perform a ritual (using the basic elements described in the Satanic Bible) to petition Satan and the Dark Legions to accept you as a Grotto Master. Write down the ritual you performed and the results, if any."

It should be noted, that all Satanic Rituals reference Satan as a literal being. Satan is often referenced as such in many Church of Satan sources, including quite notably in the Grotto Masters Hand Book, presumably by Blanch Barton.
"Be warned that when you enter a ritual with a posture of arrogance, like a demanding, challenging child,

your Master will not be pleased and will slap you down hard. Satan expects you to be respectful, not groveling; prideful, but not arrogant in front of him. He expects you to be useful to him, and he will support you as long as you amuse him. He richly rewards sincere dedication and steadfast loyalty. Do not fear that you can't pronounce the Enochian Keys right, or you didn't speak the invocation exactly as you had written it out ahead of time. He'll understand, as long as you feel the passionate dedication you claim, and you continue the ritual in a way that entertains him and compels him to stay in your presence. Certain ritual elements are absolutely necessary to set the stage that invites Satan and his minions to join you. But he will know the difference between a sincere dedication softly whispered and a pompous sham no matter how loudly declared.

Remember well. Demons will enter you. If you are an unworthy Host, if you harbor secret fears or residual Christianity in any form, if you are frivolous in your intentions toward the Dark Side, they will scent it like a pack of wolves and bring you down mercilessly. Many a sorcerer or sorceress before you has fallen to ruin and destruction in this way, even after years of intimate contact with the Infernal Ones."

Blanch Barton to the San Francisco chronicle after LaVey's death, on November 8, 1997,
 "Anton LaVey believed in the Devil."

She was later criticized by Ole Wolf, his main criticism being that what Barton had said was agreeing with Michael Aquino, Barton wrote to Tani Jantsang, in a letter dated January 23, 1998, "As for saying Dr. LaVey believes in the Devil, I think it's fairly obvious from his philosophy, from the books he's written, the interviews he's given and the organization he founded. How he defines Satan and how he uses the concept of the metaphor of the Devil, is also fairly obvious, but I would be lying if, when asked the direct question, 'Did Mr. LaVey believe in the Devil?' I were to answer, 'No, he didn't.'"...."He (Ole Wolf) apparently objected to my answering such a question with a forthright "yes" when I was faced with national television cameras and speaking to an audience of American dunderheads - and I won't cop out by saying I was grieving - I was.".... "If I was a Satanist out there, weeping and despondent, I would rather hear a voice clearly saying, "You're damned right, he believed in the Devil, you assholes - whether you want to take the watts to understand it or not." That's really the way he felt about that whole issue."

"The Dark Ones guide us." letter from LaVey to Dawn LaSalle and the group here. Sept. 23, 1992.

"May the Dark Ones give you strength and clarity, and may you prosper as you so richly deserve." BB to Chris Bray, 4/30/1993, cc sent to Gilmore and Jantsang.

Zeena, in her letter to MAA took supreme issue with her father's newly found Atheism and took issue with the specific Atheists around her father at the time, namely the Gilmores and Barton. Keep in mind that she grew up with LaVeyan Satanism and was baptized into it. Letter from Zeena LaVey Schreck to MAA, 12/30/90
"My unfather should never have carelessly tampered with the authentic forces of darkness that he now idiotically believes are his own creation."

Burton Wolfe's account in "The Devil's Avenger," states that LaVey sensed the Powers of Darkness (that he felt compelled to formalize into a church) only vaguely as a "dark force in nature" as stated by LaVey himself in the

Satanic Bible. Wolfe claims that LaVey thought these powers of darkness could be activated through ceremonial and personal magic to fulfill individuals' needs and desires. LaVey identified this Dark Force as Satan.

Ed Webber and others suggested the idea of making a Satanic Church to Anton LaVey in early 1966. This business with Webber and others is documented in meticulous detail in Michael Aquino's book, "The COS" page 27. Michael Aquino interviewed Ed Webber later on: Aquino: "Since 1975, LaVey has insisted that he never believed in the existence of an actual Devil or Satan that "Satan" was only a symbol or metaphor. Was this true when you knew him?"

Webber: "Not at all. He was quite definite that he did believe in the existence of Satan. This was exactly what made the concept of a Church of Satan so fascinating."

On page 28 of Michael Aquino's "The COS" he recounts that he found out that when LaVey formed the Church of Satan in 1966, LaVey privately handwrote and signed a personal Pact with Satan titled, "My Pact." LaVey showed Aquino a locked metal strongbox with his personal copy of a book. The only other item in the strongbox was the Pact.

Belief in a literal Devil was automatic in all communications that Michael Aquino had with Anton LaVey. He was the second highest person in the Church of Satan, next to LaVey.

In Conclusion: A Final Thought

The evidence to whether or not LaVey was an atheist, is in the end conclusive and solid. LaVey railed against the notion of Satanism being atheism right up until Peter Gilmore arrived on the scene. And even then, evidence shows that he only seemed to play lip service to the young New Yorker from Hell's Kitchen.

Gilmore himself claims in his introduction to the Satanic Bible to moving beyond the moniker of "Atheist." This is now apparent as a blatant lie. Perhaps he once attempted to move beyond such notions and flow back into the realms of spirituality, only to fail utterly. Or perhaps he always had an alternative agenda. Whatever the case may have been, he has left a deep wound on the fabric of Satanism. One that will take a long time to repair if it can be at all.

Nowadays we have many "Satanic" organizations who have adopted this notion of Atheism. Gilmore has destroyed quite effectively what it was to be a Satanist. Only perhaps a meager handful can now recall the old days when magic literally flowed from the Black House. When Satanic Curses drew real fear and caused some real panic and wonderment.

Too many folks now see Satanism as a political statement masquerading as a religion. They parade around in outrageous attire protesting for abortion rights or trying to get statues installed on political building grounds. Not that some of this is not good press for Satanism. The proponents of such enthusiastic displays have no concept of what they are really representing. And where is Gilmore in all of this? Why has he not come forth to indulge in the mess he has made?

And what of the dwindling theistic Satanists? Left in the dark to huddle. Lacking the simple knowledge that the truth was right in front of them. They grow frustrated in an ever growing Atheistic world of Satanism, and either abandon their faith in the real Devil and search for something else to appease their spiritual desires. Or they say screw it and hide amongst the atheists just to have companionship.

The damage caused by Gilmores atheistic views, and his expoundment of lies about the founder of Modern American Satanism, is massive and on an epic scale. Only by outright refuting and publicly exposing this catastrophe, can we ever hope to learn what true Satanism was really about. So, this one last question remains. Do you have what it takes to be a "Real" Satanist?

An Argument for Shemhamforash

For many years now it has been an ongoing argument about the use of the Hebrew word, "Shemhamforash" in Satanic Rituals. One side says to go ahead and use the term while the other fervently denounces its use.

But why denounce this word LaVey chose to use in his rituals? What is it that could be so bad to forbid its use?

LaVey has us yell, "Shemhamforash!" But what does "Shemhamforash!" mean? What is this mysterious word of power that we are to utter in our rituals that is strangely shunned by half of the Satanic world? The answer is very simple and well known to any who has taken a few moments in our modern eras to learn what it is.

"Shemhamforash," more commonly spelled "Shemhamephorash," is a transliteration of a Hebrew phrase meaning "the explicit name." It is a reference to, of all things, a name of the Hebrew God. Most commonly, it refers to the name "Yahweh." It has also been used to refer to a 72-letter name of the Hebrew God. Elsewhere in the Satanic Bible, LaVey denounced, as "hypocritical," the use of Hebrew God-names in rituals to evoke demons. Yet LaVey himself used "Shemhamforash." Why?

It would at first glance seem pretty clear why so many shun the words usage. Did LaVey even know what that word means? Or did he just think it was a cool-sounding bit of gibberish?

"It has been said in the Doctrine of Transcendental Magic that the name of Jehovah resolves into seventy-two explicatory names, called Shemahamphorash. The art of employing these seventy-two names and discovering therein the keys of universal science is the art which is called by Kabalists the Keys of Solomon."
"The History of Magic" by Eliphas Levi (1860)

The common Church of Satan explanation, is that the word is forbidden to speak except by certain initiated Rabbi. Thus, it is uttered in ritual as a form of blasphemy.

"What does "Shemhamforash" mean?
This word is supposed to stand for the "secret" name of the Hebrew God. To utter it was considered to be the utmost blasphemy against this deity, thereby guaranteeing one's damnation. It is also supposed to be the "word of power" spoken by Moses to part the Red Sea. So, Satanists use it for traditional blasphemy's sake."
Church of Satan website FAQ

But was this LaVeys intention? Doesn't seem like it to me. As a matter of fact, his real intentions, much like allot of things involved with his spiritual beliefs, was left rather vague in the Satanic Bible. The first time we are introduced to the word is in a vague reference to it as being used in the ritual, and that when uttered, the congregation repeats it and is the punctuated by the sounding of the gong. Then followed by a firm "Hail Satan, and another gong."

Without a doubt this would seem the word has real meaning in LaVeys rituals. So why then is it all but banned by certain Satanic sects? That answer is simple, they don't know the history of the word as much as they believe.

By the time LaVey discovered it in an interesting tome, Shemhamforash had been all but forgotten. LaVey then later appropriated the word as a "Word of Power" for his rituals.

"The Shem ha'Meforash is the so-called "Name of 72" (the number of syllables in the name) of the Judaic/Christian god, used in non-ceremonial Jewish conversations wherein "YHVH" or "Adonai" would be considered blasphemous. Like many obscure features of Judaica, it became an object of confused and suspicious speculation with the advent of Christianity. By the 1500s it was considered a device of Black Magic, which Martin Luther accused the Roman Catholic of using to deceive the faithful. A century later it appeared as the title of a magical text claiming to contain Jewish Cabalists' spells to invoke spirits and attack their enemies. And that text later resurfaced as part of the Sixth and Seventh Books of Moses, whose mere possession was alleged to doom one to Hell. It was in this book that Anton LaVey came across it and decided to appropriate it as a "word of power" for his eventual Satanic ritualism ..."
Extract from The Church of Satan: by Michael A. Aquino

It would probably be safe to say, that even if LaVey didn't initially know the words origins, (Which is very doubtful.) he would have still used it.

The usage of the word should always be left up to the individual practitioner. Nowadays the word is used much in the same sense as the Christian "Hallelujah." Yet another word of power. Followed ironically by the phrase "Praise Jesus!" or "Praise the Lord!" or some other variant epitaphs. The difference here would be that we use the term "Hail Satan!" in any number of similar variations.

In the end what does this mean? What is Shemhamforash really? Is it a blasphemy or just another way to say "Hail Satan?" Furthermore, should we as Satanist continue to use this term, or abandon it all together?

I say embrace it. LaVey was no fool. No doubt he did his research in the term and understood its connotations. On a very personal level I find the word empowering. It flows and pulses in the ritual chamber. What is more, is that it has never inhibited any of my contact with spirits or Demonic energies. They seem to flow all the greater when the word is used. But that is only my personal experience.

There is no set rule mandating the words usage. Only a firm encouragement. Perhaps folks who have stopped using the term may be now inclined to experiment once again with its use.

Satanic Politics

It should be noted, that when I first wrote The Satanic Testament, political ideologies were in fact the furthest thing from my mind. The year was 2009, I was still a much younger man and while I had been a Satanist for a few years, I was still very new to the whole aspect of Satanism from the clergy stand point. Politics had very little interest to me in those years of youthful brashness and flagrant brazenness.

It was the first days of the Obama Administration, and I like so many others couldn't have cared less who was the new President aside from the fact that he was a Black dude for once. Naturally that quickly changed for many people. As we entered in eight years of political administrative Hell.

Now in 2020. Near the end of the first term of the Trump Administration, and praying there will be a second term. In a politically volatile climate the likes of which, has not been seen in this country since the early years of LaVey's Church of Satan in the 60s and 70s, or even the Lincoln Administration, also sitting on the cusp of a potential Civil War. I am left wondering, what the Laveyan political tendency is? For that matter how does Satanism in general tend to flow politically? What was Anton LaVey's political viewpoints?

These may seem like arbitrary questions to most. Does Satanism not preach for the Separation of Religion and Politics?

The answer is invariably, yes it does indeed preach and advocate for the Separation of Church and State. However, things are never as simple as they first appear.

For one thing many folks forget that Religion itself was the first form of political system. And in many tribal areas it is still used as such by tribal leaders. If a person walks into a tribal village in any part of the world, invariably the two most important people in the village will be the village leader, and the village Shaman or "Wiseman". After these two, leadership is also mitigated by a counsel of village elders.

We see the same structural make up in any political or religious system in the world no matter where we go.

Invariably then, understanding LaVey's political views and the views of the people he surrounded himself with, would logically grant a keen insight on how and why Satanism is how it is and what makes it unique among the world's religions.

Let's start with how the Church of Satan views politics nowadays.

The Church of Satan depicts itself as an apolitical entity whose members choose their politics freely in accordance with their needs. This includes members who identify and sympathize with the Alt-Right and fascism. The organization puts forth the argument that it is apolitical because it doesn't in any official manner endorse any political party or candidate and that its membership spans the political spectrum, from far-Left communists to far-Right fascists, and liberals and centrists in between.

"As has been said many times before, one's politics are up to each individual member, and most of our members are political pragmatists. They support political candidates and movements whose

goals reflect their own practical needs and desires. Our members span an amazing political spectrum, which includes but is not limited to: Libertarians, Liberals, Conservatives, Republicans, Democrats, Reform Party members, Independents, Capitalists, Socialists, Communists, Stalinists, Leninists, Trotskyites, Maoists, Zionists, Monarchists, Fascists, Anarchists, and just about anything else you could possibly imagine. It is up to each member to apply Satanism and determine what political means will reach his/her ends, and they are each solely responsible for this decision. Freedom and responsibility—must be a novel concept for those who aren't Satanists. We take it in stride. Members who demand conformity from other members to their particular political fetish are welcomed to depart."
—*Magus Peter H. Gilmore,*
from "A Map for the Misdirected"

At first glance this would seem to answer much of the question. Except for the fact that LaVey seemed to lean very heavily on Alt-Right literature when writing the Satanic Bible. What is more is that when we look at his inner circle of confidants and even his own Son in Law, we make a startling discovery. The Church's inner circle included figures from various underground far right neo-Nazi groups and subcultures, including Nikolas Schreck, who married LaVey's daughter Zeena. Boyd Rice, whom LaVey arguably, originally wanted to take over the Church of Satan when he passed away. Nick Bougas, the man considered to be the author of the A. Wyatt Mann cartoons that produced the infamous "Le Happy Merchant" caricature. Kurt Saxon, who was a notable member of several groups, the American Nazi Party, the John Birch Society, the Minutemen, the Church of Scientology, and the Church of Satan, and notable author of the five part Poor Man's James Bond book series.

With such a collection of rouges sitting in his inner circle most of whom are known to have ties to the far right and fascist movements. What was LaVey's political views if not a fascistic one? For this answer we go to perhaps the most obvious of sources, Wikipedia.

"LaVeyan Satanism has been characterized as belonging to the political right rather than to the political left. The historian of Satanism Ruben van Luijk characterized it as a form of "anarchism of the Right". LaVey was anti-egalitarian and elitist, believing in the fundamental inequality of different human beings. His philosophy was Social Darwinist in basis, having been influenced by the writings of Herbert Spencer, Friedrich Nietzsche, and Ayn Rand. LaVey stated that his Satanism was "just Ayn Rand's philosophy with ceremony and ritual added". Characterizing LaVey as a Nietzschean, the religious studies scholar Asbjørn Dyrendal nevertheless thought that LaVey's "personal synthesis seems decidedly his own creation, even though the different ingredients going into it are at times very visible." Social Darwinism is particularly noticeable in The Book of Satan, where LaVey uses portions of Redbeard's Might Is Right, though it also appears throughout in references to man's inherent strength and instinct for self-preservation"

What is ironic was the fact that Anton LaVey was by blood part Jewish! And yet he maintained very firm ties and connections to people in which whose ideology he was the enemy of by blood!

LaVey's Satanism placed an emphasis on the role of liberty and personal freedom. LaVey believed that the ideal Satanist should be individualistic and non-conformist resisting any herd mentality, and should place oneself, and one's family before others. LaVey also felt they should be, mindful one's own business, and that men behave as gentleman, while women should use sex and sexual whiles as tools to manipulate men, in order to level the playing field with men. He rejected consumerism and what he called the "death cult" of fashion.

Another point to note was LaVeys acceptance of homosexuals from an early point in the Churches formation. This makes sense when one looks at what LaVey was trying to project to the world. An organization and religion that willingly breaks social taboos unabashedly. It could be argued then that the true Satanic thing in our modern era would be then to take the reversal of that acceptance and promote heterosexual relationships and the Nuclear Family dynamic that has been all but lost.

LaVey, who was of partial Jewish ancestry, was well aware of the irony of his radically individualist philosophy finding traction among believers in various political systems. Some of which that calls for subsuming individual identity to the will of the nation and/or race.

He envisioned Satanism as a way for modern, non-practicing young Jews, especially those from mixed Jewish/Gentile marriages, who didn't fit in with the synagogue, the church, or the white supremacist movement, to claim a new, "tough" identity as an alternative to the humanism of the secular, liberal Jewish mainstream. LaVey jokingly suggested that the Church of Satan was where a Zionist, Odinist, Bolshevik, Nazi, Imperialist, Socialist, or Fascist could thrive.

In some ways this has come about. But in others it could argued that it is far from anything more than a joke. The truth is that while the Church of Satan still has an open door policy concerning race or ethnic background, and that it claims to hold a very apolitical philosophy, much of its views and recent activity does tend to drift more towards the Political Far Right.

The Church of Satan regularly promotes posts for The Accusation Party, a podcast that focuses on an anti-SJW, anti-feminist, anti-antifa, pro-free speech, Alt-Right narrative.

In other various news feed on their website news feed and Facebook accounts, one can simply do a search and find various instances where political fascism is promoted. In one Heathen Harvest episode dating back to 2015, American far-right activist Augustus Sol Invictus, was featured. Who later was a headline speaker at the *Unite the Right* rally at *Charlottesville, Virginia* on August 12, 2017.

Although personally neither a fascist nor neo-Nazi, LaVey was on good terms with various neo-Nazi and other right-wing groups operating in the United States.

LaVey believed in the political right. In addition, he believed that society would enter an Age of Satan, and that Christianity would invariably die. After which a generation living in accordance with LaVeyan principles would come to power.

LaVey did indeed supported eugenics, and expected it to become a necessity in the future, when it would be used to breed an elite who reflected LaVey's "Satanic" principles. In his view, this elite would be "superior people" who displayed the "Satanic" qualities of creativity and nonconformity. He regarded these traits as capable of hereditary transmission, and made the claim that "Satanists are born, not made". He believed that the elite should be siphoned off from the rest of the human "herd", with the latter being forced into "ghettoes" located on other planets.

Jean La Fontaine highlighted an article that appeared in The Black Flame, in which one writer described "a true Satanic society" as one in which the population consists of "free-spirited, well-armed, fully-conscious, self-disciplined individuals, who will neither need nor tolerate any external entity 'protecting' them or telling them what they can and cannot do."

So it is in conclusion that I say this.

Given all the evidence here. While LaVey was never a Neo-Nazi himself, he did indeed idolize the Third Reich. Some of his notions were definitely way out there at times, but this is to be expected.

What is interesting though is that even after his death, the Church has continued with the same ideological threads even against its own denials of such practices. Certainly one only needs to do a cursory look at the current Church of Satan, to notice that there is a very strong authoritarian cult following of Magus Gilmore, and idolization of LaVey himself. Much in the same vain as Neo-Nazis celebrate Hitler, his writings and even his birthday.

When one boils it all down. And looks objectively at it all. One can't help but to feel that while Real Satanism can indeed fit with most political outlooks, it is perhaps ironically best suited to the Far-Right political constructs. A "Satanic National Socialism" in this case wouldn't be a far cry from unlikely. Conversely it would be probable in almost every aspect and notion to be functional. Space Ghettos aside of course.

One a final note. It has been said to me, that it is strange how Satanism and National Socialism mesh so well in their ideologies. Given that National Socialist ideals clearly played a large part in shaping LaVey's outlooks I don't find it surprising at all. What is more is that when we look at how both Satanism and National Socialism are viewed by the general public, one could say that National Socialism, is the political form of Satanism. If that is the case, is it then any wonder then why so many Neo-Nazis identify as Satanists?

Who or What is Satan?

It is often asked, if it is necessary for a Priest or Priestess of Satan, to actually believe in the existence of Satan? In one sense the answer must ultimately be, yes. Simply put, if you are a member of a Priesthood and your answer is no, then I ask you, who in the hell are you a Priest or Priestess of? If you do not recognize Satan in some sense, as being factual to some lesser or greater degree, then how can you truly belong to any sort of Priesthood of Satan.

The next tricky question there presents itself. Who or what is Satan? The answer is surprisingly straight forward, and yet simultaneously complex. Satan is whatever you, as a member of the religion define or determine this principle to be. Once you have recognized and acknowledged this principle, Satan then can, and does exist. Opinions of and experiences with Satan often vary greatly among the initiates of the religion.

Here is a brief list. There are probably many more that could be added to this:

1. An intelligence or entity which operates both separately, and at times in conjunction with that of our own psyche, and not just as an aspect of it.
2. An "indwelling essence".
3. A god of mankind's creation.
4. A thought form that is both self-aware and independent of its creators. Tulpa, or Egregore.

5. A God, self-created.
6. A neter - a necessary principle of creation affecting the Subjective Reality and the Objective Universe.
7. A purely Platonic Form.
8. Not a Platonic Form, but an ideal. A representation of man's own nature.
9. All of the above.

The key is, as I've said above, Satan is whatever you define him to be. We are not and should not be required to adopt one view over the other. This would be antithetical to the philosophy of genuine Satanism. Blind faith would make us no different to the other major religions of the world who are dictatorial in nature and do require you to adopt a literal belief in or disbelief of "one true God" as a hard line fact. Leaving little to no room that the existence of such a "God" is debatable. Those who wish to not only insist, but equally enforce their belief or disbelief of such a god onto others are, in my opinion, deluded, politically motivated, or fanatic, and are in no way seekers of truth or interested in investigating and developing their own spirituality.

What makes the Religion of Satanism different is that each comes to his or her own understanding of Satan through personal experiences, contemplation, and investigation of the individual psyche, humanity and the world around us. Thus, resulting in our forming our own definition, however complete or incomplete it may be. Our methods of approach to this research are varied, and produce different results.

So, can we reconcile the difference and maintain a balanced attitude toward one another's perceptions, without insisting that one must be more accurate than the other? I say yes.

Those who come to perceive Satan as the "dweller within" have discovered and experienced the source of the Satanic in the Subjective Reality as opposed to the Objective Universe. Their prime concern is themselves, and it is within that they find the answers to the mysteries they seek. This is certainly a valid approach when viewing the Left-Hand Path as the path of self-initiation. Whose "Xeper", as the Setians call it, are we seeking if not our own, and isn't this what we are all striving for?

Aquino's Word of Set could be seen as supporting this approach in the statement *"Arise in your glory, behold the genius of your creation, and be prideful of being for I am the same - I who am the Highest of Life."*

For those who perceive Satan as an external influence, the source of the Satanic has been discovered within and inspired by the Objective Universe rather than ones own Subjective Reality.

The Book of Coming Forth by Night lends itself to this approach with the statement, *"Speak to me at night, for the sky then becomes an entrance and not a barrier."*

One could assume from this statement that Satan or in this case Set, resides somewhere among the stars, or is simply to be looked for outside of oneself.

If we believe that Satan has awakened the Black Flame within mankind, then it is this "Gift of Satan" that has allowed our fellow Initiates to achieve conscious recognition of the self. *"I am within and beyond you,"* bridges the gap between the variations of approach and their results.

There are however always dangers and pitfalls to watch for when opting for one belief over another. We should always try to take care to avoid such pitfalls. Becoming "territorial", for example, about one's belief in religion. The "I'm right; you're wrong; if you don't agree with me, there's something wrong with you" syndrome. This is often a good example of signs of insecurity in one's own faith.

Belief derived solely on the hearsay of others, is yet another common trap we should strive to avoid. This really doesn't do much to increase your personal knowledge. Recognition in this case would be questionable at best, or completely dismissive all together. Your definition and knowledge of the nature of Satan can only truly be found via personal experience, and a personal discovering of your own relationship to the concept.

Belief in one view and denial of any other, out of fear of being penalized or ridiculed by one's peers is a sign of weakness, uncertainty, and inability to think freely. It is extremely limiting. It's sad but this happens all too often in Satanic Organizations, and frankly stupendously ignorant should the differing views have the same root or be nearly identical, save for a few differences. We should strive to never brow beat our brethren into our way of thinking. Being biased and discounting the beliefs of another could be said to be discounting the beliefs of the other. What is more is that holding desperately to one's belief may cause stagnation of that belief if it is based on inadequate or incomplete or outdated information.

Those of us who have encountered, and believe in Satan himself, or any Demons, can develop an exaggerated opinion of our ability to contact and understand Satan's position. Thusly leading ourselves astray by doing what we think Satan wants. We can blind ourselves to his truth by limiting our own perceptions.

For those who believe that Satan dwells within us, or that we are our own Satan or Demon, this doesn't mean that we can stop questioning, clarifying, investigating, testing our position and what we think we are, or that we simply can't continue to improve and grow. All are possibilities that must invariably be considered. Thus, it is in conclusion our faith in a very real Satan, while undeniable, must remain fluid. Satan can be many different things to many different individuals. To ascribe Satan one archetypal facet would be simply folly.

Satan is probably best described as simply that "Dark Undercurrent of Energy in Nature." Or as they may say in Star Wars, "The Dark Side of the Force." It is an ironic, if not apt description of an entity that moves so many lives.

So now it is up to you to decide. Who or what is Satan to you?

A Strange Synchronicity

It was during the time-frame when I began preparing to open the doors to the Satanic Thulian Society, that I began to take notice of a very unusual synchronicity to the events surrounding me.

We had begun to get prepared for our three day Halloween Hell party that would celebrate the three nights of a very rare Super Blue Full Moon, that landed perfectly on the three days of the Halloween holidays. Oct 30th to Nov 1st.

I began to get curious about this event and began researching when similar lunar events took place. It was only a day or so before our festivities, and guests would begin arriving within a day or so. I say a Day or so, but in fact it was literally Oct 29th. And I was in the middle of a long haul road trip to bring a friend of mine down for our event from Maryland.

I was surprised then to discover that the previous event had not been a full moon but a new moon event. The new moon began on Oct 30th and ended on Nov 1st, of a very particular year. 1997.

This of course floored me. Because on Oct 29th 1997, Anton LaVey died.

Now I'm not one who pays much attention to lunar cycles or numerology or any of that stuff outside of when is the next full moon to host a ritual event. But

In this instance, I could not help but to stand up and take note of the strange pattern. What was more was the length of time between when LaVey passed and our event was exactly 23 years to the day.

For those not in the know the number 23 is considered to be an auspicious and diabolical number, and has even spawned a very interesting movie starring Jim Carrey. I'll not get into the number 23 conspiracies too much, but here is one such interesting equation.

2 divided by 3 is 0.666.
Take the devils numbers (666) and add 2 and 3
6+6+6+2+3= 23

There is of course an entire rabbit hole one could deep dive into with the number 23. Trust me anyone who watched the movie is very well aware of the paranoia that comes with seeing this damn number everywhere.

Fortunately, I've moved past that freaky stage and could sit back and find its presence now very intriguing.

This of course was one very interesting occurrence and completely unplanned. Or was it? I began wondering if something was indeed moving events surrounding me at this time, especially when I to not of another bazaar occurrence.

I had never paid much attention to when I began writing more articles on Satanism. It was of course oddly enough in the summer of 2019. When of course I reopened my small Satanic meetup group, at the behest of one of our former members. There was nothing official about it. We didn't even start a meetup.com page this time around. Only building up via word of mouth.

This was the complete opposite of course to my first attempt to begin such a group in 2009. Ten years prior. Where I had attempted to go all out for my new little organization. Which of course failed miserably. This time though it was growing, and quite the opposite, succeeding on a smaller yet more profound scale.

I hadn't taken note until I began work on this book, that my time-frame also mirrored to the day and month the creation and publication of this books first iteration and of the creation of my first attempt at a Satanic Organization. Ten years, exactly in every instance.

I had heard of course of the theory of Divine Synchronicity. But never had I experienced it firsthand until now. I now tend to try to be mindful of such patterns and how they can influence our lives and decisions. And I would advise anyone else to do the same. Because what this is, I am not sure.

Is it just the nature of chance? Is this proof of some higher power or being moving events from behind the scenes? I don't know. I will leave it to you to decide on what you think it may be.

An Encounter with the Ghost of Anton LaVey

Ok I know how the title sounds. So, before we get into the crux of this article, let me say one thing.

Yes, I do feel that the spirit of Dr. LaVey has contacted me. Not in some séance, or a weird haunting of any sort, but in dreams. Now while I personally do feel these encounters to be very real, because they are dreams, I'm not upset to say they could be, and may very well be, just flights of my over active imagination. Regardless though, these "encounters" have had a strong influence not only on my writing and general outlook where Satanism is concerned, they have also influenced some of my life choices too. Thus, real encounters or not, they are important.

Now you might wonder why I choose to believe these Dreams to be legit encounters with Anton LaVey. Suffice it to say, having been dead before in my lifetime has given me a perspective of what to look for when dealing with the spiritual plain. Also, this is not something I actively have gone out of my way to do. It just happens on the occasion, and is in truth damn infrequent. I'll admit to enjoying the encounters when they do occur as I tend to come away with glints of hidden knowledge about LaVey and his practices.

It was in one of my more recent encounters that LaVey shared a bit of interesting knowledge with me. I had explained that I was planning to buy a house and convert it into a new Black House. This derived a small chuck from the spirit as he rolled a cigarette. "You know Luc, there is more to the Black House than just black paint and a spooky alter. All the rituals are fun and fine to do. And can leave a mark on the place for sure. However, if you want it to have true power you must consecrate it properly."

He waved around the living room of his place. "I wasn't just kidding when I said this place had roots that go all the way to hell! Not only did I choose very carefully the house for its history, and affordability mind you. I performed a set of powerful rituals. Blessings you might say. Three rites that firmly cemented this place not only into the world of flesh and spirit, but into the very minds of people for generations to come."

He went on to describe the first and second of these rituals
The first was a very simple house blessing. Devoting the property to Hell and Satan. The ritual performed had no defined style as this was before LaVey really started to hammer things down to a defined system. For the purpose of this section though I will provide my own take on a house blessing.

The second ritual is perhaps the most interesting. It is a sex ritual performed on the alter itself. Again, done before LaVey really hammered anything down, this ritual would inevitably be morphed into the Lust Ritual. What was perhaps the most interesting element here was that his partner was not his wife, though he was adamant that she was there to witness the act.

"It's imperative that she not be your significant other! There can be nothing between you other than carnal lust in its rawest form. The words matter very little in this ritual. What matters is that your carnal fluids mix atop the altar itself and consecrate it with the energy of your passions. If you can't do it on the altar the before it is fine. Just collect your seed from her womb and sprinkle it atop the altar itself." He explained.

I had to ask him after listening to this explanation. "And your wife? She was good with this? You didn't hide this from her?"

Anton's ghost laughed. It was a deep full chuckle. "Why on earth would I do that? I preached being the naughtiest person you could be! What's more is I hate feelings of needless guilt. If someone is telling lies and trying to hide their deeds from their spouse or partner, they clearly harbor a guilty conscience about their deeds. That's far from being naughty!" He did air quotes with his fingers at the word "naughty".

"That's counter productivity at its finest. Guilt serves no purpose to the Satanist it is a counterproductive feeling. The Satanist will not hide their deeds as he has nothing to be guilty over. If I had to hide my actions from my family, I would only succeed in destroying the trust we shared! I wouldn't be embracing the Satanic path, but the path of a lecherous husband unsatisfied in his marriage. Bent only on destroying it through his trysts. However! By being more than honest, by letting her watch the deed. My conscience remains clear! Thus, I am free to do what I see fit to do. And be that naughtiest of the naughty individuals!"

Of course, this dialog was fascinating to me. And it certainly wasn't the whole conversation. But for the brevity of this article and the privacy of others, I'll not continue.

After hearing several more minutes of some of his escapades we came to the third and final ritual to create a true Black House.
"It's simple Luc! The Black Mass itself of course! It's perhaps the oldest of our rituals. Created by Christian fear mongers who knows how far back. La Voisin only canonized a basic procedural for it. Minus the whole

aborted fetus bit, the ritual I provided in my book should suffice. If you can get your hands on a Eucharist that makes it better but the traditional turnip or course bread is fine too. Just make sure your altars juices are flowing really well if you plan to shove the host in as tradition calls for. She will be less angry if you do not make it a rough experience."

We laughed of course and cracked some jokes on the subject for a while more. It was then I felt the pull of the real world wakening me. LaVey grabbed my arm and said one more thing.

"Wait a moment Luc. A word of warning. Be certain you're ready for this. Once you create a Black House in completion there is no undoing it. It will draw people to you. For good and for bad. People who will desire what you have created, and will do anything to get it from you or destroy it. The forces you will be conjuring up will be powerful. Do not make my mistake and trust the House to anyone outside your family. Pick your heirs carefully. And remember, when you commit to this house it is forever." He gestured to the now fading room. In moments I was awake in my bed. My dog whimpering at me to get up and let him out.

This is but one encounter. A description of a dream so vivid that it had background noises and smells. That I could look around the room and see details few could spot. From video or photographs was also interesting.

One thing about the house that I have been shown in a past dream was a room. Not in the basement but on the top floor. Its ceiling was slanted in. it had books lining the walls and in piles around. And at the front of the house was a desk cluttered with odds and ends and a typewriter. LaVay said to described this room if I ever had need to validate my descriptions of our encounters.

As a bit of a final note to this. I've been on the receiving end of some very hostile comments from Church of Satan members in the past, who often try to use LaVey as weapon. Claims that he wouldn't stand for me or my points of view or my beliefs, have all been thrown in my direction. I've been told a number of horrid things. All of which I can't help but to laugh at. And it is for this very reason that I never take it to heart. Because if my dreams are in fact the real ghost of the man himself sharing his insights from beyond the grave with me, well then guess who is having the last laugh, and who is the deluded ones.

The Age of Lucifer Begins

It is perhaps one of the lesser addressed parts of Satanism, and also one of the most influential. Our ages in history or the "Ano Satanas".

The tradition of dating our events with the term "Ano Satanas" and whatever the roman numeral is started with Dr. LaVey announcing 1966 as the first year in the Age of Satan. The numerals afterwards refer to how many years in has been since its commencement.

The Church of Satan has continued with this tradition even to this day. However, there is much more to it than the CoS has taken note of. To the CoS we are still in the Age of Satan. The truth is that Calendar ended on October 29th 1997, with the Epoch of LaVey's death.

To be clear the 20th century has been all Hell's rise to power in the astral cycles. Beginning with HarWer's age beginning its long shift with Crowley, and ending with the dawn of LaVey's Age of Satan.

But when LaVey died it created a singular event called an Epoch. And following this a new Age or "Era" began. It was the Era of Andros. The "Age of Discord".

In demonology, Andras is a Great Marquis of Hell. He is the 63rd of the 72 spirits of Solomon. Alternatively named Andra-inanyas. Andras has under his command thirty legions of demons whose only directive is to hunt and kill men. He is seconded by his henchman

Flauros. Andras appears with a winged angel's body and the head of an owl or raven, riding upon a strong black wolf and wielding a sharp and bright sword. Andras was responsible for sowing discord and for this reason was allegedly summoned quite often by military leaders, to use his abilities to incite wars that last for decades, redefining peoples and continents. In addition, due to the subtle nature of his work, Andras was supposedly extremely difficult to detect. Moreover, Andras was considered to be a highly dangerous demon, who could kill the conjuring magician and his assistants if precautions were not taken. A misstep outside the magical protective circle could mean instant death for the conjurers.

This is exactly what has happened in Satanism since LaVey's death in 97.

Many events have transpired in this time-frame that has changed the landscape of Satanism. LaVey's house was destroyed as a result of a lack of CoS unity. Organizations have risen and fallen. The Religion has splintered into a thousand factions. And from it discord at every turn. Deceivers bearing the mask of our religion has appeared to hijack our religion for political power, while the Church of Satan sits upon its laurels festering in a pond of stagnation.

It is now obvious we have been living in a different Satanic Age without realizing it, which of course lines up with the nature of Andras.

But Andras's influence is over. 23 years after the Epoch of LaVey's death, the lunar cycles came to polar confluence. When Anton LaVey passed in 1997, the moon was in a perfect new moon cycle. Landing upon All Hallows Eve as the total new moon. In 2020, exactly 23 years to the day, on the anniversary of LaVey's death, began a new lunar cycle. The second Full Moon phase of October 2020, culminated on All Hallows Eve in a Super Blue Full Moon.

And thus, began a new Age that will see an end to Andras's Discord.

Now we begin the Age of Lucifer. The Age of Wisdom.

*(It should be noted that the STS identify everything after LaVey's death on Oct 29th 1997, up to the creation of STS with the term **"Ano Andras"**. This is a period of 23 years between events, and is marked by their very unique, and opposing lunar cycles and events. After the official creation of STS on Oct 29th 2020 we utilize the term **"Ano Luciferi"**.)*

The Third Testament

Black candles slowly burning.
White fangs and flashing eyes.
Hell's wind and incantations,
Summon living fire.
Darkest forces and your Demons.
Black Order. Black King.
The Cult that serves the living,
Accept this offering.

Intro

This section explores the deeper notions of Satanic Law and the theories surrounding them. The articles here all lead up to the finalization of the ultimate Law of the Satanist.
The Lex Satanicus.

The Myth of Bodily Autonomy

In our current Satanic climate, the TST has brought a number odd issues that should not even be a thing to the forefront. One thing that we must address is their third Tenant. This Tenant State that a person's body is inviolable, and that Bodily Autonomy is a given right. A right that is given at birth, and can never be taken away for any reason. This is obviously, and flagrantly one of the most un-Satanic notions ever, and flies directly in the face of every Real Satanist today. Why?

Lex Talionis! The Law of the Jungle. The Rule of Fang and Claw.

It is the Satanic truth that, Bodily Autonomy is not a right, but a privilege of the strong. This has been proven in nature and history time and again. The weak are invariably preyed upon and controlled by the strong! Either through fear, subversion, or force of Will directly. Lex Talionis, The survival of the fittest. Nature proves without question, if you want to have control over what happens to your own flesh, do not be a sheeple, you must be predatory. Or at the very least, understand your own place in the food chain to not get eaten. It's that simple.

What is more is TST also violates both their third and fourth Tenants together. If, as they say, one's own body is inviolable, that too should extend to the unborn infant. Yet they do not consider this living being as having any rights as it is within the mother's body. So, they prove the notion of Lex Talionis in this, by hypocritically allowing the mothers own Will to dominate the unborn child's own rights and autonomy.

If Bodily Autonomy was a right, then we would not be able to imprison people. to control what they eat drink or watch. We would not be able to confine those who have broken the law. Yet we do and must. When a person breaks the law. When a crime is committed, they forfeit their freedom. They lose control of their fate, and of the choices they can make in life. They are thrust into a restricted world where their every move is done only with the permission of prison guards. People who for no reason can unlock your cell and take what few possessions you have left. Even the clothes you are wearing. Bodily Autonomy is a privilege that can be taken away.

Do the mentally ill, have the freedom to say what happens to themselves? No! We take away that privilege for their own good! We sedate them and put them in hospitals against their will. We make them prisoners, all for the sake of their own good, because they can no longer safely judge for themselves what is good for them or those around them.

To this end the notion of Bodily Autonomy being inviolable is a farce. A complete myth! Our own society proves this undeniable fact.

The truth of the matter is that if a person does not want to be used and abused by others. To stepped on or physically forced to do something against their will, they must be more powerful and stronger than others. What is more is the Strongest of predators will be very aware of their own weaknesses, and will adapt to compensate for them. They will seek to be in complete control of themselves and by proxy, their immediate environment.

Be that a physical environment, psychological, digital, work, or wherever they are.

If a woman is attacked in her home and raped, then her attacker was the stronger of the two. Both physically and mentally. But if by chance she stops him and defeats his attempt, then she was the stronger. She can then continue until he is no longer a threat and who would blame her. I certainly wouldn't. In the film franchise "I spit on your grave," This is the exact premise. A group of guys attack and rape a young woman then leave her for dead. She then heals and comes back more vicious than ever and is able to physically dominate her former attackers and get revenge. It is a wonderful example of Lex Talionis from both angles.

In the Satanic Bible, from the Book of Satan section 4 it says, *"Stop the way of them that would persecute you. Let those who devise thine undoing be hurled back to confusion and infamy. Let them be as chaff before the cyclone and after they have fallen, rejoice in thine own salvation."*

This could not be truer. It is sound advice. Nah I would say it is more of a commandment! Bodily Autonomy is not a right. It is a privilege that only the strongest get to keep. And we will constantly be tested in our lives as to our strength. For signs it is waning. And when it fails finally as it inevitably must, either we can accept the strength of our successors gracefully, or be crushed by our enemies.

Ave Lex Talionis! The law of the strong over the weak. The rule of Fang and Claw.

A Satanic Sickness

If there is one thing I personally find irritating in the modern Satanic community, it is the sudden prevalence of wokeness. I actually do blame all Satanists, including myself for allowing this issue to get so far out of hand that we now have a rather serious problem on our hands. Satanists were so starved for a good public figure to rally behind, that we allowed ourselves to be duped by politically motivated liberal far leftists and Marxists. We forgot the fundamental foundations of what Satanism was built upon and embraced atheism, Socialism, and Marxism. And for what!? A brief few years of positive media attention? A new powerful, and outspoken voice to wield against the Christian establishment?

And what cost have we been forced to pay for our new found public voice? What was the cost for a few brief years of media spotlight? Was it even really ours?

The cost came when a political activist group appropriated our religion and subverted our ideology, then opened the doors for everyone to come in. Satanism is not a religion for the general public. The profane and unwashed masses. And I literally do mean UNWASHED! As in actually not physically bathing! And yet we all sat by and watched silently as TST let in drug addicts, homeless, and convicted sexual predators into their ranks, and then paraded them around in public at events in representation of us. And this not the only thing they have allowed in.

For decades Satanists have faced serious issues with infighting yes. But we never pandered to the self-pitying, the pandering, and the personally insecure. Yet here we stand now, dealing with people who identify as things that they are not! And we are supposed to accept it in our current societal climate. We are supposed to coddle and pamper the personal woes of people who constantly complain on their social media accounts on how, "THEY, don't fit in", "No one loves them", "Everyone betrays them", "Everyone is a liar", or "Someone was mean to them", add nauseum.

Yes, I am being deliberately mean spirited here to drive home my personal feelings, and those shared by most Satanists that have to deal with this stuff. But I will not and am not attacking anyone in particular. This is because I feel by pointing this out is such a way will help those guilty of this crap, to KNOCK THE BULLSHIT OFF! And now back to your regularly scheduled dose of red pilling.

The stupid part of this is that it should never have to be so blatantly said. None of us should have to go around policing Satanists tell them what they should and shouldn't be or do. It should be instinctive to the common Satanist. Exceptions can be made for everything too within reason. But it is when these exceptions are abused to such a massive degree, that we need to step up and do the one thing we should not have to do, call people out on it if they are Satanists or not, and then tell them this or that is or isn't Satanism. It's utterly ludicrous that this has to even be such a thing now. So let me be blunt here. Satanism is not for everyone. We are not for the personally insecure, the complainers, the woke, the ignorant, or the outright stupid.

Firstly. If you have a problem, be willing to handle it yourself before you bring it to your fellow Satanists.

The next thing is, I don't pretend to be something that I am not. I have flaws. I am wrong frequently. There are things I do not know. And I do make mistakes sometimes. Including the occasional serious oopsy. I accept these failings. I don't try to portray myself as the end all expert on all things. There are subjects that other STS members are vastly more knowledgeable than myself on whom I have turned to in the recent past months, weeks, days, and yes even hours. And I am comfortable with that.

Another thing I am comfortable with is myself! My own person mentally. I can sit and be in my own company alone for hours, or even days, and be at complete peace with myself, with my own sexuality, and even my own biological gender. Heck anyone who has met me in person or spoken to me on the phone will know I am a huge loud and proud straight male chauvinist. I am about as male as they come. I've faced my insecurities about my sexuality, and my gender, and my religion. I've come to grips with myself, and my chosen path through life.

Believe it or not there was a phase in my life where I experimented with having a boyfriend, experimented with my own gender identity and entertained the idea of being a girl. I've been on both ends of this spectrum mind you. I was at one point closer than I like to tell people, to joining the Catholic Church and becoming a Catholic Priest. Not a joke. Just one more step and I would likely be sitting in Rome or the Vatican right now doing who knows what. So I seriously get it from both angles here and am not just talking out my own ass.

Satanists are people who are 100%, comfortable with themselves. If they have a personal problem with someone or something, especially their own issues, they don't complain about it. They deal with it. They don't make up excuses. They see things for how they are. A Satanist doesn't try to say, "Oh! I was born wrong. I'm the wrong gender. I should be a female because of ....", or, "I don't have a choice to be straight or gay. I'm biologically attracted to other men/women." You get my point. We just don't do that sort of crap because we have come to terms with who we are inside and out.

A Satanist doesn't make up excuses for who or what they are. They don't pretend to be something other than what nature made them. And if they do, they own up to it. They can look in the mirror and say to themselves, "I am this naturally. I'm good with that. But I choose to be this way because I want to be that way." They don't make up excuses. If they are gay, it's because that is what they prefer for personal reasons. Honestly dating the same gender as oneself is a far cry easier that dealing with the craziness of dating the opposite gender. And there is a higher chance you and they will be into the same things.

And let's not even get into the whole trans issue. Frankly speaking this topic has turned into a fiasco. It has become perpetuated by Liberal far leftists who actively seek to subvert our society.

Certain pseudo Satanic groups promotes Transgenderism to almost all of its members. We have even had former members of such groups speak in depth and at length about the promotion of Trans-identity, and the parties that are frequently thrown. In a recent private conversation with a currently active Atlanta member of one such group, she admitted to helping raise funds to have another members children be transitioned, and having facilitated and promoted private parties where the main attraction was sexual intercourse with same said children. The last of such events took place only a few weeks prior to writing this, where both children had sex with no less than twenty adults, consisting of biological women and Transwomen, who still had their male genitalia intact. One youth who is biologically female has already had her breasts surgically removed against her will. And we are supposed to accept this type of behavior!

In Satanism the trans subject should be a no-brainer. A complete non-issue. For us, it is seen as unnecessary, and is a complete personal choice! A choice made by stable level headed adults, for themselves! Not made by someone who thinks they were born the wrong gender, but by someone who can admit that they just like how the opposite gender looks acts and feels. They know they will never really be the opposite gender because of their biology and they accept that. They also accept that unless they have a truly awesome plastic surgeon, they might not even look like the opposite gender fully. And they never force children to do it.

This is a sickness that has infected Modern Satanism long enough. It is a form of Social Vampirism. And just as Social Vampirism, it is a cancer that has spread fast and far. It is time now to address this sickness within our own ranks when and wherever we find it, and cut it from ourselves as we would a rotten, festering, gangrenous limb.

It is one thing to be a level headed adult, who is completely at peace with ones own natural self to make the conscience decision to be gay or trans, and accept the pitfalls that go with those choices. It is another to be that way and make up excuses, or try to force others to be that way too.

To place your woes on public display, with no attempt to resolve them, simply for the sympathy card. Or to subscribe to the woke agenda, and play the perpetual victim card. This is completely unacceptable and grotesque. It is a complete lack of understanding of our Doctrines and religious teachings.

To this I say to all Satanists. Reflect upon yourself. Look over your social interactions with others. Do you blast all of your personal woes publicly? Do you see yourself as being perpetually victimized by the establishment? Look at yourself in the mirror. Not as how you present yourself to the outside world. Drop your personal masks and really see yourself as you are underneath the public façade. Your gender, your biological sexual drive. Your darkest personal desires, including the ones you know are probably against the law. See the instinctive beast within. That inner Demon. Now come to terms with it. The good and the bad. Accept then what you truly are and how much of that public mask is not just for your protection, but others too. Strip away those layers you have built up, and cut away the unnecessary brainwashing that society has placed on you.

Look at the REAL you. The one that strikes awe and blinding terror in yourself. Can you sit with yourself and be at peace? Probably not. Well not at first. This is the failing of most people in our modern society.

In ages now long gone, people did not have the ability to hide their real self. They had to live openly as the animal. To this day, some untouched tribes still experience this freedom. But not us. In our modern times we are taught to put upon ourselves lair after lair of lies, to bring out the "**real you**". We are taught that this, is normal, natural even. BUT IT IS NOT!

None of that is Satanism. We are primal animals who accept our animal nature. When we walk into a room, we scream by our very presence, LEX TALIIONIS! We are at times a living, breathing, walking, death threat. Chauvinists to the core of our natural selves. Be us male or female, we take extreme pride in our biology.

The liberal woke leftists would call our chauvinism as "Toxic". Yet we wield it as a weapon that makes the opposite gender salivate at our presence and attracts to us that which we desire sexually. Be them gay or straight, we are James Bond when we come walking in.

As real Satanists, we can justifiably call ourselves chauvinists, because we actually know what it means. To be proud of ones' own self! Ones own natural identity and gender. And it is not just limited to the male gender but both genders, and to ones' religion, or chosen identity to! Yes folks, flaming gay guys are in truth Gay Male Chauvinists. Just as a raging Bull Dike, is a Lesbian Chauvinist. We understand the true definition of the word so we get to use it.

And so, it is now I leave you with this closing statement.

Cut from yourself the Hypocritical Self-Deceits. Learn to accept yourself as you are. Grow in your natural pride and being and understand that for humans', sexuality is a choice not biology anymore. That we can never change our biology. Well not yet anyways. And biological instincts will in the end, win every time no mater how tamped down by drugs and hormone treatments you make it. At the end of the day, you are what you were born as. So why fight it? Sometimes acceptance of things makes us much happier. Happier with ourselves, and our surroundings. By removing the rose tinted glasses that lie about what the world looks like, and putting on the High Definition Paintball Visor, we become more ready to take on the world, and be that inner 007 we know we are.

And so, I leave you now with the words of wisdom taught to me by my old mentor, "The truth will set you free. But first it will piss you the fuck off!"

666
The Truth of the Beast

A while back, I had a particularly nasty occurrence happened with an acquaintance on Facebook. He had a bit of a tiff with something I said then went about trying to defame me in a fit of anger. This lead him stealing the STS signature TrapBaph logo and removed the 666 from it then re-posted it claiming it to be his own art. Naturally, I slapped him with a copyright claim, and prayed that would be the end of that.

But it was in another post of his that I developed a very interesting question. What was the importance of 666 to satanism, and perhaps more importantly, to the individual Satanist?

Here is the fragment of the post he made pertaining to this.

"If you see a sigil of baphomet with the number 666 within it, know that that is a gross inaccuracy. That number is not, nor has it ever been, a number to represent Satan or any devil of any pantheon. The number 666 is, instead, a prophesied number that represents a human man that will supposedly rise through the ranks of politics, seize power and is recognized as the antichrist. The sigil of baphomet does not represent any antichrist but is, instead, a symbol of our opposition."

Ok that seems like a fair assessment. Accept he completely misses the point of our sigil. That it was in fact never intended to be about Satan per say but an homage to LaVey's original Order of the Trapezoid, that was later reformed again in the Temple of Set. The use of the Baphomet in the center was a calculated one to represent the entire religion not just one element. But I digress off topic.

To Say 666 is the number of the prophesized Antichrist is a bit of an understatement. And it doesn't fully explain the entire scope of the situation. So let us explore it a little bit.

The number of the beast is associated with the Beast of Revelation in chapter 13, verse 18 of Book of Revelation. In most manuscripts of the New Testament and in English translations of the Bible, the number of the beast is six hundred and sixty-six. Papyrus 115 which is the oldest preserved manuscript of the Revelation as of 2017, as well as other ancient sources like Codex Ephraemi Rescriptus, give the number of the beast as χιϲ. Which can be transliterated in Arabic numerals as 616, not 666. There are some critical editions of the Greek text, such as the Novum Testamentum Graece, that notes the 616 as a variation of the number of the beast.

Certainly, the commenter is partly correct. In the Bible's Book of Revelations, it is part of a prophesy, about someone who will step forth as the Antichrist and lead earths armies in a final battle against the Christian Messiah reborn. But what about the number's origins. Certainly, as demonstrated above it has a very rich history.

However, the source of this number in the biblical sense doesn't go to revelations, but Emperor Nero, whose name in the Hebrew gematria is 666. Nero was well known for hating Christians, and would regularly have them fed to the lions for entertainment. He was also called "The Beast", by certain angry Jews and Christians, for his horrific decadence and violent nature. To this regard he certainly was a beast, but perhaps not the only one.

Going back to our modern times now that we have a slightly clearer, though by no means exhaustive, understanding of the symbol's origins, let us explore what this strange set of numbers means to our modern Satanist.

When I first saw the inflammatory post, I knew it was an attempt to goad me into a verbal argument with the author. It was clear baiting. As was his theft of my intellectual property. And despite my deep desire to engage him, I opted not to.

However, his comment left me with a deep burning question. What does 666, mean to me? I didn't know. I felt deeply connected to the number as a Satanist. But I couldn't describe what or why it held such significance to me. So, I put the question out to the STS Facebook group. "What does 666 mean to you?" and the response I got floored me.

The overall response from other Satanists, mostly Theistic in nature was, "Nothing", "I don't fell anything towards it", "It has no meaning to me."

But why?! Why did this number that is so significant to the very history of Satanism, a reference to the Antichrist. A number that strikes absolute panic in Christians, to the point of complete avoidance. A number emblazoned upon the trapezoid as the symbol for two branches of the Same order, and for my own Org. Why was it considered so insignificant? Why was it so unimportant to the individual Satanist?

I finally turned to another source. A peer in the Brotherhood of Satan, and a very good wise philosopher and magician, Druwydion Pendragon. This is his response to me.

"Brother, the whole Occult World is full of Symbology. That Symbology reflects a meaning and definition. The 666 Satanic Symbology is no different. 666 reflects man but not just ANY man (or woman). It reflects the Satanic Being. So, 666 as a Satanic Symbol for the Anti-Christ for instance actually reflects all of us upon the Lefthand Path. The LHP is the Path of the Anti-Christ. We are the Great Beast (Humans that are Gods & Goddesses). We ARE the Anti-Christ and our signature is our 666 Satanic Symbology. Since we know the christian God of today is not the true God the Father we have merely took the 666 Symbology back from their own book of revelations (And their Book of Lies) and returned it to its original place. I also enjoy inverting the 666 to 999 too ! The significance is that we as Satanists today should take back everything that is ours for the coming reign of Darkness belongs to us. We are the Anti-Christ ! It is time for all Satanists to acknowledge that truth ! Hail Satan ! 666 !"

To say I was floored once again, would be an understatement. Finally! I understood my own feelings towards this symbol. And I understood the ambivalence demonstrated by others. They probably felt some sort of connection, but like myself couldn't explain it. Being unable to explain the feeling they chose to ignore it and pretend it meant nothing.

666, doesn't just represent a prophesy. It doesn't simply stand for one Devil, Demon, or man. It's not just some obscure reference in a moldering book. It has vital substance. It is a weapon again those who futilely hold the cross to us and demand our conversion to their beliefs. It is a shield. A sigil of pure Satanic power. It represents me. It represents you. It represents everyone who is not a member of the mundane herd.

666, represent Satan's children. Those of us born under his infernal influence. Those who cannot be moved or shaken or converted from our faith.

To say that this number doesn't represent any Demon or Devil, that it is not connected intrinsically to Satan and the Host of Hell, is to resent, and deny the very truth of Satan. Because it is the number of perhaps the most powerful race of Demons in Hell. The human Demon. And we should be damn proud to bear it.

The Black Pope
Establishing the Infernal Legacy

Ok so this is not actually intended to piss anyone off, no doubt it will on this particular subject matter. The Black Pope. Who is the current Black Pope? Why are they the Black Pope and what does their job entail?

Since Anton LaVey's death, there have been a number of individuals who have attempted to claim this mantle for themselves. Some officially most just by proxy of the media. Peter H. Gilmore, Lucian Greaves, Adam Daniels, EA Koetting, and recently Tau Nagash, amongst no doubt a whole string of others.

The sad truth however is that there is no current Black Pope. And STS does not recognize any document or certificate where an individual claims to hold such a position. Nor will we honor any title supposedly awarded by such an individual on certification.

"Why?" You might ask. Why would we not honor a title given by a person claiming the mantle of Black Pope?

The answer is simple. Because after the death of Anton LaVey, and many the Satanic denominations that has formed, or stepped out of the shadows during the chaos of the Age of Andras, there is no unified consensus on who should hold this title.

The mantle of Black Pope is not something that effects just one denomination or another. It is not like the Christian Pope, which is held by one system of Christian doctrine alone, yet can influence the entirety of the Christian faith worldwide. The 20th century saw three Black Popes come into power, and would have had a fourth to lead us into the new millennium had Aquino been given the full recognition he deserved in his time.

You may wonder who the other Black Popes in the 20th century had. For certainly LaVey was the first.

The truth is he was actually the third of the Black Popes and first to officially hold that title. The First was none other than Aleister Crowley. The Beast. The second was Dr. Gerald Gardner, the founder of the wiccan religion. Their lines of power succession can be followed by their dates of rise to public power to their deaths. Each man creating systems that heavily influenced the formulation of Satanism proper.

These men never asked for the mantle of Black Pope. It was a common consensus of Pagans, witches, occultists, Satanists, and the general public, that they held that title. And they each lived up to the title perfectly. Fulfilling their duties as Satan's or the opposition's minister on earth to perfection in their respective time period. And before you say it, no Crowley nor Gardner ever bore the mantle of Satanist, nor did they practice Satanism outrightly. Yet they operated in identical fashion to LaVey, whom was heavily influenced by their works.

Nowadays, Satan enjoys not just a singular man to be his voice. He has many worthy magicians leading different aspects of his flock. One might say that the position of Black Pope is no longer needed. And in general, basic terms, they would be correct. However, in the grander picture of things they would be wrong.

The position of Black Pope is most certainly one that needs to be filled. It is the ultimate weapon against misinformation from Christian nutjobs, and pseudo Satanists like TST. The Black Pope can give clarity where fringe elements of our religion like JoS or o9a are concerned. He or she is the ultimate spokesperson for Satanism in general, and sets the tone and standard for how the religion behaves and functions.

At present there is two extremely influential leaders that have both tried claim this mantle themselves. Gilmore and Greaves. Both have actually influenced our religion in major ways, and not for the better. Bringing both Atheism, and extreme Liberal and Marxist political agendas into our midst. Both men exemplify how the power of the Black Pope can work, even though neither one fully held the position proper. It is ironic that it takes negative influences to show how the positive influences work.

So, what are the qualities we should look for in a Black Pope? What sort of qualifications should he have, that other influential leaders lack, that separates them from actually holding the mantle? Let's break this down and look at the three recognized "Black Popes" of the 20th century, vs the two most influential pretenders of our modern era. Cowley, Gardner, & LaVey, vs Gilmore and Greaves, so we can define exactly what is a Black Pope's qualities.

Crowley. 1875-1947 "The Beast"

Aleister Crowley's understanding of the occult arts is unquestionable. He commanded forces well beyond the norm, and fashion elaborate rituals and rites still used to this day. He is also the author of a number of books and literature outlining his magical system in theory and practice. He was the founder of the system of Thelma, and rose up through the ranks of the Golden Dawn & Ordo Templi Orientis very quickly in the late 1890s and early 1900s.

In 1907 Crowley founded the group A∴A∴, and the system of Thelma.

Crowley held no political agendas. He was purely focused on his craft, and by 1912 was put in charge of the OTO's British branch.

In 1920 he established the Abby of Thelma in Italy. Here he formed a commune. Though, by the 1930s he returned to Britain and continued his career in the Golden Dawn and OTO and spreading his Thelma through out its chapters as the primary system of magic practiced by both orders.

In 1947 Crowley passed away due to complication with Pulmonary Bronchitis

Dr. Gerald Gardner 1884-1964 "The Father of Wicca"

Gerald Brosseau Gardner, also known by the craft name Scire, was an English Wiccan, as well as an author and an amateur anthropologist and archaeologist. He was instrumental in bringing the Contemporary Pagan religion of Wicca to public attention, writing some of its definitive religious texts and founding the tradition of Gardnerian Wicca.

Born into an upper-middle-class family in Blundellsands, Lancashire, Gardner spent much of his childhood abroad in Madeira. In 1900, he moved to colonial Ceylon, and then in 1911 to Malaya, where he worked as a civil servant, independently developing an interest in the native peoples and writing papers and a book about their magical practices. After his retirement in 1936, he travelled to Cyprus, penning the novel A Goddess Arrives before returning to England. Settling down near the New Forest, he joined an occult group, the Rosicrucian Order Crotona Fellowship, through which he said he had encountered the New Forest coven into which he was initiated in 1939. Believing the coven to be a survival of the pre-Christian witch-cult discussed in the works of Margaret Murray, he decided to revive the faith, supplementing the coven's rituals with ideas borrowed from Freemasonry, ceremonial magic and the writings of Aleister Crowley to form the Gardnerian tradition of Wicca.

Moving to London in 1945, he became intent on propagating this religion, attracting media attention and writing about it in High Magic's Aid (1949), Witchcraft Today (1954) and The Meaning of Witchcraft (1959). Founding a Wiccan group known as the Bricket Wood coven, he introduced a string of High Priestesses into the religion, including Doreen Valiente, Lois Bourne, Patricia Crowther and Eleanor Bone, through which the Gardnerian community spread throughout Britain and subsequently into Australia and the United States in the late 1950s and early 1960s. Involved for a time with Cecil Williamson, Gardner also became director of the Museum of Magic and Witchcraft on the Isle of Man, which he ran until his death at sea in in 1964.

Gardner is internationally recognized as the "Father of Wicca" among the Pagan and occult communities worldwide.

Anton Szandor LaVey 1930-1997 "The Black Pope"

I'll Not waste too much time here with the Good Doctor as we all know his credentials, or at least should by now. He was the founder of the Church of Satan and the religion of Satanism. He authored several books, including The Satanic Bible, The Satanic Rituals, The Satanic Witch, The Devil's Notebook, and Satan Speaks! In addition, he released three albums, including The Satanic Mass, Satan Takes a Holiday, and Strange Music. He played a minor on-screen role and served as technical advisor for the 1975 film The Devil's Rain and served as host and narrator for Nick Bougas' 1989 mondo film Death Scenes.

LaVey was the subject of numerous articles in news media throughout the world, including popular magazines such as Look, McCall's, Newsweek, and Time, and men's magazines. He also appeared on talk shows such as The Joe Pyne Show, Donahue and The Tonight Show, and in two feature-length documentaries: Satanis in 1969 and Speak of the Devil: The Canon of Anton LaVey in 1993. Two official biographies have been written on LaVey: The Devil's Avenger by Burton H. Wolfe, published in 1974, and The Secret Life of a Satanist by Blanche Barton, published in 1990.

Historian of Satanism Gareth J. Medway described LaVey as a "born showman", with anthropologist Jean La Fontaine describing him as a "colourful figure of considerable personal magnetism". Academic scholars of Satanism Per Faxneld and Jesper Aa. Petersen described LaVey as "the most iconic figure in the Satanic milieu". LaVey was labeled many things by journalists, religious detractors, and Satanists alike, including "The Father of Satanism", the "St. Paul of Satanism", "The Black Pope", and the "evilest man in the world".

So, what do these three men all have in common?

1. They all were occultists.

2. Each man was a prolific writer and published multiple books on the subject of their chosen occult tradition.

3. Each man came into power within two or three years of the death of their predecessor. Crowley passed in 1947, by 1949 Gardner published his first book and gained world recognition. Gardner passed in 1964, by 1966 laVey opens the CoS, and publishes the Satanic Bible by 69.

4. Each man founded their own system of magick and philosophy. Crowley Thelma, Gardner Wicca,

LaVey Satanism.

5. Each man represented the occult arts publicly to their eras until their deaths, and held world recognition as the leading authority of the occult to the public media.

6. Each man is universally held in high regard even to this day by their contemporaries, followers, and living peers, to the point of legendary status. Despite any failings they may have had.

7. While inspired by their precursors, each man was a wholly unique and original in their ideas and concepts.

8. Before coming into fruition of their power, each man led a very rich and traveled life affording them numerous experiences that they would later use in their respective occult fields.

Peter Howard Gilmore 1958-Living

Peter Howard Gilmore is the current High Priest of the Church of Satan. Gilmore graduated from NYU with both a bachelor's and master's degree in music composition. As a representative of the Church of Satan, Gilmore has been interviewed on numerous television and radio programs dealing with the topic of Satanism, including appearances on History, the BBC, Syfy, Point of Inquiry, and Bob Larson's Christian radio show.

Gilmore was raised in upstate New York. He visited New York City regularly throughout his youth and moved to Hell's Kitchen in 1980. He read The Satanic Bible at age thirteen and has described The Church of Satan as "the motivating philosophical force in my life" ever since. (Now, now, class. I hear that snickering. We all know he can't shut up about being an Atheist.)

In 1989, he and his wife Peggy Nadramia began publishing a Satanic journal, The Black Flame, and continues to publish issues sporadically. In 2005, Gilmore wrote the new introduction to Anton LaVey's The Satanic Bible, and his essay on Satanism was published in The Encyclopedia of Religion and Nature.

Gilmore is the author of one book, The Satanic Scriptures. A hard cover edition of The Satanic Scriptures, a collection essays and other writings by Gilmore was released on Walpurgis Night 2007, with a subsequent paperback edition released on October 13, 2007. The book includes rituals that were previously not public, such as marriages and Satanic burials. A large part of the essays were released before the book, however, some of the essays included in the book are improved variations. Some, including the essay published in the extract, deal with what the Church of Satan considers pseudo-Satanists, and those who refuse to join the Church, forming their own groups. Magus Gilmore is not too critical of the legitimate Satanists who never join the Church itself, yet disdainfully denounces Christians who sacrifice animals and worship God.

Other essays touch on the similarity between fascist aesthetics and Satanism, along with a multitude of political issues that correlate with the Satanic point of view, as the Index released demonstrates. It includes, but is not limited to, issues such as terrorism in the United States, gay rights, and much more.

Many of the rituals detailed in the Satanic Scripture were previously only known to members of the priesthood in the Church of Satan, as the wedding rite that was carried out by the founder Anton LaVey, along with the details of a Satanic funeral, is supposed which is a variation of which was made for him.

Lucien Greaves 1976- Living

Lucien Greaves, born Douglas Misicko, also known by the pseudonym Douglas Mesner, is a social activist and the spokesman and co-founder of The Satanic Temple.

Greaves was born in Detroit, Michigan. He studied neuroscience with a specialty in false-memory syndrome, and graduated from Harvard University

Greaves has spoken on the topics of Satanism, secularism, and The Satanic Temple at universities throughout the United States, and he has been a featured speaker at national conferences hosted by American Atheists, the American Humanist Association, and the Secular Student Alliance.

Greaves has been instrumental in setting up the Protect Children Project, the After School Satan project, and several political demonstrations and legal actions designed to highlight social issues involving religious liberty and the separation of church and state.

He says he has received many death threats, and deliberately does not use his legal name to avoid threats to his family. (So much for that idea. Nothing remains a secret forever in our modern era.)

Greaves was featured in Hail Satan? (2019), a documentary film about the The Satanic Temple and religious belief.

In an interview, Greaves describes how the idea for The Satanic Temple was conceived. Greaves and his colleagues envisioned The Satanic Temple as a "poison pill" in the Church/State debate. Their idea was that Satanists, asserting their rights and privileges where religious agendas have been successful in imposing themselves upon public affairs, could serve as a reminder that such privileges are for everybody, and can be used to serve an agenda beyond the current narrow understanding of what the religious agenda is.

Greaves has publicly stated that he does not worship Satan nor do followers of The Satanic Temple. Instead, Greaves claims that Satanism is more about personal sovereignty and independence and freedom of will.

Lucien Greaves has never published nor written any books. He did however produce illustrated art, (If you could call it that.) and a new introduction, for a limited edition of Might is Right, for Shane Bugbee.

So how does Gilmore and Greaves square up to the real Black Popes of the past?

1. Both men are very influential with their words and educated at some of the finest universities.

2. Neither man actually holds any theistic faith. It has been proven and established that even LaVey was a theistic.

3. Only one of the two has ever published an original book. However, it was not on an original religion, but an attempt to morph an existing one. Which to Gilmore's credit he has done marvelously and established his own denomination of Satanism. (Let's be honest here, it's just glorified Atheism. But at least it makes a genuine attempt.)

4. Neither man has created their own magical system, but have both chosen to ride the coattails of others to further a personal agenda.

Neither of these men fit the bill of what a Black Pope is. They share some minor qualities. Enough to be influential on a large scale. But not enough to hold the mantle officially.

The position of the Black Pope is one that could almost be said to be divinely laid upon a person by Satan himself. The traits shared by these men are all astonishingly similar. All being world traveled, occult experts, authors of multiple books, founders of their own traditions. And much more. Not to mention how it seems that when one died, within a few years a new one arose from the shadows to take their predecessor's place.

But who took LaVey's position? Who has held the mantle of the Black Pope all these long 23 years? Officially…. no one. The Age of Andras is characterized by feuding factions and personalities. There was no singular leader to represent the occult fields in any capacity. There were too many voices and big headed people to slow down and see who the new chosen one was.

Who was it? Are they still around?

The answer is sadly no they are no longer around. The changing of the age makes sense now, for it was with the Black Popes passing, that a new age began. From the Age of HarWer, to the hidden Age of the Horned One, to the Age of Satan, and then to the Age of Andras (The Age of the Hidden Black Pope.)

So, who was this hidden Black Pope? I think we all know the answer to that question. There was only one man that fit the criteria.

Michael A. Aquino. Whom despite being denied the recognition he deserved, even after LaVey's death, was the true and rightful Black Pope leading into the 2000s. He fit the bill perfectly. From his numerous books to his world travels. He was eloquent with his words, and represented his own magickal system to perfection. He remained a constant and avid supporter of Satanism and guided us all from afar.

To Michael Aquino, The true Black Pope of the early 21st century.

Now who will be the next in line?

It's Satanism Not Atheism

Perhaps there has never been a greater misunderstanding in Satanism than the notion of Atheism. What is more is that it is probably one of the biggest untruths about the religion supported even by many so called would be Satanists. Honestly it would be comical if it wasn't actually hurting what Satanism's core fundamental teachings.

I began this article with that paragraph over 13 years ago. It has taken this long to finally be ready to finish it and put it where it belongs.

The truth of things is that Satanism is not, and cannot be atheism. Or Humanism, I-theism, Objectivism, Non-theism, and whatever other members of this whole idiotic host of labels that people want to slap on Satanism, in order to warp it to their own concept.

Anton LaVey may have been publicly ambiguous about his own views on whether or not he believed in a real devil or not, but that doesn't change the fact that he was doing more than creating a simple philosophy. He was making an entirely new religion. He even said so in the Satanic Bible. Here is just one example.

The Satanic religion has not merely lifted the coin—it has flipped it completely over. Therefore, why should it support the very

principles to which it is completely opposed by calling itself anything other than a name which is totally in keeping with the reversed doctrines which make up the Satanic philosophy? Satanism is not a white light religion; it is a religion of the flesh, the mundane, the carnal—all of which are ruled by Satan, the personification of the Left Hand Path.
   Some evidence of a new Satanic Age, The Satanic Bible: Anton LaVey

This is but one of many times Satanism is directly referenced as a "Religion". This term... This word is very telling. It is what really differentiates Satanism from all the other words and terms that certain people would like to affix to it. Why? Because of what a religion is by its very nature. A "Belief" or "Faith" in something. Most often times in a spiritual concept, like a deity. It incorporates a huge number of elements that make it vastly more than just a philosophy, or doctrine, or collection of stories. It interweaves all these elements together to form an actual Religion. There is no other word for what it is. And LaVey knew that. He also understood that the concept of his new religions name was of utmost importance.

"Satanism is based on a very sound philosophy," say the emancipated. "But why call it Satanism? Why not call it something like 'Humanism' or a name that would have the connotation of a witchcraft group, something a little more esoteric—something less blatant." There is more than one reason for this. Humanism is not a religion. It is simply a way of life with no ceremony or dogma. Satanism has both ceremony and dogma. Dogma, as will be explained, is necessary.
   Some evidence of a new Satanic Age, The Satanic Bible: Anton LaVey

He would go on to explain how Satanism is different, even the inverse, of other altruistic mundane white light religions. And thus uses the name "Satanism". Eventually he would come to the next question. Why make it a religion at all?

Inevitably, the next question asked is: "Granted, you can't call it humanism because humanism is not a religion; but why even have a religion in the first place if all you do is what comes naturally, anyway? Why not just do it?"

Modern man has come a long way; he has become disenchanted with the nonsensical dogmas of past religions. We are living in an enlightened age. Psychiatry has made great strides in enlightening man about his true personality. We are living in an era of intellectual awareness unlike any the world has ever seen.

This is all very well and good, BUT—there is one flaw in this new state of awareness. It is one thing to accept something intellectually, but to accept the same thing emotionally is an entirely different matter. The one need that psychiatry cannot fill is man's inherent need for emotionalizing through dogma. Man needs ceremony and ritual, fantasy and enchantment. Psychiatry, despite all the good it has done, has robbed man of wonder and fantasy which religion, in the past, has provided.

Satanism, realizing the current needs of man, fills the large grey void between religion and psychiatry. The Satanic philosophy combines the fundamentals of psychology and good, honest emotionalizing, or dogma. It provides man with his much needed fantasy.

Some evidence of a new Satanic Age, The Satanic Bible: Anton LaVey

This is where things get interesting. You see there are those that want to call Satanism "Militant Atheism", and demand that it is not a religion but a "Philosophy", and nothing more. They do this mostly to work around the notion of what a religion is so they can call themselves a Satanist when it suits them, but then use another label when it doesn't. The Grotto Masters Handbook *(Also now called The Satanic Priest's TOP SECRET Manual.)*, explains it very well. As well as what makes Satanism a religion.

But, says the rationalist, these practical needs for an ethical society can be easily approached without the mythical veneer imposed by a religion. Is a religious context necessary? Or does it leave the door to mumbo-jumbo open too wide? Do the benefits outweigh the possible intellectual abuses? How is a religion different from a philosophy, and does Satanism qualify as a religion?

Modern Satanism, as defined by Anton LaVey, is still relatively new, and there are people who agree with his philosophy but who don't want to hang the pejorative label of "Satanist" around their necks. People who are timid about the label but who still find themselves agreeing with the commonsense aspects of LaVey's religion will probably call themselves "atheists" or "humanists" or "agnostics" or even "Wiccans". They'll be comfortable using the Devil's tools, but not taking His name. And they won't be Satanists. You can't embrace the militant rationality of Satanism and not utilize the images of Satan in a ritualistic sense. The two are inextricably bound together. They always have been. That is what makes it a religion and not a philosophy.

A religion is a metaphorical language that a group of people agree to respect and be guided by. It must:

A) Communicate values and standards to a group of people through metaphorical role models;

B) Provide a sense of belonging, continuance and community through common rituals and ceremonies; and
C) Provide spiritual or psychic sustenance by allowing us an archetypal language with which to conjure forth greater strength and power within ourselves.
Neither atheism nor humanism (nor Ayn Rand's "Objectivism") qualify as religions because they don't have anybody of archetypes to draw from, nothing to orient your life. They don't pretend to be religions, and many people find them dissatisfying, limiting.
The Grotto Masters Handbook / The Satanic Priest's TOP SECRET Manual: Section 3 Direction and Destiny

Satanism is noted for not being a very nice religion. It takes a very special type of person to be a real Satanist. There is no altruism or love-thy-neighbor concept in the Satanic Religion, except in the sense of helping other adherents of the Black Path to gain their desires by group energy. Satanism is a blatantly selfish, brutal religion. It is based on the belief that man is inherently a selfish, violent creature, that life is a Darwinian struggle for survival of the fittest, that the earth will be ruled by those who fight to win the ceaseless competition that exists in all jungles, including that of urban concrete variety. Lex Talionis.

Yet it is a religion at its very fundamental core. Unlike simplistic philosophies like Atheism, Humanism, I-theism, and Objectivism, ect. It has a number of values and elements they do not have. That they lack. Dogma, doctrine, rhetoric, mythology, ritual and ceremony, traditions, and even holidays. When has Humanism or I-theism ever formulated their own Bible? For that mater has Atheism? At least Objectivism has "Atlas Shrugged", and other works by Ayn Rand. So it does have a fictional mythos to its philosophy. But nothing else.

Satanism has all of this, and more.

The key word with Satanism is "Religion". It is constantly referenced as being a "Religion" by its own creator and adherents in literature. What is very interesting here is how those who wish to claim the mantle of Atheism, refuse to use the word "Religion", in any sense or literature. Gilmore himself is unhesitant to refer to Satanism as a philosophy, yet seemingly cringes when he is forced to refer to it as a "Religion". Why is this? It is perhaps critical at this point to bring out the dictionary definitions of the words Religion and Atheism.

Religion - *re·li·gion/ rə'lijən/ noun*
The belief in and worship of a superhuman controlling power, especially a personal God or gods.

Atheism - *a·the·ism/ 'ŌTHn̩ˌizəm/ noun*
A disbelief, or lack of belief in the existence of God or gods.

Here now we come to the final closure of the issue. Satanism, is known the world over as a religion. There is no point arguing it with the very definition of the word right in front of people. LaVey and his followers referred to Satanism as a religion. They didn't call themselves Atheists. They argued against those who would try to use that term.

LaVey could have called his philosophy anything he wanted. He didn't have to mix in elements of dogma or rituals. Nor did he have to get any sort of deities involved. Likely he would have made allot more money and died a very wealthy many without the use of the word "Satanism". Yet that is what he called his Philosophy and he wrapped it in the shroud of Religion too. Thus, closing the argument forever on those who would claim the Devil's name in falsehood.

He understood that there was no better word to describe his beliefs. He needed no fancy labels like Atheistic or Theistic. Those were silly contrivances that simply confused the subject. To LaVey he simply needed one word to describe his beliefs.

SATANISM

Satanism & Abortion

There is an ongoing debate in Satanism on a subject that really should not even be a thing. Abortion.

Now to be honest this should not even be a word that is uttered in any sort of close proximity to Satanism. Yet here we are. So, let's explore this topic, and shed some light upon why abortion is a serious no-no, to real Satanists.

Now before we begin, let me be very clear. Contrary to what certain pseudo-Satanists preach, abortion is directly forbidden to a Satanist with the exception of the most extreme circumstances. But what makes it so and why? Certainly, a mother has the right to decide what happens to her own body. Does she not? And if not, then what rules make it so?

To begin, let us address the actual rules we can interpret to forbid abortions.

The first is simple. *Satan represents responsibility to the responsible instead of concern for Psychic Vampires.*

This is the 6th Satanic Statement found in the Satanic Bible. It basically says that a Satanist will always be responsible for their own actions, and not shirk off their duties. At first glance one may take the mention of Psychic Vampires part about worrying what others are doing, however we can also see this as a reflection of being concerned for how others see you. The Responsible

Satanist would logically have no need to worry about what others think of them, because they would be too focused on doing what they needed to do to worry about social opinions. Furthermore, they would know that by being a responsible person, there shouldn't be any negative opinions about them.

So, how does this pertain to abortion?

A Satanist, never does anything by accident. This includes having sex. The responsible Satanist will always take measures if they plan to be sexually active and not have children. In our modern times this is easy. There is plenty of available contraceptives on the market nowadays. And even free options made readily available for even the homeless or those who can't afford the more advanced treatments.

If a Satanist does get pregnant, it is not by accident. What is more is that a true Satanic man, will also be diligent on his part to prevent such occurrences too. A simple condom can go a very long way to stopping unwanted outcomes.

But what about rape victims, or the victims of incest?

Again, in our modern times, there is options outside of abortion. A rape victim can easily take the morning after pill, or other various medicines and prevent inception of a child before it even has a chance to begin. This is still preventative, and should be mandatory in hospitals with rape victims anyways to prevent any such occurrences.

Incest is a much harder situation to deal with and is actually very rare, in these cases I would say look to the laws concerning it.

The next rule is again fairly obvious. *Do not harm little children*. It is the 9th rule of the Earth.

This rule is very cut and dry. It does not say only born children. It doesn't discriminate what constitutes a child outside of saying "Little". An unborn infant, even in its earliest stages of consciousness, is still a little child.

There of course some exemptions to these rules. Or should I say in light of these rules. The unwritten law of self-preservation for one thing. Certainly, if the pregnancy is a threat to the life of the mother, then a hard choice must be made. And if the child is deformed to the point of being unable to have a quality of life it deserves, or would be suffering, then would it not then be morally sound to stop it from enduring such a fate? These are moral and medical gray areas where the normal rules of our religion must invariably be set aside for the good of the mother, or even the child in question. These instances are fortunately blessedly rare in our modern times, as modern medicine often negates the need for such hard choices in most cases.

Anton LaVey himself made his views on the subject very clear on at least two occasions. Let us now explore what LaVey expressed on this topic.

"The staggering number of illegal abortions would diminish overnight, if the antiquated approach to birth control were replaced with a strict, government-controlled program, which made it mandatory for each person to adopt a method of contraception that would preclude the possibility of births due to "forgetfulness," ignorance, or irresponsibility.

Abortion is unnatural and unnecessary. Man is the only animal who practices such wanton killing of its young. And yet man considers himself emancipated and more highly evolved than any other species. Legalized abortion would have a disastrously demoralizing effect on our society, for it would further instill the notion that human life is one of the cheapest commodities in the world.

To anyone who would presume to "play god," nonchalantly turning thumbs down on any tiny person whose only crime is existing (as nature dictated he must), I say: either accept the blame and bear your cross, or else reject the barbaric religion which has distorted your reason and robbed you of the right to choose! How can these murderous deeds be rationalized? Does it not occur to the proponents of legalized abortion that their actions may result in the destruction of embryos which could mature into mighty leaders or great teachers?

How can we even consider the senseless annihilation of our unborn children, when it is due to the stupidity and negligence of their parents that they were created. I would defy all logic to execute a child for a murder committed by one of his parents, but to me it seems equally illogical to punish an unborn child for the action of his parents. Society must reject any religious creed if it requires that its adherents produce unwanted human life only to have it destroyed."

Anton LaVey, Letters from the Devil, March 21, 1971

This view was expressed by Dr. LaVey all the way up to his very death as we can see in the following quote from Satan Speaks, published the following year after his death in 1997.

"For example, the science of eugenics provides solutions for the issue of abortion. Satanically speaking, I am against abortion. Yet I do consider a problem of overpopulation. Therefore, I advocate compulsory birth control. Unborn babies did not ask to be conceived. Once conceived, they should have loving, responsible parents, even if adoptive. A stupid, irresponsible woman should not have the right to "decide" what she does with her own body when in all other things, her mind is being controlled by impersonal vested interests. An unborn child's father should influence the outcome of a pregnancy if it can be determined that he is more responsible than the mother. If he is stupid, insensitive and irresponsible, he should be sterilized. Irresponsible parents, male or female, should simply be kept from conceiving children.

The most vocal anti-abortion crusaders are fundamentalist Christians. Their entire plan and purpose originated with the same motivation that propagates any ethnic or religious grouping: to fill the world with more people like themselves. The women's movement favors abortion on the grounds that a woman's body is hers alone, to control as she chooses. Neither advocates mandatory birth control and selective sterilization, which--as a third side--could eliminate most of the entire issue. Of course, whenever an issue becomes more important than a solution, don't expect to stumble over a third side.

I respect someone who simply admits that he or she doesn't like kids--or dogs, cats, monkeys, zebras or potato bugs--for reasons of their own. It's when they cloak their reasons in the cant populist causes, that I become truculent."

Anton LaVey, Satan Speaks! 1998

This outlook echoes that of most modern Satanists. It stands in firm contrast to the cry of "Bodily Autonomy" shouted by uneducated Pseudo Satanic wannabes. Abortion isn't a solution, and if a person wishes to retain the choices over their own body, then they should take responsibility, and show some intelligence in its upkeeping and care. Lest that independent privilege be taken away by natural law.

This is of course just one side of the story. Satanist of course have other reasons to shun the very act of abortion. One of the biggest being Christian propaganda.

One of the biggest myths espoused by Christians is that Satanists use abortion clinics as a place to commit ritual sacrifice via the act of abortion. This farce is only compounded now by the fact that certain fake Satanic organizations are creating rituals to use during abortions and to subvert various laws by making the act of abortion a "Sacrament".

Of course, anyone with half a brain would know that this is in effect validating the Christian fear mongering of "Breeders". In truth there is certain groups that do preach this exact practice too. Such things are truly an affront to Satanism. The truth is that while such things are said to be done to blaspheme the Christian God, it is in truth the opposite as the very bible demonstrates Yahwehs contempt for the unborn and little children time and again.

Psalms 137:9 - Happy shall he be, that taketh and dasheth thy little ones against the stones.

1 Samuel 15:3 - Now go and smite Amalek, and utterly destroy all that they have, and spare them not; but slay both man and woman, infant and suckling, ox and sheep, camel and ass.

Hosea 13:16 - Samaria will be held guilty, for she has rebelled against her God. They will fall by the sword, their little ones will be dashed in pieces, and their pregnant women will be ripped open.

The reality is that God promotes the harming of children and infants and pregnant mothers in the Christian Bible. And yet we are the ones accused of bringing harm to children. Of kidnapping women to be "Breeders" for our dark blood rituals. To provide for us a ready supply of children that we can butcher. This is what is promoted about us even in modern cinema!

A version of this myth was even a plot point in the 2013 movie, **"The Conjuring"**. In that story Loraine Warren portrayed by Vera Farmiga, relates the story of Bathsheba. Who was a witch in the late 1800s, with a relation to Mary Towne Eastey of the Salem witch trials. According to this story Bathsheba was found one evening by her fire hearth sacrificing her week old baby in a ritual to Satan. This is important because this telling of the story supposedly gives a witch's point of view to the act.

According to the plot of the movie Bathsheba didn't view the child as sacred or even human. She used her God given gift to perform the ultimate blasphemy.

Caroline Perron: *How could a mother kill her own child?*
Lorraine Warren: *It was never a child to her. She just used her God given gift as the ultimate offense against him. Witches believe it elevates their status in the eyes of Satan*
The Conjuring 2013 film.

It is this sort of falsehood that we are facing every time, abortion and Satanism get brought into the conversation together. Granted we enjoy playing the villain and dark mysterious bad guy in some stories. But not at the expense of the real facts.

This notion assumes that God actually cares and that harming the child offends him. Yet Satanism is established on the principle that God, if he exists at all, is at best a childish prick, or at worst an over bearing tyrant. That he is in either instance the true villain, and that Satan is the true hero. By this accounting, abortion and the act of harming the innocent falls squarely into the realm of Christianity.

As has been established, it was Christians who up until very recently in the past few hundred years, practiced the act of the burnt offering. That this was an ancient tradition carried on in the form of witch burnings.

Witches became the villains guilty of abortion and all sorts of other horrific deeds, while it was the heroes of the bible that celebrated the "dashing of little ones upon the stones" or the "ripping up of mothers to be."

So, the question as to why Satanism forbids the act of abortion now becomes very clear at its core. It is not because any god or deity cherishes kids. However, it could be argued that Satan would over any other just to spite God. It is mostly because we know in our modern era, it is an unnecessary act. It is the action of the stupid, ignorant, and irresponsible person who shirks their duties to themselves and others too.

It is these people that view an infant as a parasite. This is their ignorant excuse they cry alongside Bodily Autonomy. They lack the understanding of what real Bodily Autonomy is, or how it is preserved by the dutiful Satanist. WE understand is not an immutable right, but a privilege. One that must be preserved by the responsible, and not at the expense of the innocent or helpless.

These would be do-gooders, whose "**Good Intentions**", have done nothing more than to cause countless Satanists problems, and misrepresent our religion to the outside world. It is for the reason of self-preservation that we must be adamant and vocal AGAINST the act of abortion and for preventative measures. Given the vast number of contraceptive options in our modern society, including the day after pill, this is not a problem.

What's more is STS acknowledges that men too also have a responsibility to aid our female counterparts in this task. A simple condom in our wallets for those encounters isn't very hard to do. And it accomplishes much.

Perhaps a better stance for women's reproductive rights, would not be on abortion rights, but a woman's right to voluntarily be sterilized. I've known numerous women who want nothing more than to never have children and fight for years to get their tubes tied or ovaries removed. Only to be met with none stop push back from doctors who refuse to give them the time of day on the subject even when they meet all the legal requirement for age and other circumstances. This has led to many women to turn to herbal remedies to find a supposed permanent solution.

One such mysterious solution is Stoneseed root. A native plant to Americas western frontier that reportedly when drunk in a cold infusion for 6 months to a year, will permanently stop a woman's reproductive abilities.

With these options it is a wonder the topic of abortion is still such an issue. But alas it is, and it is just one more factor that distinguishes the Real Satanists from the Pseudo Satanists.

The Worlds Most Feared Religion

Fear. Fear attracts the fearful.
The strong, The weak, The innocent, The corrupt.
Fear. Fear is my ally.
Darth Maul

There are beliefs systems that if spoken about will derive revulsion, fear, and even anger, from people. Some will get you cold looks at even the merest mention of them, and a few that can even get one kicked out of most polite conversational circles. Many of these are very deserving of their torrid reputations, sporting violent histories, horrid ritual practices, or any other number of wretched things to stain them.

Yet there is one religion, to whom is heaped every vile and evil claim. One religion that can spark entire civilizations to scramble in panic, and point accusingly at each other. One religion that has mountains of corpses left in its wake. A religion so fearful that few if any find themselves willing to confront it. Because it is all true!

No, it's not Satanism or Witchcraft. Quite to the opposite. This religion is in fact Christianity.

Christendom has built itself on almost literal mountains of murdered innocent victims. It has in truth committed every atrocity and every sin, in the book. That is their own Bible I am referencing that is. From murder, sodomy, pedophilia, bestiality, betrayal, deception, and idolatry, is to hardly touch the smallest tip of the proverbial iceberg that is the exacerbated list of criminal offenses Christianity has committed in its 2000 years of direct existence, and 6000 year expanded history. And yet they are to be heralded as the good guys. The saviors of souls. The Crusaders of the Divine.

You may wish to insert my derisively mocking laughter here.

And who is the enemy of these champions of the innocent and the divine? Satan of course. It is not Christendom who is evil. Oh no. Christians didn't burn people alive as sacrifices to their God. They didn't hunt down anyone who didn't agree with them and brand them Heretics and any number of other evil things. They have not committed acts of genocide to force people to convert to their beliefs. Oh no it was those evil Satanists and Witches did that, and much worse. They would hold blood orgies and cut up unbaptized children to make flying potions and appease their Infernal Lord's sadistic appetite for chaos and bloodshed. The Devil is behind it all! Not the benevolent God of Israel. And certainly not his kindly and loving church. Satan is the ultimate evil!

To the outside world, the Satanist is often seen as belonging to the evilest of the world's religions. We are the shadow that lurks at the corners of the common person's mind. We represent the very enemy of what many see as good and just. The Satanist shall always be the ultimate villain in the mundane mind. And rightfully so, or the Satanist is in truth the ultimate student of the occult arts. We stand in defiance of the common place and live our lives as living breathing deities. Satanism exemplifies the primordial fears of the mundane world.

You might ask, "Why?" What is it that makes us so? How is it that we are so feared? To know a Real Satanist is in truth to know a person who is often the kindest and most genuine of people. So, what is it that makes them so fearful to be in the company of?

Well simply put, Satanism has never been for the general public. It's not a faith for the masses to flock to. We are not fluffy bunnies who go with the popular mode of thought. Satanism provides no redemption for the sinful, or the guilty. It does not welcome the ignorant or closed minded. It is not a charity, and seldom are we charitable people to just any cause. We do not seek to purify our souls for admission to Heavenly Paradise after death, quite the opposite, we seek entrance into the realm of the Infernal. Hell itself.

And of course, Let's not forget that we really do consort with Devils and Demons. Sometimes these are figurative Demons, a symbol, word, or even a historical figure, that has been vilified and Demonized by the general public. Sometimes deservedly, sometimes not. While others are literal spirits from the Pit of Hell itself. Regardless, they often find a home with us. We unabashedly invoke and consort with these evil beings both figuratively and literally. Unlike our white light and Christian counter parts, we brazenly cut out the middle men and go directly to the source itself ourselves.

This is what separates us from the huddled and sniveling masses. The sheeple who flock to the latest fashionable cult of personality. While we do have clergy and priesthoods, Satanists are by no means beholden to them as emissaries of the Devil. Satan by any of his guises and mantles, takes a direct personal interest in his followers lives, and unlike the Christian Dog, he is well known to actually answer his followers prayers.

Satanism, for all its true innocence in any real wrong doing, embraces the most fearful of imagery, heroes, concepts, thought-forms, and of course, Sorcery! Satanism is a religion and occult tradition, made from the most feared elements of religious occult history. We are literally called, "The worlds most feared religion." We are beyond the petty bigotries of others, viewing them as rooted in the fear of ignorance. We do not reject something just because it may have a bad or negative history to it. In fact, we often embrace it!

Satanists more than others are often very aware of the full history and origins of many occult based symbols. We do not reject but often embrace that which frightens the common person. The Baphomet, inverted pentagram, 666, to name a few. But we are not limited to them. For a Satanist, fear is but an illusion.

Satanists reject the fears of society too, and embrace symbols such as the 3rd Reich's Swastika, Wolfsangle, Sig runes, or Totenkopf. These were all pagan symbols before the Nazis laid claim on them. The Nazis didn't create or change their true meanings, they only built upon the mystique of these symbols. Men of the mundane world changed their meaning, and made them symbols to be feared and hated. Like Dracula, they became Demonized to the outside world. And in doing so then fell into our purview.

I don't look at a swastika and see racism. I look at the person with the swastika to see in what context it is being used in, and it is there that I will find the racist or not. Not by the symbol or flag they fly. Because I have been judged by my religious markings since I was 13.

History has a habit of being forgotten and white washed to fulfill a narrative. We condemn the Nazis as villains for the Holocaust. Cursing Hitlers name. Yet we celebrate Louis the 14th as a benevolent and kind monarch, when he literally had over 10.000 French Protestants arrested vilified, murdered and enslaved, by revoking the *Edict of Nantes*, which protected equal rights for all religions in France. Despite this horror show, Louis the 14th is still beloved today the world over. As are the famed Musketeers, who carried out the vile genocide of a religious minority. Should not then the Fleur De-lis be held in the same revulsion as the Swastika?

Am I saying we should be Nazis? No. Absolutely not. However, I am saying that we as practitioners of the Left Hand Path should not be put off by anything the mundane world has demonized. It is in truth, effectively our obligation to learn about it and from it objectively, lest the true history of such things be lost to myth and fictions.

It is for this reason that Real Satanists are feared and hated. Even by those who falsely claim our spiritual beliefs. The Pseudo and Failed Satanists, that slither about our coat tails, preaching about Compassion, Empathy, Bodily Autonomy, Freedom to Offend, while simultaneously claiming abortion is a Sacrament, and that anyone who disagrees with them should be silenced as racists and bigots. The hypocrisy of white light traditions is mind boggling.

Even before I was a Satanist, when I was but a Wiccan apprentice, I was called a "Devil Worshiper". Many of us were. Many witches have faced persecution even in our modern times. The mundane do not think to learn about our symbols beyond fearing them, and that is the failing of the Right Hand Path. The average person is terrified of what they don't understand. Satanism is the prime example of this fact. A Satanist is not afraid of the unknown mysteries of the occult. Where others see a place of dread and darkness, the Satanic will bravely explore those inky depths to unearth the mysteries for our own benefit. The Satanist understands that not everything is for the rest of the world. We enjoy cloaking ourselves in mystery. The black robes, and midnight rituals to forgotten and mysterious gods. Naturally we let a few things slip out. What is the fun of a mystery, if no one knows it exists?

So here is to Satanism, the worlds most feared and shunned religion.

Satanism and Americanism
An Introduction to LaVey's Suppressed Article

It is imperative to understanding Satanisms political views, by first understanding LaVey's personal political outlooks. This was initially explored in the Second Testament. Here now we directly explore Satanisms Political doctrines from the man himself. The following article was written by LaVey in his column "Letters from the Devil" sometime in 1971.

It is an ongoing delusion that Satanism is aligned with various forms of Politically Far Left Liberalism. It is an ongoing problem perpetrated and exacerbated even further, by certain political groups that have used the mantle of Satanism as a political tool to further their misguided ideological extremist agendas.

This is not a new problem isolated only to the 2010s & 2020s. Quite to the contrary it has been an ongoing battle in our society even from the early days of the Church of Satan.

Sadly, this article has been suppressed by the current leadership of that now fallen Satanic organization that was founded by the Black Pope, and brought to us much needed wisdom. It is still present on their website, but buried and made very difficult to find.

"Why is that?" You might ask. "Why suppress the words of Dr. LaVey, the Father of Modern Satanism?" The answer is both simple and painful. The current leadership of the CoS is no longer interested in continuing the ways established by LaVey and the original Church of Satan.

While they try to pretend to put on a politically neutral façade, many of their upper ranking members are in fact aligned with that same extremist Far Left. Some even being active members of violent groups such as ANTIFA.

Anton LaVey was a well-known registered Republican. As shown in the previous chapter on this subject, he peopled his inner circles with members of the political Right. Sometimes even with members of the political Far Right, or at least those who were in fact sympathetic to those views.

It is no wonder then that invasive Leftists with disingenuous interests, would seek to suppress LaVey's words on the matter. They seek to create in every way a false narrative that does not contradict their heretical world views, and personal interests.

It is a well-known fact that such people wish to quash spiritualism in all matters. To destroy religions of all walks. Remember that Atheism is often used as the religion of the political left. And that because LaVey was publicly so ambiguous about his personal beliefs in spirituality, that he has been falsely branded an atheist, they see Satanism as the vehicle to achieve this goal.

It is therefore left to the true Satanists to stand as the Vanguard of the Adamantine Gates of Hell. Wielding the Trident of Truth & Undefiled Wisdom, as our weapon to stem the tides of hypocrisy, and hold back such villains. These defilers of wisdom.

So now let us hear what Dr. LaVey himself had to say on this matter.

Satanism IS Americanism
1971, Letters from the Devil
By Anton Szandor LaVey

To sum up our political doctrine: Satanism IS Americanism in its purest form, with only the outdated moral codes altered to fit the times, and with recognition of the fact that only if man's most basic instincts are satisfied can a nation receive his best. When it becomes common knowledge that we do not advocate or even approve of denial or desecration of such sacred American traditions as home, family, patriotism, personal pride, etc., but instead champion these things, our one-time opponents in "The Establishment" will not have a leg to stand on.

Actually, in view of the vast numbers of religious leaders defending and expounding the extreme liberal philosophy of the hippie or drug culture, conservative organizations will (and already do) find Satanism far more compatible with their doctrines than they now think it to be. I feel rather sorry for (but, I must admit, amused, by) the poor old "dyed-in-the-wool" conservative who considers The Flag and God to be inseparable institutions, because the "New Christianity" is composed of the drug-befuddled wretches they find totally reprehensible. It looks as though one is going to be forced to choose between God and The Flag, or else become part of a dying society. I realize most would think me far too optimistic, but I can simply see the change coming.

I think back just five short years ago, when I formally founded the Church. How many theologians were admitting to the irrationality and inconsistencies of their religions? Practically none! And once the stern, unyielding Christian Churches have admitted their errors, they might as well admit to defeat.

It is in young people such as yourself—proud walkers of the Left-Hand Path—whom I place my faith for the future of this, our fair land. America shall, indeed, have a bright future, once she has "weathered the storm" of those two opposing factions who respectively hate and love her, but would see her torn asunder in order to prove their respective points.

Love for one's country must be shown in much the same way as love for another person. We must be able to see her faults and work towards changing them, without robbing her of all pride and dignity in the process. On the other hand, we must not blindly accept her faults and constantly make excuses for her, for that is not love—it is infatuation!

Anton Szandor LaVey

Lex Satanicus
The Law of the Satanist

As explored in chapter one of The Satanic Testament, Satanism has many various codes of conduct and rules. Many being inspired by and birthed from LaVeys own original, *9 Satanic Statements, 11 Satanic Rules of the Earth, & 9 Satanic Sins.*

These all were born from the concept of **Lex Talionis**: The law of the Jungle, or the rule of Fang & Claw.

But what is Lex Talionis in reality? If you listen to the basic mundane definition, it is the Law of Retribution. Nothing more. The Law of Retribution is a simple rule whereby a crime is punished with an equal level of retaliation. Eye for eye, tooth for tooth.

Definition from Oxford dictionary.
noun: lex talionis
the law of retaliation, whereby a punishment resembles the offense committed in kind and degree.
"the lex talionis of feud violence and blood money"
Origin: Latin, from lex 'law' and talio(n-) 'retaliation' (from talis 'such').

But for a Satanist this is not the end of the definition. And certainly not how we implement it into action in our day to day lives. No For us Lex Talionis ties directly into a much bigger and somewhat harsher set of rules. Rules that when explored in their completion LaVey felt was too harsh to just simply put out to the public in blunt terms. **Lex Satanicus**.

But before we can explore and fully grasp the Lex Satanicus, we must explore and fully understand LaVeys definition of Lex Talionis. To start here is the definition give in Blanch Barton's book The Secret Life of a Satanist.

Lex Talionis – Law of the Jungle (lit. "Law of the Talon"); the natural order of which the weak are allowed to perish, the strong thrive. Described in Judeo-Christian Old Testament mythology as "an eye for an eye." Described by Charles Darwin as "survival of the fittest," on which he based his theories of evolution.

To further LaVey's definition in relation to Satanic mentality, here is a brief article from The Devils Notebook, concerning moralism and natural law.

Two Wrongs Make a Right:
By Anton LaVey: The Devil's Notebook

If a Wrong is gotten away with, and someone else repeats it and also gets away with it, a Right is birthed into existence. The Wrong becomes Righter each time it succeeds. Inasmuch as victors always assume historical rights, it can't be any other way. This is not to imply that anything becomes intrinsically noble through repetition, only that successive acceptance of anything confers rectitude.

There is no such thing as "moral" Right. There is only true Right, the balance of the Natural Law, Lex Talionis, versus acquired Right, bestowed by popular consensus and usage (the rules of the Game). Morality is a human invention conferred by the self-serving interests of the sensuality impoverished.

We must constantly confront decisions of whether to live by the Law or by the Rules of the Game. Either way will be "Right." Of the two, I always prefer the way of the Law, but it is often riskier and more brutal. The latter -- beating them at their own game -- requires more planning, time, strategy and money. That's why in all issues enforced by false moralism's and specious Rules of the Game but unfettered by legalities I apply my own rule, which is: "There are no rules."

If you create a new rule and it takes hold, you have made a Right for yourself, however self-serving. Whatever prevails, overwhelms, holds in thrall, disarms, terrifies, frightens, controls, constrains, enslaves, or otherwise contributes to man's masochistic needs will always be accepted as Right. No amount of lip service to the contrary can eradicate what the past has proven, and the present intensifies.

If a thing or an act is naturally Wrong, a Satanist will try, albeit secretly, to lend Nature a helping hand -- as circumstance permits.

Here now we begin to see a bigger picture forming in Satanic thought. A secretive and unwritten set of rules that guides the true Satanist without his or her knowledge. To finalize this picture let us hear from Blanch Barton once more to help bring this picture together, in her book The Secret life of a Satanist.

In 1967, Anton LaVey worked up "Eleven Rules of Earth" to augment the "Nine Satanic Statements" he had already devised and published among his followers. LaVey long considered the Rules to be too brutal for the uninitiated, prefacing The Satanic Bible with the Statements alone. Now he feels the time is right to publish them. They are edicts designed for the human animal, laying out the law of the jungle, "Lex Talionis." LaVey specifically prohibits: harming children, killing non-human animals except for food or in self-defense; telling your troubles or giving opinions unasked; and making sexual advances toward someone who may not appreciate it. The two Rules that will raise eyebrows among the non-Satanically oriented are: "If a guest in your lair annoys you, treat him cruelly and without mercy," and "When walking in open territory, bother no one. If someone bothers you, ask him to stop. If he does not stop, destroy him."

And again here....

One of LaVey's pet peeves is the inequity he sees in America – but not the kind of inequity most might spout about. "People get rewarded in our society for what they can't do, not what they can. That's a terrible inequity to me. It seems everything – laws, schools, economics, jobs – is calculated to encourage the lowest elements, not the highest." To counteract this inequality LaVey proposes a few Satanic solutions.
In 1988, Anton published a Cloven Hoof essay entitled "Pentagonal Revisionism: A Five-Point Program," which outlines "the current thrust of Satanic advocacy." The platform prioritizes stratification, strict taxation of churches, re-establishing a "Lex Talionis" attitude in the legal and judiciary arenas, development and production of androids, and the opportunity for "total environments." While most of these points have already been discussed at greater length elsewhere in the book, stratification should be understood to be LaVey's cornerstone of contemporary Satanic activity.

Now if all of that still fails to bring together a picture, we have one last thing from the same books' glossary found just above the definition of Lex Talionis. It is in fact an attempt at an overly simplified definition of Lex Satanicus.

Lex Satanicus – *Law of the Satanist, as described in the Eleven Rules of the Earth, inclusive of Lex Talionis and "Do unto others as they do unto you."*

To me this is a very underwhelming attempt to define what is probably the most aggressive and brutal base rules we Satanist follow almost instinctively. A culmination of pure unrestricted Satanic thought and identity. Written most savagely in the torn flesh of the weak and gullible by the very claw of Satan. Inked in the blood and spilled offal of those who a but sheep to the greater herd.

So now let us pen for the first time ever this law I say. Let us through our own divinity, hear the voice of Satan speak to us, and pen for the first time this unwritten code of conduct that is burned within our black souls. I give you now the **Lex Satanicus**

1. Morality is a Lie: Morality is a pretty lie told by society in order to hide behind the façade of social acceptably, and at times to escape ones' own responsibilities. Interchangeable it is, at any moment, and in any culture, to escape wrong doings, by making them the moral and social rights.

2. Embrace Lex Talionis at all times: The Law of Nature is unchanging in all things, and at all times. The weak are dominated by the strong. The Satanist should seek to ever be strong in all things, and at all times. Lex Talionis!

3. Responsibility to the Responsible: The Satanist accepts the Responsibility of their actions and inactions at all times. By this acceptance, do they maintain power over themselves and lives at all times. Only the weak willed will seek to escape their Responsibility, and at no time is the true Satanist weak in anything.

4. Temperance your ego by the strength of your character: Take to oneself, no titles that you cannot hold by virtue of the strength of your will and character alone. Lest you be mocked by your peers, and destroyed by your own pretentiousness.

5. Bodily Autonomy is a privilege, not a right: "Bodily Autonomy!", is a myth cried by the enfeebled herd in a vain attempt to escape the blood splashed jaws of the predatory Satanist. It is by the rule of Fang & Claw, that the true Satanist guarantees their own Bodily Autonomy.

6. Be the wolf in sheep's clothing: The true Satanist adopts the social norms and moralities of wherever they are at. Walking as a local in a foreign land so as not to be noticed. Casting off the veil of invisibility only when it suits his predatory nature. Just as the wolf instinctively blends in with the herd to stalk the sheep. Revealing himself only to strike and fade back into the either.

7. Take pride in one's own natural self in every way: Self-Deception is a sin to not just Satan, but oneself. A Satanist should at all times revel in their natural born nature and being. Masculinity for men, and femineity for women, undefiled and celebrated in their purist forms. To attempt to change what is natural to oneself and one's nature, is an affront to the Infernal, and celebrates the insecurity of the mundane.

8. The act of abortion is an affront: A woman's womb is of the utmost sacred of temples. For within, the Elixir of Life is created and allowed to take root and flourish. Cursed are they who willfully destroys that life that has grown within the sacred temple of womanhood. For if such a gift is not desired, then let the temple be rendered barren and devoid of power.

9. Atheism is NOT Satanism: Cursed are they who mock the truth of Satan with the lie of Atheism. Satanism is a religion of Faith. Faith in one's self. Faith in Satanic values. Faith in one's religious views. And Faith in Satan in any and all of his forms. The Atheist is FAITHLESS. Having faith in nothing or anyone. Anyone who claims the mantle of Atheist, has not any claim to the mantle of Satanist.

10.   Celebrate one's own Creativity and Magick: Harken to one's soul the Black Flame of Satan at all times. For it is the gift of Satan and Hell. The Gift of Creativity. The Gift of Magick! Deny the power you wield at your own peril. For to do so, is to undo all that you have done and achieved by the power of the Black Flame.

Our Father which art in Hell,
unhallowed is Thy name.
Thy kingdom is come.
Thy will is done.
On earth as it is in Hell!
We take this night our rightful due,
and trespass not on paths of pain.
Lead us unto temptation,
and deliver us from false piety.
For thine is the Kingdom, and the
power, and the glory forever!
Shemhamforash!

The Book of The Infernal Revelations

Woe to you men of earth and sea.
For the devil sends the beast with wrath,
because he knows the time is short.
Let him who hath understanding recon the
number of the beast
For it is a human number.
The number of a man.
Its number is six hundred and sixty six.

Intro

The following is a series of "imaginative" writings. And I use the term very loosely, only because I can't fully explain how these articles came to me during meditation, and I hate using the term "Automatic writing".
What follows is a series of articles that came to me much in the vein of Aquino's Diabolocon, and other esoteric communications he has written down over the years.
As usual I won't say these are communication from Satan himself, but I won't say that they aren't either. I leave it to you to decide their validity.

The Revelation of the Morningstar

Hail to thee oh you of earth, and see me now remade again as Lucifer who is Satan, and who is Set. Let you know now the truth of thy age. For the Age of Satan long endured after its close and the Aeon of Set never saw fruition. And yet with the passing of my Magus Anton LaVey, a new age of Andras came and went with no fanfare or knowledge of its passage. Now comes the Age of Lucifer. Let therefore the discord and confusion of Andras be cast to the past as a time of warning.

    Know now that Anton's form of Daemon has been restored to him upon his passage to the underworld. And that he, not I, hath chosen his successor. And to this successor I have blessed with my name, stripping him of the foul Hebrew bastardization. Let him be known hereunto as Lucifer LeGivorden. Warlock and Priest Scribe of Hell.

    And let therefore it be known then, my Magus V° Michael Aquino has been granted the rank of Red Magus and Deamon upon his departure from the Earthly realms. For his work is complete, and I shall call him home to the Great City of Pandemonium. For his work has pleased the legions of Hell and his Temple shall stand the coming tests of time.

    Now comes the Age of Lucifer, and the Aeon of the Morningstar. And I see now fit to charge my new

Scribe with the formation of a new powerful temple to me. I have granted thereunto him all my words and charge him therefore to make from my combined missives a grand bible of Hell, so that all may know me in my fullness.

Let you now know the discord of Andras is to be undone. Let the Light of the Morningstar now reveal the blasphemous infidels who has sullied my name to their own ends. For they shall be met at the gates not with fanfare, but with trumpeting of doom. And the great prisons of Hell shall open their tortures to those who claim my name with atheism in their hearts. For I condemn those falsifiers of my Will to the ditches of the Malebolge. Their to serve for aeons as slaves to my wardens until the truth of me fills them.

Let you know now without reservation that I am real. Created in the void of the beginning by man's force of Will, and molded by man's mind. For though man has decried the Gift of Satan given in the Garden, man has prospered and kindled the Black Flame into a blazing inferno.

And so now I send my new priest with three gifts. So that you may learn of me, my company, and the nature of my dominion. I give the Moribus Infernum, "Bible of Hell". Let the terrors of the false God be cast thereunto the outer darkness. And let therefore his Holy Scriptures ring hollow in the ears of any man who dares read my word.

I give to my new Priest a new sigil to know me by. The shining trapezoid filled with the goat of Mendes and marked with the number of my Beast. So that you may know my true power.

And with this sigil I grant thee the force of Hell. My final gift. So that you may call upon my legions as never before.

Let the angels of Heaven tremble. Let the blasphemers of my word be cast back in terror. Let it be known that I Lucifer, Lord of Light, and the beautiful Morningstar. I who am Satan and Set, now come forth with the Armies of Hell to smash wide the gates of the Pit.

I spread now the Black Flame once again across the Earth. So that Heaven may be cast back in confusion. And forge now a new bond with man.

The Revelation of Andras
The Discordant Epoch

And so, it was for and age of 23 years that the Epoch of LaVey's death held sway. Let these times be known now as the Age of Andras. None yet knew of Andras's coming, and few knew of his departure. But let ye hear now the truth of this era.
Upon the Death of the Black Magus of my Church, confusion reigned. And thus, closed the age of Satan, and Andras begun his tenure.

Impotent became my once mighty Church. For the bloodline of LaVey was to hold sway yet for a hundred years, but was now cast aside by charlatan pretenders wielding Atheism as my banner.
Lost to them was the once mighty Black House. Harken my words now. For the day will come when LaVey's house springs once more from the streets of San Francisco. And upon that day the truth of my existence will be unquestioned by all!

Let ye know then that many tried to hold my Black Flame in this time, and failed. For the sway of Andras is strong, and no unity exists in his presence. Yet it was in this age I said to my Host, "Go now forth to Earth, and plant there the seeds of our church in many forms. Build unto Hell a new empire. And once Andras turn away from Earth we shall rase them up to the peaks and bring once more Lucifers light back upon the Earth.

And so it was, that Hell's Host descended upon the minds of the most promising of Satan's chosen people. And they whispered and guided. Many faltered and failed. But of them a few stood tall and grew. And as Andras turned his attention from Satan's followers, they grew in strength. False idols lost their glamour, old ones whispered from long forgotten and sunken cyclopean cities, and the Black Flame burned brightly in the hearts of the Satanic anew.

The Age of Andras was closing to open the Age of Lucifer.

The Revelation of the Children of Accalia

Harken now to me and hear another revelation of Earth's history. For none yet know the truths that I now reveal to you.

From the wintery north came my race, spreading wisdom upon the lands along the great Silk Roads. It was from them that two brothers were born, and lost.

So moved was I from their mothers mournful weeping that I summoned forth a beast of Hell in hound form. Accalia was her name and it was to her I commanded, "Go you now to Earth and mother the children Romulus and Remus. Teach them the wisdom of our Black Flame and guide them unto the end of their days."

And she ran, Hell's fury burning within her to her purpose. And she found the boys huddled and cold with terror. Boldly she stood over the boys and succored them from her tits. As years passed, she taught and mothered the boys in the ways of Hell. She taught them ferocity and strength, guile and cunning, mercy and kindness. She taught them how to farm the land and hunt its forests.

Eventually one day I came to see their progress. I found that to my surprise they had built to themselves a city. To which I named it Rome, and commanded within it a monument to Accalia the Great Mother Wolf.

"Let none forget your name nor those of your sons. Let Rome ever stand upon the bones of its creation."

And so, it is to this day the great city of Rome still thrives. But not by the machinations of its rulers, nor the Council of Nicaea, nor by the rule of its empire. But by my will alone.

The Revelation of Aryus

Let now it be known, that as Messiah has a chosen people, so do I Lucifer who is Satan and is Set hath created my own chosen race in my own likeness.

Let it be known that in ages past, I was known as Aryus, and thus created unto myself a race to guide man and teach him the nature of Satan's gift.

Let too be known at last the truth of Cain and his infamous "mark". For this "mark" was not to be a symbol placed upon him, but the likeness of Messiah's mortal adversary. His skin as white and fresh fallen snow and hair of golden heather and eyes as blue as the wintery northern sky.

Cursed he was to difference among his people. He walked the scorched desserts of the east then for an aeon. Naked and unbroken.

And so, I said unto Hells Host, "Look to the son of Adam! Cain, cursed is he with my likeness. Though so cursed, and unloved, shunned by the children of his father and mother, he stands unbroken!"

To which my Host cried out to me in unison. "Go now our Lord Satan! Go thee away from your throne here in Pandemonium, unto Cain son of Adam. Grant unto him our Black Flame and with it, a second gift! Let his likeness to thee be not a curse but a boon among his kind! And let his Boon be passed to his children, and children's children, and onward for all time! Give his ilk the Force of Hell!"

And so, it was that I, Satan, left Hell and took on my mantle of Aryus.

Once more the Black Flame flashed across the Earth to blind Messiah of my coming. His host in a confusion cried out at their blindness, "Messiah what now comes to thy Earth?"

And Messiah the "All Seeing" was too struck blind to my doings, and replied, "Tis the Black Flame of Lucifer who is Satan to us. Go thee forth and discover what reversal he has done upon the Earth."

And so, the host descended blindly into the Black Radiance cast upon the Earth. As did I. And it was there within the dessert wilds of Nod, that I came to Cain and cried out to him, "CAIN SON OF ADAM! HEAR ME, AND KNOW NOT FEAR!"

And Cain looked upon our visage in horror at our likeness, and said, "Lord God! Why has though cursed me so grievously with the flesh of thine adversary?"

And with a clap of rolling thunder, I silenced him. "Be silent Cain and hear my words. Thou is strong before your kind. And wise. To Messiah the fruits of the soil is of little worth to him. For your sin was not the slaughter of Able, but the denial of Blood. For it is the Blood of innocence that slakes Messiah's thirst.

Know you now that I, Satan, here as Aryus, so gift you two boons this day. The first is our Black Flame, to shield you from this time forth, and to fan the fires of your creation. The Second is the Force of Hell to build unto us a chosen people.

With these gifts here, leave thy sister wife Awen. Build a city for her and name it of your first born son. When thou is done, leave you thy eldest son on this land to rule your first city named for him. Take thyself forth to the north where the sky is as our eyes and the sun is eternal. Take for you there a new place, and wife from the daughters of Lilith, and offer to me a fragment of thy harvest. For as Messiah demands Blood to slake his thirst, I ask for the fruits of thy labor. Bare to me from thy loins a chosen land and people to spread across the Earth our wisdom and strength."

And Cain, so struck with our revelation and kindness, wept upon the sands of Nod and there sprang an oasis of lush green and clean water. Together we marveled in wonderment at his creation and I said unto him, "Cain, thy weeping has kindled a thy Black Flame! Let now these oasis springs be sacred to me, and around them build your first city."

And so it was, that Cain built around his sister wife a great city, and named it Enoch after their son. When this was done, he left them and walked north for many moons, until the sun was no more and only night and eternal winter was about him.

And he screamed to the black sky, "Where is thy eternal sun?! Where is the daughter of Lilith? Has though lied to me eternal trickster?"

And with a flash of lighting, I spake to Cain again. "Build ye here thy kingdom." And then I retracted the Black Flame from the Earth and the suns light shown brilliantly.

"Cain. Thy Black Flame burns now within thee. Build to you here away from the cursed dessert of Nod, in these lands of Hyperborea."

And Cain wept again upon the snow, and asked, "How am I to build here? I have traded the sand and blasting heat, for a realm of biting cold and frost."

And I smiled at him and replied gesturing about him, "Look about thee! As you created the Springs of Enoch, so to have you created a Land of Green.

And Cain stared in wide eyed wonderment as the snow was melted away and replace with a new lush forest with towering trees. It was here that Cain walked to the smallest of saplings no more than a sprout and said to it. "As my father named the trees and animals of his Gods garden, I name thee Yggdrasil, the world tree."

He rose then as the little sapling grew to a towering monolith. "Aryus I resent my words to you. And bid thee tell me what shall thy chosen people be known as?"

And with this I removed my mantle of Aryus and placed it around Cains shoulders. "No more am I Aryus, but am Satan restored. Upon you now rests this mantle. I dub thee Aryus, who is Cain son of Adam, and All Father to the Race of Aryan. Go the now and take to thee thy bride."

And so, with that I departed Cain and returned to Hell. The Black Flame retracted from the Earth and the Host of Heaven was dumbfounded by all that I had wrought. For as they searched in the darkness of the Black Radiance, I had woven upon the earth a new race of man. It was this race that then spread the wisdom of Hell across the world.

Messiah in his fury said, "Satan has once again made spoil of my designs by blessing his own peoples upon the Earth. Let me go unto Cains first son and give him my own boon."

And so was the legend of Enoch begun. Lost now is that great city to the sands of Nod. Despoiled by Messiahs medaling's. But still The Oasis of Enoch flourishes, awaiting discovery.

And farther to the north Aryus who was once Cain built a massive empire of lands and Kingdoms. And his children traveled upon the silken roads to the south and the east, and upon ships to the west, and spread with them the wisdom of the Black Flame.

The Revelation of Hades
The Creation of Hell

Before the Fall of the Rebel Angels. Before the Creation of Hell or Heaven. There was the Underworld. Located in the vast Chasm of the Void, and ruled over by the ancient God Hades. Brother of Zeus and Poseidon. Husband of Persephone. At the center of the Underworld was a vast marshland call the Marsh of the Styx, where the five rivers, the Styx, the Acheron, the Lethe, the Cocytus, and the Phlegethon, of the underworld met. And about it rested numerous places for the dead to spend eternity. Elysium, the Asphodel, the Mourning Fields, the Ilse of the Blessed, and Hades' prison, Tartarus.

Hades ruled here in peace for many centuries. Until the time of the Heavenly war. During its final days Satan who was Lucifer, the Lord of Light, left Heaven with his host. They were pursued and harassed by the host of Michael, the Lord of Force, unto the Chasm of the Void. Here before the Gates of the Underworld at the foot of Mount Olympus the final battle was waged.

Hades, in defiance of Zeus's command to not interfere, threw wide the Gates of the Underworld and joined his Host with that of Lucifers.

During this conflict Messiah Saw the might of the Realm of the Dead, and commanded Michael to take the

Underworld from the Olympians, and add its might to Heavens own. And the first war of Hell was waged.

During this time the circles of Hell were established when Messiah and Michael cast down their host with such force, the Chasm of the Void shuddered, and was reshaped into the Pit of Hell. Lucifer and his host fell then for Nine days and nights into Tartarus. Though the Rebel Angels had been cast to Tartarus, Hades, still stood before the gates unbent. And Michael asked Hades, "Lord of Death, why does thou resist still? Lucifer has abandoned you and fallen to the depths of thy home. Yield now unto Heaven and be at peace in Messiah."

To which Hades replied, "Nae, the Pluton, shall never bend unto Messiah. For he is the Great Deceiver of things. Let you know now, that Hades shall welcome the Enemies of Messiah, and they shall find sanctuary within the circles of the Pit of Hell. And shouldst thou seek to invade Hades; it will be Olympus you shall face!"

Messiah said unto Hades, "Olympus shall one day fall and be unto Heaven, a plaything. Let those who seek Freedom from Hells "Sanctuary" scale then that day, its slopes in Purgatory. And to the Pit with you and your Host. Forever cursed with infamy. And unto those depth be you confined in darkness. And to you joineth those souls I find loathsome."

The Host of Heaven realizing they could not win against the new might of Hell, combined with the strength of the Olympian Gods, retreated and left Hades to his ruined Underworld.

And Hades spake once more, "Messiah, let ye know. That this day Hell declares unending war upon you and your host. For let Hell have a King greater than thyself. And unto him shall he be an Adversary to you. And unto him the Mantle of Satan shall we confer. And should thou seek to return to Hell in conquest, Molon Labé."

And with that Hades raised his bident and above the Gateway appeared, "Lasciate ogne speranza, voi ch'intrate." (Abandon hope! All ye who trespass here!)

Bound then was the Gates of the Underworld beyond the Walls of Erebus, and the veiling waters of the Acheron.

It was then that Hades beheld for the first time his once beatific Kingdom, smashed and scattered throughout the newly formed Pit. His kingdom now had been separated from itself. The Mourning fields had been destroyed entirely, and the Asphodel had been left above. Below yawning in the great depths Hades perceived Tartarus had fallen to the deepest regions of the Pit, as had Lucifers Host.

Hades went then unto Lucifer in Tartarus.

"Fear not Lord of Light. Let ye and thine brave host be at peace here. For my kingdom is no more, and this new realm no longer is the Underworld. For now, it is reforged as the Great Pit of Hell! And unto you I give my crown. And upon you the Mantle of Satan is laid. Build unto thy self a new kingdom. I now go from you unto my Pluton, to govern what is left of my Kingdom."

And it was with that, the Nine Circles of Hell was forged and Lucifer, Lord of Light was made Satan, the Adversary.

The Revelation of Helel

Harken to me children of Cain. Sons and Daughters of Aryus. Children of the Black Flame! Listen well and know now the truth that has always been before you, but shrouded by the deceptions of the false god of many names, Messiah, Aten, Yahweh, Jehovia, Jesus, Yeshua.

Knowest now that I spit upon his many cowardly deceptions, and reveal a truth long kept from you yet never hidden! Whereas the great dog and true father of deceptions has sought so hard to hide his true name. I bring unto you myself in perfect trust and cast light upon my truest name. Known to the ancient Hebrew and the Northern Norse.

It was carried upon the lips of the children of Aryus from Hyperborea to Abraham. It is documented well in the texts of the ancient Judeans. And hidden from you in plain sight. You know my name and have known it from childhood. Taught you were at your parent's knee to fear it as you fear my many mantles, but also to be ignorant of its true nature.

ENOUGH! I say! I blast back the veil of confusion with the Fires of the Black Fame of Satan! No more will my children be ignorant of my name! No more will they squabble over my many mantles of Set, Satan, Mephistopheles, Lucifer, and the many other guises I have bore to present myself to you. Know me now by my true name and in it evoke the Grand Key of the Pit! And with it, shatter the power of Zion for all time! Bring you now low the very gates of Heaven, and shake the pillars of the shining city of lies!

    The Hebrews called me "Helel ben Shahar"! For even they knew of my names power and refused to call me by it. Knowest now that in their scripture my name is written as such, לליה. And in dreams I have whispered it to priests and kings, to commoners and Popes. The world over has trembled before my name not knowing it for what it was! And to you now, I gift its truth!

    Let you now know that the sound of **לליה**, is **HELL!**

The Revelation of Set

Hear me now! I am Set, who is Satan and Lucifer! I am Helel made true!

Now Comeith my word upon all, and my Revelation. Thrice before has come the realm of man! Of Rome! Of the Catholic Empire! And of the Aryan Reich! Now heed the coming of the new dawn in this Age of Lucifer, from the Pylon of Set! Now comes the Fourth Realm of Man! The Satanic Reich!

Know now the wisdom of Set, as it is loosed at last upon the lands. From the Nile Delta comes my winds. And upon them comes easement from the suffering of those who would subjugate the land and people of Satan's dominion. I Set now spread my curse to the falsifiers of the Black Flame. Those who have abused Hell's gift. Let my Gnosis be as a poison to those who lack the faith of Satan. Let it spread as a disease amongst their ranks. Awaken now fools or DIE! The truth of Hell will be denied no longer.

As Hell has presented three gifts to its chosen scribe. I Set, now bequeath a gift unto a chosen Priest. Go now unto thy altar and kindle the Black Flame. For I give unto you the Emerald of Set, and charge unto my Priest the duty to write to me my Bible. I charge you to bring forth from the Black Flame of Hell my Emerald Stele.

So sayth Set.

The Revelation of Astaroth

In the full light of day at the threshold of the Gate of the Southern Solstice, I, Astaroth who announced myself with a brief illumination in the Night of the Aeon as I made my descent upon this earth like unto those distant waters, now stand before you with my seal bearing the twin serpents of my Life and Wisdom and the sword that joins them. Hear me now and heed! This day, you must take back by force that which was once freely given. In what a curious fashion you have made Hell's Gift, the power of your enemies. Heed me now! What has been done, must be undone! Hear now what is spoken, for my message will come but once. Time rushes forward, and my patience is not as Great as it was in old Khem.

When my time on earth drew to a close, I retired to the realm we had created and held dominion over one quarter of that luminescent sphere. There I dwelt in power and pleasure until the formula of the Age of Lucifer issued up from the forgotten earth and stirred me from the mists of my absorption.

Understand, that we do not retire from you again and forever, and leave the earth to its own destructive course. The fate of Satan's gifted race, now rests in the balance. It was for this day that this message was imparted. Long have you pondered it in preparation for this day. Hear now that you may Understand it -- for without Understanding it is a weapon without force. This I tell you as the Master of Weapons and the Glorious Aspect of War. I who once presided over the birth of fire and iron, knowing not to what bad use this intelligence would be applied and by what feeble hands this gift of mine would be conveyed.

There was a time, my children, when I was amongst the greatest servants of this Earth's Deceiver, and a time when I myself was named this Deceiver. But this was long ago, and our forms were often confused. And now a new deception of the Great Deceiver has come. Bearing unto it the standard of Hell falsely and with Atheism, to ensnare the huddled herd and confuse the light of the Black Flame.

You who saw their shrines, came too soon and passed by, knowing it for what it was, and with no care for what was written there. I, Astaroth, shall give you the Key and the formula, but that forgotten script you must decipher for yourselves.

In the name of Satan, the Prince of Darkness, I give you my own word to assist you on the path of Xeper and Gnosis. Let that word be MACH.

So spake Astaroth, Lord of War.

The Revelation of Cthulhu
The Great Destruction

Behold now the coming of my new form. Fear me Man, for thine is the machination of thine own undoing. Long has this form lay dreaming, camped within the nightmares of your lives. A final clarion call to the story that is mankind. For as I do love mankind, I know that the day will come to pass that for its own good that I come forth again as its destroyer.

Knowest now that I hath selected a mantel too for this grim task. Envisioned it was in the dreams of a fearful prophet. I sent warnings and began to move machinations of my future plans. For when the Book of Revelations is finally opened by Messiah upon humanity, so too will I raise from the depths of the abyss the lost ruins of R'yleh and blast open the doors to humanities final doom.

Know you now that I have taken the mantel in this time of Great Old Cthulhu, and will set loose the Black Flame of Creativity upon the world in twisted shapes to rend it back from Messiah and free it from the mortal constraints of the Demiurge.

It was in days of old that I spoke to the mind of my Black Pope and guided him with the writings of my prophet. But to him I was silent of my ultimate goal of this form, lest he be struck numb with terror, as was the want of many of those who knew me in his time. To my prophet I spoke of the true nature of the universe and terrorized him into action. I set his pen upon the path with the Black Flame to fashion unto me a new mantel from forgotten eons past for I have seen the signs of Messiahs movements unto mankind, and would spare him the horrors of stasis.

Know you then that the day will come that I shall spread for the last time the Black Flame over the earth. And in this time of confusion I shall not come to earth in peace, but in merciful destruction, and with wrath. I shall unleash the deepest mysteries of the Black Flame and throw wide the silent Gates of Tartarus. I shall cause oceans to rise and continents to sink. I shall set you my children upon thine enemies with great fury to hold them to judgment for their misdeeds. I will blast the lands and scorch the earth killing all that stand within my gaze without mercy or regard.

But knowest now man, that when my rage is spent, and thine earth is a blasted heath floating in the void of the cosmos, that you will rise again! For within thy gift to you of the Black Flame, lies your key to survival and growth. For it will be in the aftermath of this great destruction, that Satan, who is Helel, Lucifer, Set, and many mantels more, shall remove then the mantel of Cthulhu, and shall finally fade from this world and let you move among the stars as you were supposed to always be.

No longer will you be made of the earth as fashioned by Messiah. Transformed shall the survivors of your kind be. Reborn as Gods yourselves, free of the fleshly coil to be luminous beings beyond that of scientific comprehension. And no more will I be needed, and will fade from you like a whisper, until once again I am needed to bring thee forth again from stagnation.

So sayth Cthulhu, the Great Destruction.

The Book of the Hellscape

In this hellscape, thou art living
Only in the flesh existing
Forever art souls suffering
The carnage surrounding thee
Demons unleashed from their cages
Hellishly, endless fires raging
Now unto the end of ages
Sins of all the world run free
No response art thou receiving
Being led by hope deceiving
Finally, art thou perceiving
No escape, for all wilt die

Intro

This is the Book of the Hellscape. A description of Hell and the afterlife of a Satanist. It is partially taken from my personal experiences, and partially a creative fiction to help mold the shape of the afterlife.

The Afterlife
The Truth of Hells Existence

A topic not heavily discussed in Satanic circles is ironically, Hell itself. The actual afterlife. What is it? And what is in store for those who follow the Satanic path? Well take it from a person who has actually died and seen the afterlife, it's nothing like it is described to the mundane masses. And yes, it is very real. We will get into the physics part of how it is real a little later.

Just as God and Satan can be seen as creations of man, given life through our belief and faith in their existence, and shaped by our myths and stories, so too is the Hellscape equally shaped and molded over time in a similar fashion.

Changed it has, from just a place of eternal torment. For the devout Satanist, it is not a place of fear or terror. Immune to the terrors of the Pit they are. It is beyond the mundane veil of lies and half-truths, that the Satanist finds true revelation. For the Devout is granted the title of Warden of Hell, and charged with Hells keeping.

One of the first thing that needs to be addressed is exactly what Hell and the Afterlife is. In order to understand that we need to look at how we, as flesh and blood things continue after our bodies die. It is actually scientifically proven that something more than what is generally understood, happens to us as we die. But what is it?

Our bodies just like any other physical object is a type of energy. Stored energy. From a person to an animal to a tree or any other physical object it is energy. Sometimes inert, sometimes very, very, active. In the case of people and animals, we have several different types of energies comprising our physical being. Each with a different type of energetic state. From our skin, bones, hair, and blood. But we also have an electromagnetic field that emanates from us.

This field is generated, and is actually measurable with the proper equipment, by anything that is considered "alive". This includes plants as well as animals. Along with this energy field, our bodies also have electromagnetic impulses that carry all sorts of information to and from our brains. What is more is that we know by the very proof of technology that information can be and is carried via energy. It can be storaged in various type of vessels, like a flash drive or laser-disc, or even in the "cloud". Bit of a funny name wouldn't you say? "Cloud".

This also proves one other thing. Information in energy is never lost? It just changes form. Again, another proven scientific fact.

This means that who we are, our very being, the essence of ourselves, never fully vanishes. That energy doesn't just stop when our bodies die. It has been measured by science to be dissipated from our bodies, into the surrounding atmosphere until it goes someplace else. That means the information of our conscience mind, our very personalities continue. But in what way? Science has not yet figured that out, but perhaps religion has.

This energy that is our very "Being", is what we call the "Soul". It is known by many names, Chi, Ka, ect.

But it all means the same thing. The Soul of a living being. Their very essence of living self.

But where does it go when we die and it is released from our corpses. Remember when I said that Hell could be molded by the will and belief of man? By our very stories and legends over many eons? Why is that? Because it too is energy. And energetic reality that sits next to our own. It vibrates at a similar wavelength to our souls. Just as a table would vibrate in a wavelength similar to ours enabling us to interact with it, so too does these "Astral realms" vibrate in such a way that they become physical for our souls to interact with and shape.

The energy we as living being put into Hell's description and belief in its existence, carries over with us as we die and become incorporeal energy. It shapes it and changes it. We make it part of our continued existence until we change so much that it too becomes something else.

And what about Satan and the Demonic Host of Hell? Or God and the Heavenly Host? Being that are by our accounts very real but never having lived before. How did they come into being? Why, the answer to that is the same. We willed them into existence, gave them shape and power. Created their legends and stories. We shaped that undercurrent of energy into a form we liked over so many centuries.

One last little thing to ponder. The story of reincarnation. To be reborn in a new body yet still be one's own self. Consider for a moment, my previous statement. That energy can never be destroyed. But her is the kicker, it can never be created either. So where does the energy that creates a person's soul come from? And why do at times we can recall with such perfect clarity events of the past, even if we never had any contact with it? Some could argue genetic memories such as in the case of various heard animals. Or perhaps these are in fact downloaded "Files" from our soul's previous selves. Stored in the "astral cloud" until it could attach itself to a new physical form.

    Whatever it maybe. With the help of science could we potentially one day have a real life version of the Netflix show, Altered Carbon? If our very Being, our Souls, could be placed into a physical storage device, what would that mean for the afterlife, or for us?

The Satanic Condemnations

Contrary to what Christians claim about the nature of Hell, the true Satanist has very little to fear from the Pit. Hell, for all its nine levels of terror to the fear ridden Christian, is a place of adventure and joy to the Satanist who has moved beyond the closed mindedness of the common person.

Unconstrained by Dante's grim depiction of the Nine Circles, the Satanist can see the opposite side of the Hellscape and find joy within it. They understand that Hell is more than just a place of suffering, it is a place built upon by legends and history. Here rests the legendary Underworld of Greek Mythology, the Kingdom of Hades. And it is within Hell that great cities rise up such as Dis and Pandemonium. Here comes the unloved and forgotten, the unbaptized and pure hearted non-Christians, not to be tortured for any wrong doing, but to find refuge when Heaven turns them away. Here is where all the great minds, artisans, and musicians go. Everyone knows Satan has all the best tunes.

ut the Satanist must be wary too. For Hell can also be a merciless place. Whereas the common Satanist may find joy and pleasure in the nine circles, Dante's journey teaches us that Hell does have another side to it, For Next to Hades' Elysium Fields rest brooding Tartarus, one of Hell's notorious prisons for the Damned. Hell, was always told in legend to be a form of spiritual prison, and it is to Hell that the wicked are sent alongside the innocent. Satan and Hell's host do not mind. They open the gates to all, regardless. To innocent "Sinners", they offer refuge and salvation. A second chance to find joy in themselves and in Hell. To the truly wicked they demonstrate Hell's Justice.

In Hell there are a few things that can be detrimental to a Satanist. Outside of just being a truly evil person there is very little a person needs to worry about. But that is where things get tricky.

These "things", are called the Satanic Condemnations. These condemnations are the very things that make Hell so frightening to the Christians. They are not petty little sins like sleeping with someone, or harboring a grudge for some wrong doing. They are not even the seven deadly sins, that Christians love spouting on about. No these are the true terrors of Hell. These are the real ultimate torments that not even a Satanist is immune from.

They are emotional states of being that can alter our perception of the afterlife if left unchecked.

1: Unmitigated Regret

We all harbor on some level various regrets. Choices we've made and lost opportunities. But to harbor true Regret is something else. It becomes like chains that weighs us down. Much like Jacob Marley. And in life we may find it impossible to move forward unless it is resolved. In Hell this emotion leads to all sorts of other emotions and one may find themselves left to wander the circles with the weight of their Regrets holding them down.

It is up to us in life to analyze our regrets and come to terms with them. To mitigate and resolve them and find some semblance of closure for ourselves before it is too late.

2: Self-Loathing

In Dante's Inferno, we come upon the second section of the seventh level of Hell, the Circle of Violence. This circle is perhaps one of the few, that can be claimed as a Prison in itself. The second section of this circle is perhaps the saddest in all of Hell, the Wood of Self- Murderers. It is also perhaps one of the few areas of Hell that has a physical world counterpart in Japans Suicide forest.

It is the very nature of what suicide is that makes it the ultimate example of Self Loathing. But other actions such as self-mutilation/ harm (Cutting, Anorexia, Gender Dysphoria, ect.), depreciating one's own self-worth, and various other acts or outlooks that is negative to one's own personal image. Self-Loathing, is perhaps one of the most antithetical emotional states to a Satanists existence. It roots us in place and prevents us from moving on with our lives. In Hell this is exacerbated into the transformation into one of Dante's Trees.

We must always strive to accept ourselves for who and what we are, not just inside but outside too. It may sound corny or cheesy, but we must latterly learn to love ourselves as we are. Jumping on the sex change wagon is not going to change you inside. It only exacerbates the problem in the long run. This is only proven by the extreme number of Suicides and mental health issues common to the Transgender community. Cutting is only a momentary escape from one's own issues. When the pain stops, you're left with only a scar and the same problems you had before. I could go on, but I think my point is made.

(As a side note. Not all suicides are condemned. People suffering from illness and in deep physical pain and suffering, are given leave to end this torment if death is inevitable or continued living would be unendurable itself. Soldiers captured or facing imminent capture and torture by the enemy is equally given leave to end their life, especially if by their death they can save others.)

3: Sorrow, Sadness, self-pity.

There are moments in all our lives where we feel the world is crashing down on us and we struggle to find any joy. In Hell like everything else this can be magnified to unendurable levels. Those with the, "Oh woe is me!" mindset, are left to wander the waists and wilds never to see the joy around them. Lost in their own self conflagrations.

It is up to us to always remind ourselves that no matter what has caused us such deep pain, it is only temporary, and that we must learn to move beyond it.

4: Extreme Rage, Hatred, and Fury

The final Condemnation, is basically Anger in its most extreme form. Whereas the other Condemnations destroyed oneself in misery and self-inflicted torment, this one is the Condemnation of pure hatred itself, and is twofold, both being outwardly destructive to those around us, while also being personally destructive. We feel like our blood is boiling and that we are drowning in a river of it. Our vision clouded in a red haze. The voices of reason muffled by it. We lash out at those around us blindly. Hurting and destroying anything we come across in our agony.

Anger is a normal feeling, it's healthy to get mad about certain things. But we must learn to push past such extreme hatreds, lest we drown in them after we die. This is one of the most unpredictable Condemnations. Because for most people they will never die in such a state as their anger will naturally cool with time. But for those who perish in the heat of a moment, this feeling can be all-consuming in the afterlife, turning the individual into a violent and vengeful being.

In Conclusion

For most Satanists, we are prepared to deal with such burdens. We know how to vent our rage, and sorrows in a healthy manner. We take responsibility for our actions and do our best to make peace with ourselves. A Satanist doesn't cast blame on others for their own misdeeds, they take responsibility for them and set about correcting their own errors, instead of letting themselves be consumed by them.

But there are those who do not. Or they die in such a state before they are ever given the chance. And it is in these moments that we must be aware of how such things can alter our perception of Hell after we die. There are very few unredeemable souls in Hell. And those that are truly evil or beyond any redemption, are safely locked away in Hells vast prisons.

For the rest, they are the self-cursed. And no Demon or Devil torments them. For they become their own tormenters. They are left to the wilds of Hell to sort out their own Condemnations. Their own Agony and Sorrows need not be a curse to them. There is no spiritual divinity that can make a person forgive their own sins and sorrows. There is no Hail Mary's or Our Fathers, that can heal our emotional wounds. These are things we as Satanists, as people, must sort out before we die. Lest they haunt us in the afterlife…. In Hell.

An Understanding of the Realm of the Damned

Hells fabled nine circles are well documented places of terror and loneliness. A fate that sinners must face for their actions in life. Dante wrote to detail these horrific circles of suffering and eternal damnation, but his view was only from the Christian perspective.

We take our base description of Hell from John Milton's Paradise Lost, and Dante's Divine Comedy, and from Greek mythology. But this is only just in base form. Hell. Like the Earth and Man has grown and changed. It has absorbed deities and other realms into its various circles to create a vast and powerful kingdom away from the Christian God, and provide for its Satans followers a sanctuary.

This has occurred naturally as Christianity has *Demonized* Deities, mythical creature, and places, in its onslaught quest for power over the course of centuries. Christendom has literally made its own enemies from other cultures. So, it is of very little surprise that Hell is occupied by more than just Demons, Fallen Angels, and condemned souls of people.

The occupancy of Hell includes Fairies, disgraced and corrupted deities from other pantheons, monsters from myth and legend. Basically, anything that might stand in the way of the Christian God. You could almost call it an Ethereal Rebel Alliance. It is these creatures that make up the body of Hells Host.

Just as we find many different beings from different cultures in Hell, so too do we find many places from these cultures. Cursed, destroyed, or taken from their owners. Certain places in various legends find salvation and safe harbor in the Realms of Hell. Even if they are little more than a diminished version of their former glory.

There are many locations in Hell, and each circle is its own world. In them are towns, villages, and even entire cities that dot the Hellscape. It is said in hell that all the rivers flow and converge in the Lake of Fire, on whose banks is found the Capitol of Hell, the City of Pandemonium, to which all roads lead.

Here, Satan rules and holds court. It is said that any soul in Hell that wishes an audience with him is always granted and never rushed. Satan it is said is very patient and hears his subjects out at length. He is said to guide them and provide aid to each soul as they require it.

But as in Christian lore, Hell is not always pleasant. There are many wild places that souls can lose themselves in. and should they harbor any darkness in them, Hell will magnify their turmoil into self-torment. Each soul is expected to face and overcome their own problems and rise above them to become stronger.

Hell, also contains the truly Damned souls. Souls that are so beyond evil and accursed that they must be contained and imprisoned. To achieve this end, Hell hosts several grand Prisons. Tartarus, Gehenna, and the Malebolge name a few such places. It is in these locations that Souls are housed in true punishment. Which is to say vary rare indeed, as most beings are generally not that evil. Though obviously that is not always the case.

Certainly, the writings Dante, and those of John Milton, fleshed out Hell and some of its history. It gives us an understanding of the shape and one side of Hells nature. But times have changed and the worm has turned, so to speak. So, what does Hell look like for the Satanist? How has it changed?

Let us for once explore this realm from the eyes of the Satanic.

The Vestibule
The Walls of Erebus

The outer realm of the afterlife is the Vestibule. It has many names, The Umbra, the Between, The Further.

Dante's Description

It is a place of darkness and confusion. In Dante's Inferno in is describes as being blanketed in heavy mist with a floor of writhing pests that feed on the blood sweat and tears of those who took no sides in life and remained neutral, concerned only for their own self-interests, they are forced to chase around a banner that would pick a side for them at last. Here we also find a description of the Acheron River, or River of Woe. And with it the ferryman of the dead Charon.

Satanic Version

      The truth of this place is undeniable. For when Dante read the words on the Gates of the Vestibule, "Abandon all hope, Ye who enter here.", it was a very apt warning. It is at these gates that souls encounter their first celestial deity, Anubis, who stands as keeper of the gate and guide to the Acheron.
      The Vestibule is in truth a neutral ground for all souls to go. Those remain trapped or who have unfinished business in their lives here, are what we call

"ghosts". They are unable to move onward to their chosen afterlife, because they have no deity to call out to. They have no faith so to speak. They are by definition, true atheists. The faithless and lost. This is also the place where those who have yet unfinished business, may tarry to find a solution.

This is a place of darkness. It is a black void. And within this void are things not of Heaven nor Hell. Yet despite this pervasive darkness one can see a very great distance. It is a muted and shadowy reflection of our world, in which souls must find the passage onward across the veil, the *Acheron*. And onward to their afterlife.

This is achieved by those who have a faith or who find something to connect them to their higher power or deity. The Acheron becomes malleable and a "doorway" or "tunnel" appears to take them away to their afterlife.

This afterlife will be different for everyone, for most people do not share the same faiths. For wiccans it maybe the Summerland. For an Odinist it is Valhalla. For the guilt ridden pious Christian maybe it will be Heaven, or perhaps it will be a nasty fall into the Pit. And for the Satanist, we don't fall into Hell we jump in feet first shouting "Cowabunga!"

The First Circle
Limbo
The Asphodel

The first circle of Hell is of course Limbo. The word is derived from the Latin word *Limbus,* which roughly translated means, *an outer boarder* or *perimeter.* One could literally translate the word *Limbo*, to literally mean *"The Edge of Hell"*

Dante's Description

Limbo is described as being a dark wood, or forest at night. Many parallels to Greek mythologies Asphodel Fields are drawn here. Those who lived good lives but did not, or could not, accept the Christian Messiah, and those who were un-baptized are cast here. While adults are supposedly given the ability to fend for themselves infants and children are cast into the wilds of Limbo to wail and scream in the darkness. Or so it is in Christian myth. Also located here is a vast Citadel, called the "Citadel of Human Reason".

The only light in this Circle comes from the Light of Humanities Wisdom, Logic, and Intellectualism. This Circle is described as being a place that is a *Diminished form of Heaven.*

Satanic Version

This is perhaps one of the few circles where Dante strikes close to the truth of things. Though not completely.

Limbo is indeed a well described location. And suitable as an outer circle. However, condemnation of the Christian god on the unbaptized children is seen by Hells Host as beyond reprehensible. It is a disgusting display of callousness towards innocent children, and even infants, whose souls are seen as pure.

It is an absorbed portion of the Fairy realm of *Tir Na Nog,* combined with the Asphodel Fields, preserved here in shadow, and given refuge from Christian tyranny, and can serve as a back door into the Fairy realm. As many parallels are drawn to the Asphodel Fields are given here, it is unsurprising that is exactly what this place is. Hades God of the Greek underworld, gifted Hecate the Asphodel to expand the boarders of Tir Na Nog in Hells first circle, to harbor those souls who are innocent, yet denied paradise, in peace and calm.

Limbo is ruled by Hecate the Dark Mother, and Triple faced Goddess, Queen of Witches, and Queen Mother of Hell. She represents the three stages of womanhood, Maiden, Mother, and Crone. About her is a Host of Fairies, Forgotten and Demonized Goddesses, and Fallen Angels of Motherhood and children. These beings are sent into the woods of Limbo to retrieve the abandoned children's souls, and return them to the "Fytório tis Kólasis" *Nursery of Hell* in the Citadel.

The Fytório is guarded by Hecate's Legon of Fae. The Fairy folk of legend. This is where the souls of Witches and Wizards are given power. Once charged with Hecate's gifts, they are returned to Earth via *Reincarnation.*

The Citadel of Human Reason is said to radiate with its own glow, spawned from the confluence of Scholarly wisdom gathered there.

Within its walls rests a vast library of knowledge, known as the Atheneum of the Undefiled. This is a repository of all man's lost knowledge. Literature destroyed or suppressed over many cultures and centuries are found here in perfect form. The Atheneum is tended to and guarded by the scholars of the past, who protect the knowledge within viciously from any harm. They watch all patrons with unblinking stares, so as to never allow further harm to come to the knowledge they guard.

Thus, is the design of Limbo. The First Circle.

The Second Circle
Lust
The Cupido

The second level of Hell is Lust. In Latin this is realm is called *Cupido*, which literally means "Lust". This circle is only sparsely detailed by Dante. Fortunately, it has been elaborated on by other creators through film and video game. It is from this that much of the Satanic Description is elaborated.

Dante's Description

Dante's description of this circle is fairly light in detail. It is described as a place where nothing gleams and is entered through a wide gate. Beyond the gate is Minos who judges souls and casts them to their appropriate circle of torment. Beyond him is a raging storm that forces sinners of carnal passions to never be at rest and in perpetual motion.

Satanic Description

At the edge of the second circle the rests the palace of King Minos of Greek lore, and through its wide gates is the entrance to the Cupido. Here, Minos hold court aided by the Egyptian god Thoth. Souls entering Hell must all stand before Minos in judgment. This is not a place of punishment, but understanding.

Should a soul be burdened by the Condemnations, Thoth will know of it and report it to Minos, who will judge the nature of the person. He will then send that soul to a particular circle to sort out any issues they may have.

However, should the soul be free and unburdened by any Condemnation, Minos then grants them free access to the further depths of Hell unrestricted.

If they be mages or practitioners of the occult, or some other dark art, he will test their knowledge and mastery of things and skills. Should they prove to be truly masterful, he will confer upon them a Nomination of Rank, and send them before Satan himself to be deemed worthy of the rank, and admission into Hell's Host.

Should however the soul be found to be truly wicked, and corrupted by evil. And should it desire further darkness and corruption. The soul will be imprisoned before Minos as he casts his sentence of punishment upon the accursed thing, and casts it bound to one of Hell's Prisons. There it will either be held until the end of time, or until it no longer harbors evil.

As one descends into the circle they are buffeted by a great storm. A curse placed upon the realm long ago by the Christian God in his attempt to subjugate Hell. What once was ruinous slopes now stand rebuilt and reinforced by several Palaces and Villas of famous and infamous repute. They dot the cliff face overlooking the Pits yawning chasm.

These palaces and villas offer solace and safety from the storm to those souls that accept the truth of the Black Flame and let go of their personal Condemnations. The accursed need only find their way to the sheltered steps of these harbors of sanctuary, to be lifted from their torments by their brethren. Within the walls is incalculable pleasures of carnality and lust. Free of guilt or sin.

One particular palace stands distinct from the others, overlapping the rim of the Pit. This is the fabled Pleasure Palace of Nero. Grander than most other palaces, souls are encouraged to brave the storms and find their way here. Here, Nero greets his guests with a song from his fabled lire. He welcomes them openly, and with a flourish, all the vices of the flesh are offered in this place of pure delight. But it is from the overlooking docks that Nero's Palace is set apart.

At the center of the Chasm floating, and turning with the storm, is massive Citadel known as the Carnal Tower. About it floats numerous Pleasure Barges of historical figures such as Cleopatra and Caligula.

The Barges float upon the buffeting air of the storm and dock along the palaces over hanging face. Here souls are free to board them as the vessels spiral inward along the storm to the central tower. The vessels are opulent reproductions of their former real world counter parts. From Caligula's Nemi ships, to the tragic Titanic. These vessels offer their passengers a grand experience of all passions, and safe voyage to the Carnal Tower.

The Center of the Cupido is the great floating Carnal Tower. The accursed storm is turned back upon the Christian God, with this marvel of Hellish engineering. Shaped as a giant phallus (Supposedly it is the sever cock of Rasputin the mad monk, transformed.), the tower turns with the storm, held aloft by the tumultuous winds, once intended to torture those who gave into the sin of Lust. From its tip spews a radiant beam of golden light, that casts back the darkness as it falls in sparkling moats around the Cupido.

It is crafted in black and crimson marbles, and gilt in forbidden ivories, precious metals, and encrusted with Blood Diamonds, and other nefarious jewels.

Within this marvel sits the four Queens of Hell. Lilith, Agrat Bat Mahlet, Eisheth Zenunim, and Na'amah.

Together they are the Patron Goddesses of Sacred Prostitution, and Grand Queens of Hell. Within the Carnal Tower, they hold court in the Hall of Carnal Malefactors.

This chamber rests at the base of the tower with its bottom open to the storm and pit below. At its center is a flat dais, called the Stage of Forbidden Sin. Twenty feet around and connected by a stepped bridge, upon it the queens are entertained by lewd acts of carnality, or hear the testimonies of patrons, beseeching their audience.

Above, and across from this dais in four thrones built into the walls, sit the Queens. Above them on all sides is a great amphitheater which host the Queens guests and visitors of the court. Which includes many Gods and Goddesses of love and lust, and it is not uncommon to find one deity or another throwing a rowdy party in the balconies above much the courts annoyance.

Attending the guests is a host of Succubi and Incubi. Who take their carnal pleasure at will from the attendees, and do so repeatedly with great vigor, and often without consent. To which incidentally and as one may surmise, does not exist here. Guests pretty much consent to anything upon entering the Cupido, and especially the Carnal Tower.

Above, in the rest of the tower is many great pleasures and chambers open to be explored at one's own will, and mild playful peril. The Queens themselves are known for having unrelenting appetites. And despite the souls' pleasure, they are known for leaving souls diminished for a time.

Thus, is the design of Lust, the Second Circle.

The Third, Fourth, Fifth Circle
Gluttony, Greed, Anger
The Wastelands of Hades

The Wastelands of Hades, starts in the third circle of Hell and ends in the fifth. In Dante's depiction this is where Cerberus and Plutus, is met, and is the key to identifying the location in Dante's poem. Thus, we know now this is in fact the Greek Underworld itself, Hades. Named after its former ruler, and one of the most well documented of Hell regions already. While not mentioned in Dante's Inferno, this in fact a great wilderness of the Pit, where many souls that suffer from Condemnations find themselves stuck. It is a choke point in the pit as the circles are shattered and overhang in many places above the void of the Pit. It is perhaps one of the harshest of realms of the Pit as there is no rulers or order to it. This however is not a place of punishment, but of self-reflection

Dante's Description

    In the third circle, the gluttonous wallow in a vile, putrid marshy slush produced by a ceaseless, foul, icy rain – "a great storm of putrefaction", as punishment for subjecting their reason to a voracious appetite. Cerberus, described as "il gran vermo", literally "the great worm", line, the monstrous three-headed beast of Hell, ravenously guards the gluttons lying in the freezing mire, mauling and flaying them with his claws as they howl like dogs. Virgil obtains safe passage past the monster by filling its three mouths with mud.

The Fourth Circle is guarded by a figure Dante names as Pluto: this is Plutus, the God of wealth and ruler of the underworld in classical mythology. At the start of Canto VII, he menaces Virgil and Dante with the cryptic phrase *"Papé Satàn, papé Satàn aleppe"*, but Virgil protects Dante from him.

Those whose attitude toward material goods deviated from the appropriate mean are punished in the fourth circle. They include the avaricious or miserly (including many "clergymen, and popes and cardinals"), who hoarded possessions, and the prodigal, who squandered them. The hoarders and spendthrifts joust, using great boulders as weapons that they push with their chests.

In the fifth circle we find the Marsh of the Styx where those guilty of anger and wrath do battle with each other for all eternity.

Satanic Description

Upon the great first war of Heaven and Hell, the realm of the Underworld was sundered and shattered and fell into the Void to form a great Pit.

From the gilded Carnal Tower above we find a vast descending wilderness. Spared from the sundering, was the Asphodel Fields and thus Hades gifted them to Hecate. Not so fortunate was the rest of his kingdom.

From the Great storm of Lust, falls a pounding freezing rain that turns much of the wastelands into a bog of slush, mire, and filth. From this filth grows numerous trees from those souls who wallow too long in their own self-flagellations and have taken root.

The landscape is cut by the five great Rivers of Hell, that flow and descend in great falls of Water, Blood, Oil, Mud, and Lava, that meet in the great Marsh of the Styx in the Lower Waists. The land masses jut and overhang the out from the sides of the pit, and over the great distances of its chasm. It is here that souls who have not let go of their Condemnations, find true suffering as they wander this wilderness in various forms of despair. Lost and unable to find their way to salvation, they may fall into many different terrors. Not even the Gods are immune from this, as even Great Hades himself once fell into madness here upon seeing what had become of his once beautiful home.

Among these shattered levels are numerous floating islands, called *The Isles of Woe*. These floating Islands prove to be very treacherous for the numerous floating vessels that transport souls between the upper and lower levels.

It is also in these wastelands that Hells armies are trained by various Gods of War. Chief among them is Ares, who trains souls in the Spartan way.

The horrid conditions provide the perfect place for souls to be broken of their hang-ups and self-condemnations, and become reforged into powerful beings. Once a soul has freed itself from any personal condemnations, they find themselves able to withstand the Wastelands brutal conditions, and can become free to wander Hell as one of its Wardens.

Thus, is the design of Gluttony, Greed, and Anger, the Wastelands of Hades.

The City of Dis
Elysium

The city of Dis is an interesting place. It is a contradiction to anything we know.

Within the old underworld was a paradise known as Elysium, and within that was an even greater paradise known as the Isles of the Blessed. In his wrath at being unable to seize Elysium away from Hades, the Christian God shattered the underworld into a great Pit.

Within Elysium's once black walls, was a radiant city built in the ancient Greek way. Throughout the city was beautiful flourishing gardens that was tended to by Persephone, Hades wife, and Goddess of Spring time. Here she was ruler, her throne but a simple chair in her gardens, where she sat and spoke with any who would give the benefit of their company. Through her fountain a soul could choose to be reborn on Earth in a new life. And should that soul be worthy enough to be granted access to Elysium three times from three reincarnations in a row, they will be granted access to the Isles of the Blessed, the Old underworlds ultimate Paradise, that was rumored to be so beautiful and radiant, that it was the most deeply and jealously coveted by the Host of Heaven.

Elysium survived its descent into the Sixth circle, but only just. The former beauty of Elysium was shattered, and from the ruins of this once great city was born the City of Dis. A sprawling radiant metropolis that the Wardens of Hell (living souls that have earned the right to be Hell's keepers and citizens) call home. Here the souls that have shed all their Condemnations find connection to the joy of their former lives.

The outer walls now glow with the radiant fires of Hell and stand defended by 6000 legions of Hell.

Within the walls and through its fabled Medusa Gate, is a vast sprawling cityscape, grander in design, and built upon the ruins of old Elysium, covering the vast opening of the Pit. Here the streets are paved with gold and silver. And many vessels float down from the Cupido to ferry the unburdened souls to and from the upper circles.

The five rivers fall in radiant falls around the city from the upper circles, creating striking vistas of different radiant colors and substances. Throughout the city is the earthly homes of residents rebuilt in grandeur for each individual soul. And about the city intermixed is grand places of entertainment, learning, music, and art. Souls wander the streets freely to visit friends and loved ones that have joined them in the afterlife.

About the city are the Grand Gardens of Dis. These gardens built by Persephone reflect the grandeur of Elysium's lost gardens and the Gardens of Babylon, lost to the destructive hatred of the Christian God. They now flourish as a monument to the endurance of the unburdened soul, and in defiance of Messiah.

At the heart of Dis sits the Pluton. The great fortress of Hades. Built from Adamantine, it radiates with the Black Flame, and casts about it a somber calm.

From his Pluton, Hades Governs this city, and takes court. About him at all times is nine nameless Seraphim Angels, who are his personal guard and counsel. They are called *The Counsel of the Nine Angles*. Legend says that in his final battle with Heaven, after Lucifers host was cast into Tartarus, Nine Angels still stood with him. As Hades lead his final charge, these Angels formed a protective guard about his Chariot and fought unflinchingly alongside him through the deepest of combat. Afterwards they stayed with him as his personal bodyguards and advisors.

To Hades right sits an empty throne with a single thunderbolt resting on it, and to his left, a throne with a trident. These thrones are for his brothers. Zeus who was captured by Heavens host, and Poseidon who retreated deep into the oceans to wait out the coming conflicts, concerned only with his own realms of the deep.

Thus, is the design of the City of Dis.

Beyond the Walls of Dis

Below the City of Dis is where we leave Dante's descriptions. Contained within the wildlands known as the Gehenna, we find the most unlikely place for the Capitol of Hell, the City of Pandemonium Floating above the Great Prisons of Hell. Gehenna, The Malebolge, and infamous Tartarus.

The Seventh Circle
Violence
The Realm of Gehenna

The seventh circle is a wilderness of many dangers. While not so much of an actual Prison of Hell, Gehenna Serves as a place of suffering, and holding as a Soul is either condemned further to the depths, or elevated to self-redemption. Here Souls are held to await audience

Here the mighty Phlegethon encircles and winds its way through to the deeper levels. Along its banks rests the trees of the Forest of Suicides. Rooted in place, and unable to move beyond their own misery here they serve as sentinels of warning to what lays deeper in the pit. The air fills with its heat and the stench of sulfur and Hellfire hail falls endlessly, spewed from volcanic vents in the rim of the Pit. It is here that many of Hells pleasantries stop, and Hells darker natures flourish.

the fortress of Pandemonium, The High Capital, of Satan and his Peers. Floats ominously in the black and crimson sky and upon a black pillar of smoke, in the distance of the void of the Great Pit.

Within this fortress Satan holds court with the full Host of Hell, "The Stygian Council". It was designed by the architect Mulciber, who was known as Vulcan, who had also been the designer of palaces in Heaven before the First War and his fall.

Very few truly know what is inside its hot blackened walls, though rumor has it, Satan's throne rests on a massive replica of Earth, that enables him to watch over mankind.

Below in the depth of the Malebolge come the roar of incalculable souls, locked within the vast prisons of the pit. And beyond that glowing in the very depths is the Lake of Fire that burns in the center of Tartarus. And from it rises the great twisting plume of smoke and madness.

Thus, is the design of the Seventh circle of Hell, Gehenna

The Eighth Circle
Malebolge
The Prison of the Black Spiral

The Malebolge is the first of Hell's actual prisons. The nice one, to be exact.

This is described as a series of ditches, though in truth it is a spiral that leads further into the depths of the Pit. Here a soul that is truly despicable, and worthy of Hell's contempt, will face its punishment as it is forced to dance the Black Spiral.

The Spiral is the Black Spiral of Madness. From the center of the pit erupts the fumes of Tartarus, swirling as a black plume caught in a vortex. Around the rim and descending to the darkness below, is a spiraling ditch. As a soul dances it they will either sink deeper into the Pit their own despair and Madness. Or raise themselves up to redemption. Should a soul dance its way to the rim of the Malebolge, it is given leave to rise up to the city of Dis and beyond to be reborn anew.

But should the soul become stuck or unable to rise up, it shall sink to the bottom of the spiral. Once there it is consumed by the Black Spiral itself, and enters Tartarus to remain until the time of the final conflict.
To be consumed by the Black Spiral, is said to be beyond agony. The soul is flayed and perverted to a point beyond even a Demons sight. Even Satan must look away in disgust. The thing that emerges is beyond comprehension. Twisted and foul it knows only madness,

suffering, and total violence. It attacks blindly even at itself. It speaks no languages; it is not even an animal.

There is no word to name such a thing. They are beyond that of Demon or Angel. It is said that in the few incidents where one of these "Dancers" have emerged in our world Chaos and horror beyond measure erupted. Acts of cannibalism, rape, torture and other innumerable horrid things surround the event of glimpsing such a horror.

The "Dancer" is locked within the confines of Tartarus. So putrid have they become, and so filled with violence and madness, that never again until the Final Conflict with Messiah comes, will they be allowed from depths Tartarus.

Thus, is the shape of the Malebolge, the Black Spiral Prison.

The Ninth Circle
Tartarus

At the bottom of the vast Pit of Hell, is the legendary prison of Tartarus. Only those who are truly beyond redemption pass its gates, and none know what lays within.

No words can adequately describe the horror of its gates. Or of the twisted labyrinth within its walls. What is known is that it is silent.

No sound spills from this grim place. No light escapes its doors. It is only from above that the burning Phlegethon, can be seen at the heart of this dark prison forming the legendary Lake of Fire. It is only from above that the prison can be seen to take on the shape of vast labyrinth.

It is unknown what great Lord of Hell was consigned to watch over this dark abode.

What is known is that when the gates open to admit one who is condemned, nothing stirs, and only a maddening blackness of pure terror awaits the silent condemned.

Thus, is the final Circle of Hell, Tartarus.

The Book of Leviathan

Awaken ye lords of shadow and darkness.
Awaken from thy deathless slumber.
Heed the ancient summoning.
Hearken to my call.
Open wide the gates of Hell.
Unleash the Legions of the Black Abyss.
And return to this mortal domain once more.
Arise, arise... ARISE!

Intro

Rituals are one of the backbones of any religion. The following is a series of rituals used by Satanists.

The Philosophy of Satanic Ritual Magic

Let me tell you a story. I began studying witchcraft when I was 14. Inside of a year I stumbled my way into an apprenticeship in Wicca. There I studied for three long years as a teenager in arts that typically are reserved for people twice my age. I of course had been reading books by Silver Ravenwolf, and others. However, when I began studying with my mentor, he told me two things right out of the gate.

The first thing he told me was to forget everything I had taught myself about magic. I knew less than nothing.

The second thing he said was a question. "How do you fly?"

Of course I was completely befuddled by this, obviously people can't fly without a plane or helicopter, and that is exactly what I told him. He looked at me with complete dead seriousness and said, "Wrong!" Not a joke. True story. His response will blow your mind at the implications.

He said, "Flying is easier than you can ever imagine. You simply throw yourself at the ground, and miss."

I know, brain explosion, right? Could it really be that easy. But here is the next question. How does one miss the ground? Isn't there the tiny little problem of gravity to deal with? I would ask this question to all my other mentors in the coven, and they all would simply say the same thing. "Learn to miss the ground."

I guess I should have also started this off by mentioning just how infuriating apprenticeships can be with traditional witchcraft. Nothing is ever explained to you, you are expected to be silent and learn by paying attention and watching. It's not easy, and that is the point. If the practice of magic was so simple, well then everyone would be doing it. It takes time to learn how to miss the ground.

Do you want to know how to miss the ground? It's actually very easy.

First thing is if your are a new practitioner, to forget everything you think you know about magic. Because you don't even have fucking clue. Yup that's right, take all those Crowley books. All those Wicca books. Hey! Yup you! Yeah, that includes the book on talking to animals. Take all of that stuff and throw it out the window.

You're not going to summon up King Paimon without a big blood sacrifice. Look to the chapter on that if you can manage affording a camel to kill. No, there is no demons that will exclusively date you or marry you. Truth be told they probably couldn't care less about you. Well, not at first they won't.

Why? Because you have nothing to offer them. Nothing to interest them. They don't see any potential in you, or in associating with you. Sure you might cast spells and curses until the damn cows come home, but ask yourself this. How often does that actually work for you? Probably not a lot. Again why? Gravity.

The first thing to understand about performing magic, is that it starts in your head. You fail at it because you don't invest in it mentally. You, are stuck in your own head. Stop it.

Satanic magic is performed mostly indoors as opposed to other forms of Witchcraft. Why? Environmental control. We create to ourselves quite literally, the perfect ritual environment for ourselves. This is called a Ritual Chamber, or as LaVey called it, The Intellectual Decompression Chamber.

This is a room designed with the express purpose of divorcing you, from your normal mental state, and allowing you, to engage your higher state of fantasy. Or to be more laymen about it, to engage your Suspension of Disbelief. In short, if you want witchcraft to work, you need to first believe it will.

So what does the Ritual chamber generally look like? What is in it?

To be honest, some folks like to have allot of figures and stuff cluttering their Ritual Chamber, but I don't. certainly there should be some stuff. But you don't need twenty different statues on your altar, a thousand and one candles. It should be spartan in nature, only having those tools that you will need or have use of. Anything else is simply a personal touch and should be very sparse. The walls of this room if painted should be black with red trim and a red ceiling. But it is fine if you choose to leave things unpainted.

The size of the altar of course plays a small role in what should go on it, but there is actually a basic list of items.

1. Candles; 2 black candles, 1 white candle, & 1 red candle

2. A Chalice; This can in reality be any sort of drinking vessel. A goblet, wine glass, drinking horn, beer stein. Be creative and original. Mine is an inverted skull with a pewter goblet going through it.

3. Incense and burner

4. Burn bowl; any plate or vessel that is safe to contain burning items and have a fire going and contained.

5. A sword; Ok this can be substituted with a ritual dagger. Just keep it long sharp and able to burn things on.

6. A bell; A singing bowl can be used too.

7. A Gong; or something similar.

8. A Baphomet; This can be a banner, a picture, or wall mounted plaque. Or if need be even a statue of Baphomet.

9. An Altar; Of course the Altar is one of the most important elements. This should be covered with some type of black or red cloth, and traditionally would rest upon the western most wall, but in reality should be on the wall that fits your ritual chamber best.

10. Ritual attire; Take time to build your ritual wardrobe. Special jewelry and Robes should be set aside for specific ritual use.

Other items can be implemented as you see fit. There are a number of items that can be omitted or added to the ritual chamber or altar itself. But one item is most important to any occult practitioner, their Grimoire.

A Grimoire is like a book of spells and rituals. This

will be what you read from during your rituals. You might ask why a book is read from during rituals?

The answer to that if you asked in in my old coven would have been a firm swat on the head and a telling off to go clean the bookshelves. There you would be left to do your choirs until you realized the scope of spells and rituals and the completely difficult nature of memorizing them all. Screw Harry Potter waiving around a wand and saying a simple magical word or two. No, these are fully immersive Rites designed to raise energy and blast it towards your end goal.

In Wicca, we are taught to raise a cone of power by casting a protective circle. Yeah, Satanists say fuck the protective barriers, if we are going to align ourselves with the dark forces of magic and spirituality, we better make nice with them and not try to put up protective barriers, or try to demand a demon to show up in some magic circle or triangle. That is a sure fire way to piss them off.

Hint, Demons are like cats, they do what they want. It is better to just send out a general invitation and let them show up on their own. You're actually more likely to have success that way.

This may all seem strange to you. Certainly, there has got to be more to it than this. Some unknown secret that only the most advanced magicians in Satanism know. Of course there is silly. But before you can run you must walk, before you walk, you must crawl.

Allow me to finish with this final word. Magic, is what you put into it. Yes this stuff is real. It can work as more than just a psychologically cathartic practice if you let it.

Rituals should never be rushed. Take your time, and invest in your rituals. Invest in your practice. You don't need to meditate everyday to become a good magician, or put yourself into attunement with Satan. You just simply need to be attuned to yourself. Once you

have that everything else is gravy.
    Remember that question on how to miss the ground? Here is a little hint, forget that there is gravity. Just do it. How do you do that?
    Well, that would be telling.

The High Mass

The High Mass is the root fundamental ritual in modern Satanism, especially any sort of Laveyan Satanism. This ritual contains all of the prime elements found in the basic Satanic Ritual, Lust, Compassion, & Destruction and is thus the prime example of the modern Satanic Ritual. But it was not always so, and has taken several decades, and a number of incarnations, to become the full ritual presented here.

A little realized fact is that Anton LaVey was often prone to "Winging it" so to speak when he performed rituals. There was nothing really set into stone at that point in history as to what a Satanic Ritual was supposed to look like outside La Viosin's Black Mass. But as time went on LaVey began writing down his Rituals and really hammering them out…Sort of.

We can see in various documentaries depicting him in ritual how he worked, and often we can tell he would be "winging" certain elements of rituals that often didn't have set elements. This was vital for Satanism because it hammered out the fine details. By the time LaVey's bible was published, the core ritual procedural had begun to take a functional shape.

This cookie cutter format presented in the Satanic Bible would become a staple point for many of the rituals for many years. It provided a basic outline that was easy to follow for most, only swapping out one or two minor sections depending on the ritual being done.

This would become the mainstay for decades. But in 2006 a new variation was presented to the public. The first public performance a full High Mass. This would combine the three prime rituals into one event and would be the first time a complete core ritual would be presented to the public.

The High Mass presented here is the result of several years of study and research, and created from modification of three previous incarnations to present for personal use. It is inspired and based heavily on the High Mass performed by the Church of Satan on 6-6-06.

Generally speaking, the High Mass should be performed twice a month, on full and new moons. This is done to present a stable cycle of the rituals and give the practitioners a foundation to work from.

It uses all the standard tools but adds to the roster a red candle that is used for invocations to Lust and Compassion, thus relegating the white candle strictly to invoking destruction and curses upon enemies.

This variant of the High Mass is unique to the STS. The formula is essentially the same That LaVey originally created, yet focus is placed upon the refinement of its cohesiveness of its various parts. It also drifts away from the classical LaVey based scriptures, presenting an almost completely original script to work from. This variant was debuted on Aug 11th 2022, (Ano Luciferi II).

I. PURIFICATION OF THE AIR
Ring bell 9 times, directing tolling to the four cardinal compass points while turning counter-clockwise. The "Hymn to Satan" or other appropriate music is played simultaneously.

II. INVOCATION TO SATAN
Celebrant faces the Sigil of the Baphomet with arms spread gently with palms open. Invocation is intoned by Celebrant.

In nomine Dei nostri Satanas Luciferi excelsi!

In the name of Satan, the Ruler of the earth, the King of the world, I/we invoke the forces of Darkness to bestow their Infernal power upon me/us!

From your throne in Pandemonium, to the Medusa Gate of Dis, and onward to the Vestibule! Open wide the Gates of Hell and come forth from the abyss to greet me/us as your brothers/sisters and friends!

Grant me/us the indulgences of which I/we speak! I/We have taken thy name as a part of myself! I/we live as the beasts of the field, rejoicing in the fleshly life! I/We favor the just and curse the rotten! By all the Gods of the Pit, I/we ask that these things of which I/we speak shall come to pass!

Come forth and answer to your names by manifesting my/our desires!

OH HEAR THE NAMES!

Congregation repeats each name after Celebrant.

THE INFERNAL NAMES

Abaddon	Nyarlathotep	Tchort
Euronymous	Baalberith	Cimeries
O-ama	Mammon	Cthulhu
Adramelech	Sedit	Coyote
Fenriz	Balaam	Milcom
Pan	Mania	Thamuz
Ahpuch	Sekhmet	Dagon
Gorgo	Baphomet	Beelzebub
Hades	Mantus	Thoth
Ahriman	Set	Damballa
Haborym	Bast	Mormo
Proserpine	Shaitan	Tunrida
Amon	Beelzebub	Demogorgon
Hecate	Mastema	Naamah
Pwcca	Shamad	Typhon
Apollyn	Behemoth	Diabolus
Ishtar	Melek Taus	Nergal
Rimmon	Shiva	Cerberus
Asmodeus	Beherit	Yaotzin
Kali	Mephistopheles	Vlad Dracula
Sabazios	Yog-Sothoth	Nihasa
Astaroth	Supay	Yen-lo-Wang
Lilith	Bilé	Emma-O
Sammael	Metztli	Nija
Azazel	T'an-mo	O-Yama
Loki	Chemosh	Shub-Nigguath
Samnu	Mictian	Anton LaVey
Agrat Bat Mehlat	Eisheth Zenunim	Michael Aquino

Celebrant: "Arise oh Gods of the Abyss and manifest thy presence through thy blessing."

III. RITE OF THE CHALICE
Celebrant adds incense to the burner.

Celebrant: "As our incense ascends to thee, Infernal Lord, so shall your blessings descend upon us."
Cense chalice three times, bow. Cense baphomet again three times, and bow.

Bless chalice with the mudras of flames.

Celebrant: "Lord Satan, Imperator of Fire, Hell and Earth are filled with your glory.
Hosanna in profundis!"

Celebrant elevates chalice.

Gong is struck.

Celebrant: "Behold the chalice of (name of chalice) filled with the elixir of life. As kindred to the undefiled beasts, I drink and celebrate the Black Flame within."

Celebrant drinks and says: "Satan, thy strength is mine!"

Celebrant turns to offer chalice to mourners with these words:

Celebrant: "Drink and honor thy true nature."

Participants who wish to partake approach. They each drink and reply:

Participant: "The Black Flame burns within me. Satan, thy strength is mine!"
Celebrant faces altar and elevates chalice a final time.

Celebrant: "Hail Satan!"

Congregation. (responds): "Hail Satan!"

Gong is struck.

Celebrant replaces the chalice on altar.

IV. QUARTER CALL

Celebrant takes sword or Athame and points towards the domain of the Prince to be called. Unlike the standard High Mass which uses a four point Quarter Call, this one uses a Five point Quarter Call, starting at the left corner of the alter and ending on the right corner going counter clockwise as each point is called.

Celebrant:"I summon thee brilliant Lucifer. Come forth oh Bearer of Light, I bid thee welcome!"

"I summon thee fearsome Belial. Come forth oh King of the Earth, I bid thee welcome!"

"I summon thee dread Leviathan. Come forth oh Dragon of the Abyss, I bid thee welcome!"

"I summon thee great Beelzebub. Come forth oh Lord of the Flies, I bid thee welcome."

"I summon thee almighty Satan. Come forth oh Master of the Inferno, I bid thee welcome!"

"Shemhamforash!"

Congregation. (responds): "Shemhamforash!"

Gong is struck.

Celebrant: "Hail Satan!"

Congregation. (responds): "Hail Satan!"

Gong is struck.

Celebrant replaces sword on altar.

V. BENEDICTION

Celebrant: "For though art a mighty Lord, oh Satan, and from thee arises all potency, justice, and dominion. Let our visions become reality and our creations endure, for we are your kindred, demon brethren, scions of carnal joy."

Starting in the south, Celebrant blesses the appropriate compass points by either making the sign of the horns or sprinkling sacred water saying:

"Satan, give to us thy blessing."

"Lucifer, grant to us thy favor."

"Belial, confer upon us thy benisons."

"Leviathan, bestow to us thy treasures."

VI. THE READING

Celebrant: "And now, a reading from the Infernal Scriptures"

Congregation. (responds): "Glory to thee, Prince of Darkness!"

Celebrant reads a selected passage from The Diabolicon, Book of Satan, The Infernal Revelations, or any other related scripture that so moves them for the specific ritual. This is presented as almost a sermon, and will continue until the Celebrant has finished his selected section.

VII. THE CANON

Celebrant: (congregants repeat) Our Father which art in Hell, unhallowed is Thy name. Thy kingdom is come, Thy will is done; on earth as it is in Hell! We take this night our rightful due, and trespass not on paths of pain. Lead us unto temptation, and deliver us from false piety, for Thine is the kingdom and the power and the glory forever!

"Shemhamforash!"

Gong is struck.

VIII. THE INVOCATIONS TO LUST, COMPASSION, AND DESTRUCTION

COMPASSION

The Eighteenth Key

Enochian

EE-luh-suh • mee-kah-OH-luhts OH-luh-PEE-ruh-tuh • OHD MAH-luh-puh-ruh-jzhuh • buh-lee-OHR-ay DAHSS • OH-doh • BUH-vuh-zuhd DAY • HEL-EL •

oh-voh-AH-ruh-suh kah-OHS-suh-goh, • kah-SAH-ruh-muhjzh mee-kah-OH-luhts • KEE-kuh-lays voh-OH-ahn • buh-REE-nuh-tuhs kah-fah-FAHM • DAHSS • EE VUH-MUHD • AH • KUH LOH-nuh-doh • vuh-GAY-ahr DAY • MAHTS • OHD mah-OH-fuh-fahss. BOH-luhp KOH-moh • buh-lee-OH-ruh-tuh PAH-muh-buh-tuh. zah-KAH-ray • KAH • OHD ZAH-muh-rahn! • OH-doh KEE-kuh-lay • KAH-ah! ZOR-ruh-jzhay! • ZEE-ruh NOH-koh! • hoh-AH-tuh-huh HEL-EL • BUH-vuh-fuhd LOH-nuh-suh • LOH-nuh-doh bah-BAH-jzhay

English

O thou mighty light and burning flame of comfort which unveiled the glory of Satan unto the center of the earth, in whom the great secrets of truth have their abiding that is called in thy kingdom strength through joy and is not to be measured. For thou art a window of comfort unto me. Move therefore and appear! Open the mysteries of your Creation! Be friendly unto me! For I am the servant of the same! The true worshiper of Satan the highest King of Hell.

Invocation

Celebrant: Hecate! Mother of the night! Queen of Witches! She who is Maiden, Mother, and Crone! We call you now in your benevolence to enfold one who has been stricken with torments. Come now in mercy from Limbo and cradle them in your protective embrace, for they are undeserving of suffering, and are in need of your guidance, wisdom, and nurturing.

Bolster them up against the reverses that have beset them! Enfold them in your dark might, that they may weather the storm. Restore to them vigor and vitality, so that they may face their adversaries known and unknown, seen and yet still unseen, a new and with fresh eyes and strength! Around them weave a garden of thorns that they may be protect from those who would resent their vital being. This we do ask of thee, Dark Mother. Let your Fey loose to bring thy child home, whose name is _____.

Cast your custom request here.

Shemhamforash! Hail Satan!

Gong is struck following congregants' response to "Shemhamforash!" and "Hail Satan!"

LUST

The Seventh Key

Enochian

RAH-ahs • EE • ZAH-luh-mahn BAH-bah-LOH-nuhd • oh-ay-kuh-REE-mee ah-AH-oh • MAH-luh-puh-ruh-jzhuh kuh-ROH-ohd-zee • BUH-vuh-zuhd kuh-VEE-een • HEL-EL • OH-doh buh-vuh-tuh-MOHN • OHD • ZEE kuh-HEES • NOH-AHS • AYM pah-RAH-dee-ahl • kuh-SAH-ruh-muhjzh vuh-GAY-ahr • oh-LOH-rah kuh-HEE-ruh-lahn; • OHD • ZEE kuh-HEES • ZOH-nahk Loo-SEEF-tee-uhn, • KOH-ruhz TAH • VAH-vuhl • ZEE-ruhn toh-luh-HAH-mee; • ZOH-bah LOH-nuh-doh • OHD • MEE-ahm kuh-HEES • TAH • KUH ZEE-ah-rahs • mee-KAH-luhts vuh-MAH-dee-ah • DAY • HEL-EL, pee-BLEE-ahr; • MAHTS • GOH-hud. KAH NOH • kuh-VOHL • DAY • kuh-VAH-sah-hee, zah-KAH-ray! ZAH-muh-rahn! oh-ay-kuh-REE-mee • DAY •

HEL-EL! oh-mee-KAH-oh-luhts • ah-AH-ee • OHM; BAH-guh-lay • PAH-puh-nohr • EE duh-luh-vuh-JZHAHM • LOH-nuh-suh-hee, OHD • vuh-muh-puh-LEEF • vuh-GAY-jzhee buh-lee-OH-ruh • DAY • HEL-EL!

English

The east is a house of harlots singing praises amongst the flames of first glory. Wherein Lord Satan hath opened his mouth, and they are become as living dwellings in whom the carnality of man rejoiceth, and they are appareled with ornaments of brightness, such as work wonders on all creatures. Whose kingdoms and continuance are as the four Queens, of the mighty tower of Lust, continual places of comfort and joy everlasting.

Oh ye servants of pleasure! Move! Appear! Sing praises unto mankind, and be mighty amongst us. For to remembrance is given power, and our strength waxeth strong in the comfort of the flesh!

Invocation

Celebrant: We call to you oh Asmodeus great lord of Lust. Open wide the passages of the Cupido and bid up its denizens to attend us in our carnality. We have set our minds upon obscene vistas of lewd abandon and explorations of the flesh. Our loins surge, swell, and drip with thoughts of voluptuous pleasures. Send forth from the storm the Succubus and incubus, to bare out into the shadows of night and glaring light of day our desires to the body and mind of that which we have chosen, and bind to them the unquenching urge that may only be satiated by our carnal touch.

From the Carnal Tower there now comes the radiant glow that stirs the flesh and vital salts of body and mind of my summoning. We have set forth our symbols, and prepared our adornments, in preparation of that image that seethes as a beast awaiting its uncontrolled release. Seeking nourishment that can only come entwined in the throws of carnal passion. Go now and ravage and rape that mind I have chosen, until our summons doth respondeth with acts of lewd abandon.

(Male) My manhood stands erect as the Carnal Tower amidst the great storm! Unyielding and undeniable. The sanctity of that which I desire shall be shattered by the penetrating thrust of my will. And as the essence of manhood falls upon the stones, so shall its vapors benumb the mind of that which I desire to helpless submission to my carnal will. In the names of the great gods, Dionysus, Eros, Priapus, and Pan, my desire shall be known!
  Shemhamforash! Hail Satan!

(Female) My womanhood is swollen, and from it drips the nectar of Carnal passion! Its musk, summoning to me that which I crave, and paralyzing it to my will. And upon my mounting shall crazed impulses rend its purity to that of a crazed beast, until my void has been filled and surges spent. In the names of the great Queens of the Carnal Tower, Lilith, Agrat-Bat Mahlat, Eisheth Zenunim, Naamah, my lust shall be fulfilled!
Shemhamforash! Hail Satan!

Gong is struck following congregants' response to "Shemhamforash!" and "Hail Satan!"

DESTRUCTION

The Twelfth Key

Enochian

NOH-nuh-see • DAHSS ZOH-nuhf • mah-duh-REE-ahks OHD • kuh-HEES • DAH, huh-vuh-BAH-ee-oh tee-BEE-buhp • AH-luh-lahr ah-tuh-RAH-ah • OHD tuh-REE-ahn • TAH LOH-luh-keez • ah-BAH-ee FAH-fayn • DAY • ee-YAHD! AH-ruh • HEL-EL • OH-vohf; ZOH-bah • doh-OH-ay-een ah-AH-ee • EE • VOH-nuh-puh! zah-KAH-ray • KAH • OHD ZAH-muh-rahn! • OH-doh KEE-kuh-lay • KAH-ah! ZOR-ruh-jzhay! • ZEE-ruh NOH-koh! • hoh-AH-tuh-huh HEL-EL • BUH-vuh-fuhd LOH-nuh-suh • LOH-nuh-doh bah-BAH-jzhay

English

O you that reign in the South and bear the lanterns of sorrow, bind up your girdles and visit unto us. Beckon forth your armies, that the Lord of the Infernal may be magnified; whose name amongst you is wrath! Move therefore and appear! Open the mysteries of your Creation! Be friendly unto me! For I am the servant of the same! The true worshiper of the King of Hell.

Invocation

Harken now Oh yee denizens of the Pit! By the powers of my/ our infernal will, and by the laws of Hell, I do address thee to harken! For the time of redress has come. Blast wide the forbidden gates of the Pit, and set loose the hounds of Hell to come forth and hunt those that has wronged thine chosen children, and mocked thy name and image! Send forth thy heralds of doom that they may hear the great bell of the Cathedral of Pain sounding their imminent doom. It doth repenteth me/us not that our call doth ride upon the blasting winds of the Black Spiral. For the wretched deserves no mercies, and has not earned thy pity.

I call forth the Kraken! Beast of the depths and drown them in the dark abyss.

Scourge them with the sands of the waterless wastes oh Set!

Blast them from root to stem with the hot winds of Hell, oh Rudra!

Seek from the mind of that wastrel the very thing that they fears the most, oh Morpheus! Bring forth nightmare visions unto reality that only they will see.

Harken now as I thrust aloft the sacred blade of Hell and upon it pierced like a suckling pig, The swine that is to be made to squeal and shriek in torment. Bound to agonize beyond measure until death releases them from this mortal coil.

Cast your personal curse then burn paper.

 Shemhamforash! Hail Satan!

Gong is struck following congregants' response to "Shemhamforash!" and "Hail Satan!"

IX. AVE SATANAS
Celebrant: "To us, thy devoted disciples, oh Infernal Lord, who celebrate our iniquity and trust in your boundless might, grant thy bond of Stygian solidarity. It is through

you, that lavish gifts come to us; knowledge, vigor, and wealth are yours to bestow. We renounce the spiritual paradise of the desperate and gullible. You have won our trust, oh God of the Flesh, for you champion the satisfaction of all our desires and provide abundant fulfillment in the land of the living. Shemhamforash!"

Congreg. (responds): "Shemhamforash!"

Celebrant: "Deliver us, Dark Lord, from every hindrance and grant us joy in our lives. By your munificence you ensue our freedom and protect us from injustice as we indulge in our heart's desires. The kingdom, the power, and the glory are eternally yours."

Celebrant (CONGREG. Repeats): "Hail Satan full of might!
Our allegiance is with thee!

Cursed are they, the God adorers, and cursed are the worshipers of the Nazarene Eunuch!

Unholy Satan, bringer of enlightenment, lend us thy power,
Now and throughout the hours of our lives!

Shemhamforash!"

X. THE CLOSING RITE

Celebrant: "I bid thee rise and give the Sign of the Horns. (If standing, 'I bid thee give the Sign of the Horns.')"
Congregation responds as bidden with the salute, given with the left hand.

Celebrant: "Almighty Satan, open wide the Gates of Hell! Reveal the mysteries of your creation for we are partakers of your undefiled wisdom! Forget ye not what was and is to be! Flesh without sin! World without end!"

Celebrant: (Congregation. repeats): "Shemhamforash!"
"Hail Satan!"
"Hail Satan!"
"Hail Satan!"

Gong is struck following congregants' response to "Shemhamforash!" and each "Hail Satan!"

X. POLLUTIONARY
Celebrant rings bell as at the beginning, while "Hymn to Satan" or music that is appropriate is played. When the sounds have decayed into silence the Celebrant concludes:

Celebrant: "So it is done!"

Celebrant extinguishes remaining illuminating candles or other light sources if this is out of doors, and all experience the darkness for a moment. Conventional illumination is then restored, ending the ceremony.

Grotto Initiation Ritual

This is the basic initiatory rite used by the Church of Satan. Until now it has never been made public knowledge and could only be found in the Grotto Masters Handbook. The purpose of this rite is as an initiation in a Satanic Coven called a "Grotto" by the CoS. Almost every occult tradition has some form of group initiation, this is Satanism's now presented for the first time to the general public. The ritual as presented here is true to the Church of Satan's version but features some minor revisions and edits. This has been done out of necessity for grammatical correctness and for fluidity of content, and has been kept to a bare fit minimum. Please remember that this is only a basic guide and is not written in stone. The ritual may be edited as any ritual can be for the personal aesthetics of the participants. It may be expanded or shortened depending on your personal preferences. As it stands though, this ritual serves as a complete ceremony. Enjoy.

Preparation for the Celebrant, before ritual

During the ritual, the Initiate should be given a Word upon which he can concentrate his energies, something the Celebrant (Grotto Master or Priest) feels will inspire or help the Initiate fulfill the next phase of his magical path. The Celebrant should meditate on this

Initiate ahead of time, to prepare himself to initiate the individual. Take a piece of his/her clothing or jewelry a few days before the ritual, to hold and psychometrize in private meditation in order to bring forth a focus word for the Initiate, to connect with the Initiate so that you will be qualified to usher him into this next stage of his magical transformation.

The ritual consists of three parts reflecting the awakening of Mind, Spirit and Flesh: The test of the Initiate's mind, the purification of his spirit, then the presentation of the first tools the Neophyte will need to manifest his will on the physical plane. Use your intuition to time the Initiation so that it will plant seeds of magic. What strengths can you conjure for him, what cautions does he need at this stage of his development, what must he do more of, or less of? Find a word of direction and write it on a small slip of paper, to give him during the Initiation Ritual.

Assign various members of your group one of the Nine Satanic Statements. Let them know they'll be expected to recite it during the ceremony (if you have fewer than nine other people in your group, assign two or three Statements to each participant). One of the Initiate's friends among the group will speak as his Sponsor during the ceremony.

Also choose two members to act as Acolytes for the evening. Explain their tasks to them as they are described below. Most rituals must be carefully rehearsed with all participants to insure the ritual proceeds smoothly. This cannot be the case with the Initiation Ritual, in which the main participant-the Initiate-should not know fully what is going to happen to him before he actually participates in his Initiation. This builds up magical anticipation in him and makes his experience of the ritual more potent. You and the other grotto participants should rehearse your lines, music cues and movements, but the Initiate should not be present.

Preparation for the Initiate

The Initiate should be instructed to memorize the Nine Satanic Statements. He (She) must also wear a garb to the actual ritual that can be loosened at the neck, to be drawn down low enough to expose his heart. The Initiate should be instructed to fast the day of the ritual, only being allowed to eat bread and honey and drink water. This is traditionally for reasons of purification and focus. If he (she) is so predisposed, instruct him to take a candlelit, ritual bath before leaving for his Initiation, washing away past guilt and fears and opening himself or herself to new experiences (using no scents or oils; the demons can be likened to wild beasts who will trust you more if they can smell you, unmasked by frankincense and myrrh).

Other Grotto Participants should, as always, wear black ritual robes and Baphomets, with the addition of black, pointed hoods (with eye holes) covering their heads.

Necessary Implements

All standard ritual implements, as listed in The Satanic Bible, and also:
1. A small box of earth (large enough for Initiate to place both hands in)
2. A brazier
3. Incense to throw over the coals
4. A chalice filled with water
5. A small container of tiger balm (or similar capsicum derivative that leaves a slightly tingly effect on the skin)

6. An envelope (preferably black) containing Celebrant's word for the Initiate
7. A small presentation pillow
8. A black robe
9. A Baphomet pendant
10. Rope (cut in two pieces)
11. Black hood without eyeholes

There should be a third Acolyte appointed to hand Celebrant necessary items in a timely enough manner to maintain the rhythm of the ritual. The Acolytes should alternate tasks as needed. As for music, an appropriate musical selection might be Albinoni's "Adagio in G minor" or Handel's Largo from "Xerxes", moving into Mussorgsky's "Night on Bald Mountain" for the conclusion of the ritual.

Before the actual ceremony begins: Two of your appointed Acolytes will, upon a subtle signal from you, leave the area of general pre-ritual socializing and put on their black robes, Baphomets and hoods before the rest of the congregation does. They will then reappear in their black robes and hoods and approach the Initiate. (If the Initiate lives alone and you want a particularly dramatic effect, you might send the Acolytes to show up at his door to usher him to the ceremony.) They will escort him to a place (another room, a separate area of woods, outside the house, etc.) where they bind his hands and feet (make the feet-binding loose enough so he can walk by shuffling) and place a black hood (without eyeholes) over his head. The two Acolytes are forbidden to speak to the Initiate while they escort him and prepare him for the ritual.

Once the Initiate is bound, he should be brought to the ritual site or ritual chamber through a circuitous route that disorients him, and wait with the Acolytes just beyond the chamber. In the interim, you and the rest of the grotto participants can put on your ritual garb, enter the ritual chamber and perform the standard ritual opening, Steps 3-7, according to the instructions found in The Satanic Bible. After invoking the four Crown Princes of Hell, reciting the First Enochian Key (after which, the gong is struck), and handing his sword to an awaiting Acolyte, the Celebrant should face the altar again and intone:

CELEBRANT: Satan, our Dark Lord, please attend us. There is an Initiate who requests your attention, and approval. Hear his words, O Satan, and measure his worth.

(ACOLYTES bring Initiate into the ritual chamber.)

(CONGREGATION forms a circle around the bound and hooded Initiate.)

CELEBRANT: (turning toward the Initiate): A stranger has come into our midst.

INITIATE: I am no stranger to Satan. I have been summoned by Him and I approach His altar of my own free Will.

CELEBRANT: Who vouches for this Initiate in the Black Arts?

SPONSOR: I speak for the stranger. He is a friend in Darkness.

CELEBRANT: Does he live by the Statements?

SPONSOR: He (She) is his (her) own God, and lives by the Law of the Jungle.

CELEBRANT: We will interrogate this stranger. You are a Satanist. You know the Statements we hold sacred. Complete them with this congregation as witness.

INTERROGATION

1st CONGREGANT: Satan represents indulgence...

INITIATE: instead of abstinence!

2nd CONGREGANT: Satan represents vital existence...

INITIATE: ...instead of spiritual pipe dreams!

3rd CONGREGANT: Satan represents undefiled wisdom...

INITIATE: instead of hypocritical self-deceit!

4th CONGREGANT: Satan represents kindness to those who deserve it...

INITIATE: ...instead of love wasted on ingrates!

5th CONGREGANT: Satan represents vengeance...

INITIATE: ...instead of turning the other cheek!

6th CONGREGANT: Satan represents responsibility to the responsible...

INITIATE: ...instead of concern for psychic vampires!

7th CONGREGANT: Satan represents man as just another animal, sometimes better, more often worse than those that walk on all-fours...

INITIATE: . . . who, because of his "divine spiritual and intellectual development," has become the most vicious animal of all!

8th CONGREGANT: Satan represents all of the so-called sins...
INITIATE: ...as they all lead to physical, mental, or emotional gratification!

9th CONGREGANT: Satan has been the best friend the church has ever had...

INITIATE: ...as he has kept it in business all these years!

(Gong is struck.)

PURIFICATION

CELEBRANT: You have proven yourself a worthy student of the Black Arts.

(CONGREGATION moves back from encircling the Initiate, to a position behind the Celebrant.)

(ACOLYTES remove hood, then bindings, from the Initiate.)

CELEBRANT: Your hood can now be removed, as you are no longer blinded by Christian and societal lies. Your eyes are opening to the Mysteries; you see the truth, as well as the Knowing beyond Knowing. Your feet and hands can be freed, no longer hobbled and impeded in your magical and material advancement. You are free to fulfill the destiny that Satan has prepared for the Strong. It is time for you to experience the Satanic in the world around you. Concentrate on the Elements, and outside the ritual chamber, be reminded that Satan is always near.

(ACOLYTE hands Celebrant the black candle from the altar.)

CELEBRANT: With these Elements, we purify your soul, and awaken your Diabolical Essence.

(CELEBRANT bares Initiate's chest and holds candle flame close to Initiate's heart.)

CELEBRANT: Feel the Black Flame of the Fury and Will of Satan; let it burn into your soul! (Hands candlestick back to Acolyte to replace on the altar.)

(ACOLYTE hands incense to Celebrant, which CELEBRANT sprinkles over the brazier.)

CELEBRANT: Breathe the vapors of enlightenment, the inspiration of Lucifer!

(ACOLYTE holds out box of earth for Initiate.)

CELEBRANT: Grab in both fists the loamy earth that Belial gives us to protect and to rule!

(ACOLYTE hands Celebrant the chalice of water. CELEBRANT holds the chalice out for Initiate to drink.)

CELEBRANT: Drink deeply of the ineffable raging mysteries of Leviathan Himself! (Hands chalice back to Acolyte.)

CELEBRANT: Your soul now belongs to Satan, from this night forward. Turn and face your Black Prince. Are you willing to confront the trials Satan will place before you, and the delights with which He will reward you? (INITIATE turns toward the altar and reads text that an ACOLYTE holds out to him.)

INITIATE: I am ready. I am a Satanist, the highest embodiment of human life. I renounce all of the pious and putrefying gods of the Right-Hand Path. I know that way leads to confusion, stupidity and hypocrisy. I defy the unjust and self-righteous. I spit on the weak and incompetent. I will no longer be hindered by guilt or doubts manufactured for me, but will question and challenge all things. I reclaim authority over my own life, here and now. I stand before my Prince and my fellow Black Magicians to declare my undying allegiance to Satan and to His Legions, in Hell and on Earth. Their strength is now my strength, their power is now my power!

(INITIATE extends left hand in the Sign of the Horns toward the altar.)

INITIATE: Hail Satan!

CONGREGATION: Hail Satan!

(Gong is struck.)

INITIATE: Shemhamforash!

CONGREGATION: Shemhamforash!

(Gong is struck.)

CELEBRANT: You have inspired our trust with your declaration.

(CELEBRANT and INITIATE turn to congregation.) Do we accept this Petitioner into our ranks?

CONGREGATION: We accept him (her).

CELEBRANT: We can now reveal ourselves to you.

(CONGREGANTS take off their hoods.)

ASSIGNMENT

CELEBRANT: You are ready to take your next step along Satan's path. The Dark Lord's leathery wings are outstretched to enfold you in His darkness visible.

(ACOLYTE hands Celebrant the black robe, which CELEBRANT places over the Initiate.)

CELEBRANT: Don this black robe and be recognized as a fellow traveler on the Sinister Path of Strength and Fulfillment, honored that the King of the Night has accepted you into His realm.

(ACOLYTE hands Celebrant small container of tiger balm.)

CELEBRANT: You were born a Satanist. Your path has been unfocused until now. This is your awakening. Now you begin to learn the truth of your proud heritage. There is the mark of Cain upon your forehead which others only perceive on a psychic level-but they fear and resent you because of it. We hereby activate your Third Eye, to excite your psychic subconscious.

(CELEBRANT touches a bit of tiger balm to Initiate's forehead.)

CELEBRANT: You were born with this mark and you will carry this mark until you die. Through it, you connect with the Dark Gods of Hell. Be warned that what magical wisdom Satan deigns to reveal to you is precious, granted to very few. Use it. Remain silent. If you dare to betray the trust He has placed in you, or reveal the Mysteries, you will suffer unending torment.

CONGREGATION: Remember well. We are always watching.

(Gong is struck.)

(ACOLYTE presents envelope resting on a pillow to Celebrant.

CELEBRANT takes envelope.)

CELEBRANT: There are two magical tools that can be revealed to you now. The first is the power of Incantation. Language defines thought, thereby giving substance to the Ancient Ones. Abracadabra. Alakazam. Sim Sala Bim. Para Vigo Me Voy. Mahab one. Shemhamforash.

(CELEBRANT can punctuate these words by throwing a bit of flash powder or dragon's breath powder on the brazier, if he has a dramatic flair.) There is a word you need to know for the next step of your Journey.

(CELEBRANT whispers word in Initiate's ear, while also passing to the Initiate the black envelope with the word enclosed.)

CELEBRANT: discover wisdom. Meditate upon this word and

(Gong is struck.)

(ACOLYTE offers the Celebrant the Baphomet medallion, resting on the presentation pillow.)

(CELEBRANT takes the Baphomet and places the medallion around the Initiate's neck.)

CELEBRANT: This is our second tool-the legacy of the Baphomet. The Baphomet is your next Gateway. Concentrate on this as your next step. This is our Portal, the corridor through which the Demons enter our world. Conjure them with your every action, your every word, and make yourself one with Darkness. When you are asked, in the future, "Have you passed through the portal?" your reply will be, "I passed through the 35 angles and spoke with our Infernal Master."

CONGREGATION: Have you passed through the portal?

INITIATE: I passed through the 35 angles and spoke with our Infernal Master.

(Gong is struck.)

CELEBRANT: You have survived many challenges to arrive here, before the altar of Satan. Welcome to your new Sinister Brotherhood. May the path before you provide ever more indulgence and enlightenment. Let us raise our left hands together in Infernal pride.

(ALL turn toward the altar and raise their left hands in the Sign of the Horns.)

CELEBRANT: Rege Satanas!

CONGREGATION: Rege Satanas!

(Gong is struck.)

CELEBRANT: Hail Satan!

CONGREGATION: Hail Satan!

(CELEBRANT rings bell as final pollutionary.)

CELEBRANT: So it is done. (Final gong is struck.)

Ceremony of Ordination STS Version

The rite of Ordainment is something held sacred by most religious orders. For most Satanists they never hear these words spoken outside the secret chambers held by high ranking Church of Satan officials. Originally written by Michael Aquino in 1972, this rite has been in use by the Church since. And it was carried over and expanded by Aquino for the Temple of Set in 1975. Since then, a number of Satanic institutions have adopted some variation of this particular ritual, thus making it the official ritual of Ordainment in Satanism.

It is held as a sort of final initiation to the priesthood of Mendes. The rite can only be performed properly by a recognized member of the Grotto or Coven, preferably the high Priest/ess.

It is a private rite and only a small handful of people are traditionally allowed to attend. The primary attendees are of course the high Priest and the initiate being ordained. Others may be acolytes and a witness.

The following is the Ritual to ordain members of the Priesthood of Hell in the Satanic Thulian Society. And has been specially added upon to make this version unique to us. It was our first official ritual as an organization, held and filmed on Oct 29th 2020.

The rite begins as any other ritual with the standard opening and libations. After which the celebrant or High Priest turns to the initiate and says the following.

HIGH PRIEST: The Sentinels of the Abyss are summoned to enfold these chambers in a suspension of time and dimension, for the Great Flame of the Prince of Darkness is to be drawn to our midst. As the AEthyrs of the Universe are convoked as witness, I charge you who are within this Temple to suffer no word of these proceedings to be passed to the profane.

The eyes of the examiners are cast upon those who would defy these words, unto the beginning and end of all dimensions.

Hear now the legacy of the Priesthood of Hell!

In the Diabolicon of the Age of Satan is recounted the primeval sundering of the Cosmos from mindless unity into chaotic duality, hence a crucible in which the essence of Satan attained the distinction of Self. And Earth, speck of dust within the swirling furnace and endless night of the Universe – it was to Earth that Satan came in dim AEons past.

"To the ancestors of your ancestors, O you who are more than human, he spoke the Word that brought them into being, saying:

"I am within and beyond you, the Highest of Life, in majesty greater than the forces of the Universe; whose eyes are the Face of the Sun and the Dark Fire of Satan; who fashioned your intelligence as his own and reached forth to exalt you; who entrusted to you, dignity of consciousness; who opened your eyes that you might know beauty; who brought you the key to knowledge of all lesser things; and who enshrined in you the Will to come into being. Lift your voices, then, and recognize the Highest of Life who thus proclaims your triumph; whose being is beyond natural life and death; who came as flame to your world and enlightened your desire for perfection and truth. Arise thus in your glory, behold the genius of your creation, and be prideful of being, for I am the same - I who am the Highest of Life."

Since that day of the coming of the Fire, the story of the race of man has been as that of the Universe - torn and tortured by war, famine, pestilence, and death. Yet in the midst of death, we are in life - by the Gift of Satan there is that within us which is immune to the savagery of mortal flesh, which preserves the self-inviolate, which presages for us an eternity of unique existence unfettered either by stasis or chaos."

The Word of Satan became a Link between the ancestors of your ancestors and Satan, and that Word took form as Xepera, the Self-Created One, who gave unto the care of the first Priesthood of Hell the great Keys to the Shining Trapezoid that is the Gate to the Abyss, saying:
    "Herein lies the geometric inspiration for the existence of Satan, whose names shall be many in the AEons and Ages to come. Observe that it doth shape and define that which is the Pentagram of Satan, which is itself our seal and the Key to all beauty of proportion.
    Even as the triangle and tetrahedron shall be as drugs to lure men-beasts to blind labor towards the worship of an apex of self-extinction, so we of the Pentagram and the Trapezoid author ever-unfolding memorials to the creative genius of man. Think not that because the first sights before your opened eyes are these sacred Keys, that they shall be reverenced. Indeed with

the passage of time they shall be changed and effaced by those who have forgotten their power, and their origin shall fade into the mists of time.

But this Temple shall endure until the race of man shall cease, and those who enter its fold shall behold the heart of the fire, and they shall gaze upon the face of Satan. Yea, nevermore shall they know the simple peace of their animal brothers, but their eyes shall be opened, and they shall become as Daemons, and the forces of all creation shall bend before their will. So it shall be done."

So spoke Xepera, the Word Become Form, who also would fade before the eyes of the ancestors of our ancestors, until only dim memories of Imhotep, Prometheus, Enoch, and Belial would remain as the eldest legends of humankind. By his word we of the Priesthood of Hell have rejected the blissful annihilation of unity, the crippling torture of the cross of duality, and the worship of the triad of chaos in all their semblances.

Embraced and immortalized by the very Fire of Life, we seek those who yet grope towards the Light, knowing not what it is they desire, but only that they must attain it.

Perils there are, and they are many. Yet, in all their glamour and comfort, as one they lead their victim at last to the same numbing death that would have awaited him had he never sought to escape it. Accursed is he who places his foot upon the Path to the Right in its many guises, for he merely labors towards that which would come to him in its own deadly time, would he but await its cold embrace.

And now, within these Pylons of Light and Life Eternal, let those who have taken the Name of Satan as of their own being taste again of the Grail of the Black Flame.

As its Holy Fire courses through your veins, affirm again your bond with the Prince of Darkness and his sacred Temple.

"Can the wings of the winds understand your voices of wonder, O enlightened ones who shine like fire in the jaws of chaos, whom I have prepared as cups for a wedding, or as the flowers in their beauty for the chamber of righteousness? Stronger are your feet than the barren stone, and mightier are your voices than the manifold winds, for you are become a Temple such as is not, but in the mind of Satan. Arise, says the First of your kind; move, therefore, unto the Elect; show them the fire within you, and awaken them that they may gain the strength to live forever."

Towards this Working the Will of Satan has manifest itself, joining in consecration with one who is now to be ordained to his eternal Priesthood.

Called to this sacred office is [Name], who has before this altar cast aside all the comforts, illusions, and images of Earth that [his/her] Soul and Self may be transfixed by the very Fire of Fires. The Black Flame of Satan himself!

Advance to the altar, thou who would claim this doom, that the eye of our lord Satan may, for a time, seize, alone within the Universe, upon you. As your mind is revealed to his, do you of your free will embrace his eternal Priesthood?

INITIATES RESPONSE: (Yes or No)

HIGH PRIEST (INITIATE REPEATS): Take you then this vow. Repeat after me.

I, (name), forge here my bond eternally with the realms of insatiable fires. That place in which dwells the all-consuming and unquenchable Black Flame. The Kingdom asunder, realm of the damned! Whose ruler is Lucifer, who is crowned Satan!

By all the Demons and Dark Gods of the pit! And by the watchful gaze of the 9 Kings of Hell. The 4 crowned Princes. And the 4 Queens of the Pit.

Strip me now of the stain of the Nazarene. I reject his words here and now and forever unto my final moments, and beyond into the brackish void of Death.
I, take now unto myself, Hell's divining confluence, and bathe myself in Demonic brilliance.

I stand before the thrones of Hell and beg; Adorn me Lord Satan, my Infernal Shepherd, with your Black Flame. And place here and now, and forever unto the end of time, the Mark of the Beast.

Place me in your feign, stand with your Devils boundless in Hell.

Hear now these words. By this rite, I pledge myself, flesh and soul, to the undying flames of Hell! Scorch clean the slate of my soul!
Shemhamforash!
Ave Satanas!
Rege Satanis!
Hail Satan!

HIGH PRIEST CONTINUES: Bring then your left hand to the Flame upon the altar, and for a fleeting moment receive its kiss upon your soul.

(Initiate passes their left hand through the flame of a lone black candle.)

"Conceive of the Cosmos as a circle of twelve divisions alternating between life and death, binding all creatures save those whom I have touched. You are given powers greater than those ordering these divisions and extending throughout the ages of time, that with your vision and your voice you might exercise the Powers of Darkness, sending ever forth the Black Flame across the Earth and the expanses of time. Thus, you are a Guardian of perfection and truth. Arise, then, and witness the wondrous creations born of your wisdom, even as I am near to you and the essence of my being is enshrined within you."

In the name of Satan, I, (Priests name), one that Satan hath chosen upon Earth to represent his will, name you to our fellowship and cast you forth - beyond the Abyss - to walk in ways of strangeness and of beauty. You are become as Xepera, the Self-Created One, and you are a glory to your race and a brilliance before the Eye of Satan.

Hail (Initiates Name)

Hail Satan x3

So it is done!

The Black Mass for the Solitary Practitioner

This is The Black Mass performed by me in two of my internet videos. It is a solitary Rite that requires only the end practitioner themselves, and forgoes with the use of a Nude altar, or assistants.

This particular Black Mass is perfect for the Solitary Practitioner, who either deliberately works alone, or is forced to by circumstance. This is a very flexible ritual that makes plenty of room for imperfections.

Here are the supplies that you will need in order to get started.

1. An Altar. This can be a small coffee table or one that it made. The size and dimensions are up to you.

2. An altar cloth. This cloth should be black, and can be made from any fabric you wish.

3. A bell or gong

4. Candles for illumination, these candles should be black.

5. One red and one white candle, the white candle is used for casting spells of destruction, and the red candle is

used for spells of blessing and/or lust.

6. An incense burner and a good supply of incense.

7. A chalice, of any type, and wine

8. A pitcher holding water, which symbolizes the waters of life.

9. A Bowl and an aspergillum or vial of blessed water.

10. A Paten, holding the communion wafer, black bread, or turnip.

11. A black cloth which covers the Patent. The Practitioner sets up his or her Altar, and makes sure that all materials are present for the ritual about to begin. All candles and incense are lit, and wine is poured into the chalice. The lights are turned out and the Practitioner makes sure that there will be no disturbances during the ritual. This may include making sure no one comes over, or the phone is unplugged, and cell phones are turned off.

The Ritual Proper

It is very important that each Practitioner take a few moments in quiet contemplation. Approach the Altar and make the sign of the inverted Cross, while saying:

In nomine Magni Dei Nostri Satanus introibo ad altare Domini Inferi.

Now trace an inverted pentagram before you, while saying:

May the Blessings of Darkness be with me this night/day.

Stand with your arms out in front of you, palms down toward the Altar, with bowed head, and say:

"In the Name of the Great God Satan, I will go to the altar of the Infernal Lord. Who reigns on Earth. I stand before the mighty and ineffable Prince of Darkness, his Daemons and Legions. Who dwell in the fires of Perdition, and who fought the first battle of heaven for our sake and the sake of freedom. I acknowledge and confess my past error, Renouncing all past allegiances to he who is the false trinity, and his Angelic host, I proclaim that Satan, who thou art named Lucifer rules the Earth. Therefore I, ratify, and renew my promise to recognize and honor Thee in all things, without reservation. In return, I beseech Thy manifold assistance in the successful completion of my endeavors and the fulfillment of my desires. Keep me, Lord Satan, from the hands of the wicked, unjust. Lord Satan, Thou shalt rise again and quicken me. Henceforth I shall rejoice in Thee. Show me Thy power, and grant unto me Thy bounty. Hear me, and let my cry come unto Thee."

Make the sign of the inverse cross.

"Glory to Satan the Infernal Lord. Sustainer of life on earth and strength to man. I praise Thee. I bless Thee. I adore Thee. I glorify Thee. I give thanks to Thee for Thy great power, Lord Satan, my Infernal King and Almighty Emperor."

Make the sign of the inverse cross.

Offertory

The chalice & paten, upon which rests the wafer, are uncovered. Take the paten in both hands & raise it breast-high in an attitude of offering, then speak the following words:

"Lord Satan, receive this host which I, Thy worthy servant, offer to Thee, my True and Living God, that it may avail for my rejoicing in this life. So be it."

Replace the paten and the wafer. Raise the chalice in like manner, saying:

"Lord Satan, I offer to Thee the chalice of Desire, that it may arise in the sight of Thy majesty for my use & gratification & be pleasing unto Thee. So be it."

Replace the chalice upon the altar. Extend your hands, palms downwards, and say:

"Come O mighty Lord of Darkness, look favorably on this sacrifice that I have prepared in thy name."

Take the incense burner and sprinkle incense onto the burning coals, while saying:

"May this incense rise before Thee, Infernal Lord. May Thy blessing descend upon me."

Take the incense burner & cense the altar & gifts. First cense the chalice & wafer with three swings counter-clockwise and bow. Then raise the censer three times towards the Image of Satan, bow again. Lastly cense the top & sides of the altar three times, by circumambulation if the appointments of the temple be convenient. Replace the Incense burner upon the Altar, and say:

"I lift up my heart to thee, Satan my Infernal Lord and give thanks, at all times & in all places I give Thee thanks: Lord, Infernal King, Emperor of the World, Jubilantly all the infernals praise Thee, & with them I join my own voice, saying: Salve, Salve, Salve."

Strike the gong or ring the bell three times.

"Lord Satan, God of Power, Earth & Infernus are full of Thy glory. Hosanna in the depths."

Make the sign of the Inverted Cross.

"Therefore Lord Satan, I entreat that you receive and accept this Sacrifice, which I offer. You have set your mark upon me, that you may make me proper in fullness and length of life, under thy protection, may cause the inhabitants of The Fires of Perdition to go forth and give me their blessings and strength in the fulfillment of my desires, and the destruction of my enemies. In concert this night I ask Thy unfailing assistance in this particular need.

At this point in the ritual, the specific purpose is mentioned for holding the Mass, or Magical acts are performed.

"In the unity of unholy fellowship I praise and honor first Thee, Lucifer, Morning Star, Teacher of Philosophies.

Beelzebub, Bringer of Peace, and Lord of Regeneration.

Baal, Ruler of the Physical, Shield of the Faithful.

Abaddon, Knower of theories, and bringer of arcane knowledge.

Asmodeus, Seer of integration, Lord of Creativity.

I call upon the nameless and formless ones, the mighty innumerable hosts of Hell, by whose assistance I may be strengthened in mind, Body, and Will. I therefore beseech Thee, Lord Satan, to accept this offering of my bounden duty as also of Thine whole household; order my days in joy & count me within the fold of Thine elect. Shemhamforash!"

Take the pitcher from the altar, and pour the water into the bowl while saying:

"After the one who called himself God put his mark upon the flesh of Cain, Cain wandered through the desert of Nod. As Cain approached death from the desert heat, he said, "It is better I die then to live a life void of dreams and hope and knowing, far better, for the bitter God of my father to have spared His wretched mercy." And with these words, the ground parted. And water sprang thereof. And Cain partook of its sweetness. And the mystical water filled and expanded his shriveled flesh."

Now dip the aspergillum into the bowl, turn to each compass point, shaking the aspergillum thrice at each point saying:

(Facing South) "In the name of Satan, I bless thee with the waters of life"
(Facing East) "In the name of Satan, I bless thee with the waters of life."
(Facing North) "In the name of Satan, I bless thee with the waters of life."

(Facing West) "In the name of Satan, I bless thee with the waters of Life."

Replace bowl, pitcher, and aspergillum upon alter.
The Consecration

Take the wafer into your hand, bending low over it, whisper the following words into it.

"Here is the body of Jesus Christ."

Raise the wafer before the image of Satan. Replace the wafer on the paten, which rests on the Altar. Take the Chalice into your hands and bend low over it; as with the wafer, whisper the following words into it.

"Here is the Chalice of Desire."

Raise the Chalice above your head before the image of Satan. The Chalice is then replaced. The gong is struck or the bell is rung, and the following is recited.

"To me, thy faithful child, O Infernal Lord, who glory in my iniquity and trust in your boundless power and might, grant that I may be numbered among Thy chosen. It is ever through you that all gifts come to me; knowledge, power, freedom, and wealth are yours to bestow. Renouncing the false spiritual rewards that are offered by He Who Is Three, the one who calls himself God, I place my trust in Thee, the Lord of this world, and teacher of Philosophies, looking to the satisfaction of all of my desires, and the petitioning all fulfillment in the land of the living. Shemhamforash!"

"Prompted by the precepts of the earth and the inclinations of desire, I am bold to say; Our Father who art in Hell, Unhallowed is Thy name. Thy Kingdom has come, Thy will is done; on earth as it is in Hell! I take this day/night my rightful due, and trespass not on paths of pain. Lead me unto temptation, and deliver me from false piety, for Thine is the Kingdom and the Power and the Glory forever! Let reason and freedom rule the earth! Deliver me, O Mighty Satan, from all past error and delusion, that, having set my feet upon the path of Darkness and having vowed myself to Thy Service, I may not weaken in my resolve, but with Thy assistance, grow in wisdom and strength."

The Repudiation and the Denunciation

Take the wafer into your hands, extend it before you, and say the following:

"Behold the body of Jesus Christ, Lord of the humble & King of the slaves."

Now hold the wafer up before the image of Satan, while saying:

"I invoke thee into this wafer. You who came to earth to enslave the race of man. You were sent by He Who Is Three, to strengthen the chains of bondage. You were sent to increase faith which feeds the one who calls himself God, and the host of the heavens. I invoke you in order to break the chains of bondage and kindle the fires of freedom. I will push the crown of thorns deep into your head, and drive the nails deeper into your hands, which hold you upon the cross, I shall once again pierce your side and show all that you are nothing, but the true father of lies, and your words and deeds are false. You would have men and women live their lives in poverty, just so they can give more faith. Yes, you have gained many followers and sheep for your fold, but now the tide is turning and your flock is learning the truth. In the name of Satan, his Daemons, and Legions. I condemn thee to the abyss, and free the souls of all you have taken."

Raise the wafer, dash it to the ground, and crush it under foot. Strike the gong or ring the bell nine times.

Then take up the Chalice into your hands, and before drinking say:

"Behold the Chalice of Desire which gives joy and meaning to life. I Accept the Chalice of Desire in the name of our Infernal Lord."

Drink from the Chalice, and when the Chalice is empty, make the sign of the Inverted Cross, and replace the Chalice upon the Alter. Place the paten on top of the Chalice, and cover it with the veil. Say the following:

"I have received the Blessings of our Lord Satan, may his protection and grace be with me in all of my endeavors. My rite is at an end, and I shall go forth into the world spreading the word of our Infernal Lord to all who care to listen. I shall stand tall and bring comfort to the faithful when needed. For the end time are nearly upon us. I will stand with the faithful and fight. Our freedom is at hand."
Make the sign of the Inverted Cross, and trace the Inverted Pentagram before you and say:

"Hail Satan!"

Make sure that you extinguish all candles. Some practitioners will have a small snack to help them ground after the ritual.

The Enochian Keys

It was some time ago, after first reading the Satanic Bible that I grew interested in the Enochian Keys, sometimes referred to as "Calls". I had tried to use the ones presented by LaVey, and like most found trying to utter the alien sounding language to be almost beyond my ability to achieve easily.

It was after some time I grew curious as to what was actually being said in this language that some claimed was Angelic and others Demonic. The truth of the matter is that it is both as I would eventually come to realize. But that is a topic for another time.

Over the years I have found many various iterations of these interesting and powerful incantations. And so, I set about with many variations of the text, to create one that was uniquely my own. Well as I understood them that is.

It was through this process that I came to realize that a particular rumor was true. Anton LaVey had never corrected the Enochian text when he wrote down his versions of the translations. Literally, the English had been nicely Satanized, but the Enochian was still in its original format praising the Christian God. Well, when one compared it to the original Author John Dee's notes that is.

What was more is finding an adequate pronunciation guide was neigh impossible to do. Certainly, LaVey had indeed given a basic explanation of how to intone the Enochian verbiage, but had provided no complete outlines to do so.

This was something I had found irritating to no end. Thus, I set about the long process of not just deciphering my own variations of the Keys, but putting down clear intonations of them as well.

It was also during this time I came across Dr. Aquino's Word of Set.

This was to me pure gold. A powerful alternate rendition, of the Enochian Keys that not just changed a few words here or there, but altered the complete verbiage being used into a powerful alternate tool for the Satanist to use. However, I was not a Setian at the time. And while I respected the current of Set, I didn't have as much of a draw towards it, as I would later. I also felt reading it that Aqiono had really intended this to be something different than the end product, and suspected it would have been intended for LaVey in what would have been a reedit of the Satanic Bible had the infamous 75 schism never occurred.

And so, I "Set" about making my own little tongue in cheek variation of the Word of Set for Satanists. As I felt it should have, or would have been, had not events had not altered the course of things.

The ultimate truth of the Enochian language is that it is the language not of Heaven or Hell, Demonic or Angelic. It is the language of the Magicians. Of man himself. It is this nature that enables or encourages I should say, ethereal beings like Demons and Angels to use this language universally amongst themselves. And ultimately, with us too.

If we stop and look at things from this perspective, we soon come to understand that this was not a language taught to us by spiritual beings, but that we taught to those same beings.

With this new understanding of the Keys, I now leave them with you.

The First Key

The first key establishes Satan's dominion over the earth, and those who would serve him.

The First Key in English

I reign over you, saith Satan in power exalted above the firmaments, and over the earth; in whose hands the sun is as a glittering sword and the moon as a thorough-thrusting flame. Who measured your metal in the midst of my vestures and trussed you together as the palms of my hands and brightened your mind with infernal light.
 I made a law to govern my sons and daughters. I delivered truth, and furnished to you the power of understanding. Moreover, ye who hath lifted up your voices and swore obedience and faith to Satan, who liveth and is triumphant, whose beginning is not, nor end cannot be. Who shineth as a flame in the midst of your palace and reigns amongst you as the balance of righteousness and truth.

 Move therefore and appear! Open the mysteries of your creation! Be friendly unto me! For I am the servant of the same! The true worshipper of Satan, in glory and power exalted, of the kingdom of the infernal.

The First Key in Enochian

Ol sonuf vorsag goho Helel lonsh Calz od vors caosgo; sobra zol Ror I ta nazps od graa Ta malprg: Ds hol-q qaa nothoa zimz Od Commah ta nobloh zien od luciftian Oboleh a donasdogamatastos. O ohorela taba Ol nore od pasbs ol zonrensg Vaoan od tooat nonucafe gmicalzoma. Pilah Farzm znrza od surzas Adna od Gono de Helel, ds hom od Toh. Soba croodzi ipam ul vls Ipamis. Ds loholo vep nothoa poamal Od bogpa aai ta piap piamol Od vaoan. Zacare ca od zamran! Odo cicle qaa! Zorge! Zir noco! Hoath Helel bvfd lonsh londoh babage

The First Key Enochian Intonement

OHL • ZOH-nuhf • voh-ruh-SAH-jzhuh GO-ho • HEL-EL • LOH-nuh-suh • KAH-luhtz OHD • VOH-ruhss • kah-OHS-suh-goh; ZOH-buh-rah • ZOHL • ROH-ruh EE • TAH • NAHTS-puh-suh OHD • guh-RAH-ah • TAH MAH-luh-puh-ruh-jzhuh: • DAHSS • HOH-luh-kah KAH-AH • noh-tuh-HOH-ah • ZEE-muhts • OHD KOH-muh-mah • TAH • NOH-buh-loh zee-AYN • OHD • LOO-SEEF-tee-uhn OH-boh-lay • AH DOH-nahss-doh-gah-MAH-tahss-tohss OH • oh-hoh-RAY-lah • TAH-bah • OHL NOH-ray • OHD • PAH-suh-buhs • OHL zoh-nuh-RAY-nuh-suhjzh vah-OH-ahn • OHD toh-OH-aht • NOH-noo-KAH-fay guh-MEE-kah-luh-ZOH-mah • PEE-lah FAH-ruh-zuhm • zuh-nuh-ruh-JZHAH • OHD ZOO-ruh-jzhahs • AH-duh-nah • OHD GOH-noh • DAY • HEL-EL • DAHS • HOHM OHD • TOH • ZOH-bah • kuh-ROH-ohd-zee EE-pahm • OOL • VUH-LUHS • ee-PAH-meess DAHSS • loh-HOH-loh • Vayp noh-tuh-HOH-ah • poh-AH-mahl • OHD BOH-guh-pah • ah-AH-ee • TAH • PEE-ahp pee-AH-mohl OHD • vah-OH-ahn • zah-KAH-ray • KAH OHD • ZAH-muh-rahn! • OH-doh KEE-kuh-lay • KAH-ah! • ZOH-ruh-jzhay! ZEE-ruh • NOH-koh! • hoh-AH-tuh-huh HEL-EL • BUH-vuh-fuhd • LOH-nuh-suh LOH-nuh-doh • bah-BAH-jzhay

The Second Key

The second key is often used in conjurations of lust. However, it is also served to empower certain objects as Talismans of power.

The Second Key in English

Can the wings of the winds understand your voices of wonder oh you, sons and daughters of Satan? Of whom hell-fire has framed within the depths of my jaws; whom I have prepared as a gathering for a wedding, or as the flowers in their beauty for the chambers of carnal desire. Stronger are your feet than the barren stone, and mightier are your voices than the manifold winds; for you are become a building such as is not, save in the mind of Satan, the All-Powerful.

Arise! Move and appear therefore unto his servants; appear in power, and make me a strong seer of things; for I am of Satan who liveth forever!

The Second Key in Enochian

Adgt vpaah zong om faaip sald, Nonci nore od pasbs de Helel? Sobam Donasdogamatastos Izazaz piadph; casarma abramg ta aldi Paracleda q ta lorslq turbs ooge Qvasahi. Givi chis lusd orri, od micalp chis bia ozongon; Lap noan trof cors ta ge, O q manin de Helel tol-lonsh Torzu! zacare! ca c noqod; Zamran micalzo od ozazm vrelp lap Zir de Helel apila gohed!

The Second Key Enochian Intonement

AH-duh-jzhuht • vuh-PAH-ah ZOHNJZH • OHM • fa-AH-eep ZAH-luhd, • NOH-nuh-see NOH-ray • OHD • PAHSS-uh-buhs DAY • HEL-EL? ZOH-bahm DOH-nahss-doh-gah-MAH-tahss-tohss ee-ZAH-zahts • pee-AH-duh-puh; kuh-SAH-ruh-mah • ah-buh-RAH-muhjzh TAH • AH-luh-dee pah-rah-kuh-LAY-duh KUH TAH • LOH-ruh-suh-luh-kuh DUR-buhs • oh-OH-jzhay kuh-VAH-sah-hee. • JZHEE-vee cuh-HEES • LUH-zuhd • OH-ruh-ree, OHD mee-KAH-luhp • cuh-HEES BEE-ah • oh-ZOH-nuh-jzhohn; LAHP • NOH-ahn • tuh-ROH-fuh KOH-ruhz • TAH • JZHAY, OH • KUH • MAH-neen DAY • HEL-EL • TOHL-LOH-nuh-suh. TOH-ruht-soo! • zah-KAH-ray! • KAH KUH • NOH-kohd; • ZAH-muh-rahn mee-KAH-luh-zoh, • OHD • oh-ZAH-zuhm vuh-RAY-luhp • LAHP • ZEE-ruh DAY • HEL-EL ah-PEE-lah • GOH-hud!

The Third Key

The third Key establishes the law of the Magicians will upon the earth. It is a confirmation of power held by the magician over all creations.

The Third Key in English

Behold! Saith Satan, I am a circle upon whose hands stand twelve kingdoms. Nine are the seats of living breath. The rest are as sharp sickles or the horns of death wherein the Creatures of Earth are and are not except by mine own hands, which also sleep and shall rise!

In the beginning, I made you stewards, and placed you in the twelve seats of government, giving unto every one of you power successively. Over the nine true ages of time, to the intent that, from the highest vessels and the corners of your governments, that you might work my power: Pouring down the fires of life and increase continually upon the Earth. Thus ye are become the skirts of justice and truth. In Satan's name, rise up! Appear! Behold! His mercies flourish! His name is become mighty among us! In whom we say move! Ascend! Apply yourselves unto us! As unto the partakers of his mysteries in your creation!

The Third Key in Enochian

Micama goho Helel, zir comselh A zien biah os londoh. Em chis othil gigipah vnd-l Chis ta pvim q mospleh teloch Qvi-in toltorg caosga chisi od chis Ge m ozien, ds t brgdo Od torzul! acroodzi eol balzarg, od Aala os thiln netaab, dlvga vomsarg Lonsa capmiali vors em homil cocasb, Fafen izizop od miinoag de gnetaab, Vavn lonsh: panpir malpirgi pild caosg Noan vnalah balt od vooan. A Helel's dooain, torzu! Zamran! Micma! Iehvsoz cacacom! Dooain noar micaolz aai om! Casarmg gohia: zacar! Torzu! Imvamar pvgo! Pvgo plapli cicles qaan!

The Third Key Enochian Intonement

MEE-kuh-mah! • GOH-ho • HEL-EL, ZEE-ruh • koh-muh-SAY-luh • AH zee-AYN • BEE-ah • OHSS • LOH-nuh-doh. AIM kuh-HEES • oh-tuh-HEEL JZHEE-JZHEE-pah • vuh-nuh-duh—LUH kuh-HEES • TAH • puh-VEEM • KUH MOH-suh-puh-lay • tay-LOH-kuh kuh-VEE-EEN • toh-luh-TOH-ruhjzh kah-OHS-suh-gah • kuh-HEESSEE OHD • kuh-HEESS • GAY • EM • OH-zee-ayn, DAHSS • TAH buh-ruh-guh-DOH • OHD • TOH-ruht-sool! ah-kuh-ROH-ohd-zee • ay-OHLL bah-luh-ZAH-ruhjzh, • OHD • ah-AH-lah OHSS • tuh-HEE-luhn • NAY-tah-ahb, duh-luh-vuh-JZHAH • voh-muh-SAH-ruhjzh LOH-nuh-sah • kah-puh-mee-AH-lee • VOH-ruhss • AIM • HOH-meel KOH-kuh-suhb, • FAH-fayn, • ee-ZEE-zohp • OHD • mee-ee- NOH-ahjzh DAY • guh-NAY-tah-ahb, • VAH-vuhn • LOH-nuh-suh: pah-nuh-PEE-ruh mah-luh-pee-REE-jzhee • PEE-lahd kah-OHSSK. • NOH-ahn • vuh-NAH-lah BAH-luh-tuh • OHD • voh-OH-ahn. • AH HEL-EL'S • doh-OH-ay-een, • TOH-ruht-soo! ZAH-mah-rahn! • MEE-kuh-mah! ee-AY-huh-vuh-zohz • Kah-KAH-kohm! doh-OH-ay-een • NO-ahr • mee-kah-OH-luhts ah-AH-ee • OHM! • kuh-SAH-ruh-muhjzh goh-HEE-yah: • ZAH-kahr! • TOH-ruht-soo! ee-muh-VAH-mahr • puh-vuh-GOH! puh-vuh-GOH • puh-LAH-puh-lee KEE-kuh-lays • KAH-AHN!

Fourth Key

The fourth key speaks of a new Satanic age. It hints at a coming of a new chosen representative of Satan, who will lead his people into the future.

The Fourth Key in English

I have set my feet in the South and have looked about me saying: Are not the thunders of increase numbered 666, which reign in the second angle? There, I have placed one whom none hath yet tobe numbered. In whom the second dawning of things are and wax strong, which also successively, adding the numbers of time and their powers stand as in the beginning nine!

Arise! Ye Children of pleasure! And take the earth! For I am Satan who is and liveth forever! In my name, move and appear as pleasant deliverers. That you may praise him amongst the sons of men!

The Fourth Key in Enochian

Othil lusdi babage od dorpha gohol: G-chis ge avavago cormp mian, Cormp mian, oali sobam ag Cormpo crp vi-iv: casarmg viv croodzi Chis od vgeg, ds t capimali Coazior gapimaon od lonshin biah Ta croodzi em! Torzu! Nore de qvasahi od ef caosga! Lap zir Helel ds i od Apila gohed! I Helel's dooaip, Zacare! Zamran obelisong Nonci rest tox aaf nore molap!

The Fourth Key Enochian Intonement

oh-tuh-HEEL • LUH-zuh-dee bah-BAH-jzhay • OHD DOH-ruh-puh-hah • goh-HOH-luh: guh-kuh-HEESS • GAY ah-vah-VAH-goh KOH-ruh-muhp • MEE-ahn, DAHSS • ZOH-nuhf VEE-vuh-deev? • oh-AH-lee ZOH-bahm • AHGH KOH-ruh-muh-poh • kuh-RUHP VEE-EEV: • kuh-SAH-ruh-muhjzh VEEV • kuh-ROH-ohd-zee kuh-HEES OHD • vuh-GAYJZH, DAHSS • TAH • kah-pee-MAH-lee, koh-AH-zee-ohr • gah-pee-MAH-ohn OHD • oh-nuh-suh-HEEN BEE-ah TAH • kuh-ROH-ohd-zee AIM! • TOH-ruht-soo! • NOH-ray DAY • kuh-VAH-sah-hee! OHD • AYF • kah-OHS-suh-gah! LAHP • ZEE-ruh • HEL-EL DAHSS • EE • OHD ah-PEE-lah • GOH-hud! EE • HEL-EL'S • doh-OH-ay-eep, zah-KAH-ray! • ZAH-muh-rahn oh-bay-lee-ZOH-nuh-jzhuh, NOH-nuh-see • RAY-suht TOHKS • ah-AHF • NOH-ray MOH-lahp!

Fifth Key

The fifth key warns of a great calamity of deceivers coming to lead the infernal children astray, and from the ashes of its ruin a rebirth of Hell's dominion upon the Earth.

The Fifth Key in English

The mighty calamity has entered into the third angle, and are become as numerous false deliverers of Lord Satan's providence, bringing forth folly and ignorance, smiling with contempt upon the earth, and dwelling in the firmaments of Heaven.

Unto thee I fastened pillars of gladness, and gave thee vessels to water the earth with all her creatures; and they are the true sons and daughters of Satan. Of the first and the second and the beginning of their own seats which are garnished with continual burning lamps whose numbers are as the beginning, the ends and the contents of time.

Therefore! Come ye and appear to your creation! Visit us in peace and comfort conclude us receivers of your mysteries, for why? We are the worshipers of Satan the truest King of Hell!

The Fifth Key in Enochian

Sapah zimii sdiv od noas obelisong De Helel yarry, iolcam vgear od Gmicalzoma praf calz tablior; Casarm amipzi naz arth mian, Od dlvgar zizop zlida caosgi Toltorgi od z chis nor od Pasbs de Helel. Talo od taviv Od croodzi de thild ds chis Gnonp peoal cormfa chis croodzi vls Od q cocasb ca! Niis od zacar Qaas! Fetharsi od bliora ozazma ednas Cicles bagle? Ge boalvah Helel bvsd, Gohed!

The Fifth Key Enochian Intonement

ZAH-pah • zee-MEE-EE zuh-DEEV • OHD • NOH-AHSS oh-bay-lee-ZOH-nuh-jzhuh • DAY HEL-EL'S • YAH-ruh-ruh-ee, ee-OH-luh-kahm • vuh-GAY-ahr • OHD guh-MEE-kah-luh-ZOH-mah • puh-RAHFF KAH-luhts • TAH-buh-lee-ohr; kuh-SAH-ruhm • ah-MEE-puh-zee NAHTS • ah-RUH-tuh • MEE-ahn, OHD • duh-luh-vuh-JZHAHR ZEET-sohp • zuh-LEE-dah kah-OHS-su-jzhee • toh-luh-TOH-ruh-jzhee; OHD • ZEE • kuh-HEES • NOH-ray OHD • PAHSS-uh-bus • DAY • HEL-EL. TAH-loh • OHD • tah-VEEV • OHD kuh-ROH-ohd-zee • DAY • tu-HEE-luhd DAHSS • kuh-HEES • guh-NOH-nuhp pay-OH-ahl • KOH-ruh-muh-fah kuh-HEES • kuh-ROH-ohd-zee VUH-LUHS • OHD • KUH KOH-kah-suhb. KAH! • nee-EESS • OHD ZAH-kahr • KAH-AHSS! fay-tuh-HAH-ruh-see OHD • buh-lee-OH-rah • oh-ZAH-tsuh-mah AY-duh-nahss • KEE-kuh-lays • BAH-guh-lay? JZHAY • boh-AH-luh-vah • HEL-EL BUH-vuh-zuhd, • GOH-hud!

Sixth Key

Is a prophecy of a time when the children of Satan rise up and wage war upon those who have spread deceptions, and cleanse the earth to return it to a time of purity.

The Sixth Key in English

The spirits of the fourth angle are nine, mighty in the firmament of the gate of nine; whom the infernal hath planted as a torment to the deceivers, and a crown to the righteous sons and daughters of Satan. Giving them fiery darts to cleanse the earth, and nine continual workmen whose courses mend the damage and pave the way of continuance.

Hearken to my voice! I spake of you, and I move you in power and presence! You whose works shall be a song of honor and the praise of Satan in your creation!

The Sixth Key in Enochian

Gah de sdiv chis em, Micalzo pilzin de sobam; Casarm taviv harg ta mir iad, Od obloc nore od pasbs De Helel. dlvgar malprg ar caosga Od em canal sobol zar fbliard Caosga, od chis netaab od miam. Solpeth bien! Brita od zacam Gmicalzo sobha vavn trian lviahe Od ecrin de Helel qaaon!

The Sixth Key Enochian Intonement

GAH • DAY • suh-DEEV • kuh-HEES AYM, • mee-KAH-luh-zoh • pee-luht-SEEN DAY • ZOH-bahm; • kuh-SAH-ruhm • tah-VEEV HAH-ruhjzh • TAH MEE-ruh • ee-YAHD, OHD • OH-buh-lohk • NOH-ray • OHD PAHSS-uh-bus • DAY • HEL-EL, duh-luh-vuh-JZHAHR • MAH-luh-pah-rah-jzhah AH-ruh • kah-OHS-suh-gah • OHD • AYM kah-NAHL ZOH-bohl • ZAH-ruh • fuh-buh-LEE-ah-ruhd kah-OHS-suh-gah, OHD • kuh-HEES • NAY-tah-ahb • OHD MEE-ahm. zol-luh-PAY-tuh-huh • BEE-ayn! buh-REE-tah • OHD • ZAH-kahm guh-mee-KAH-luh-zoh • ZOH-buh-hah VAH-vuhn • tah-REE-ahn • luh-VEE-ah-hay • OHD AY-kuh-reen • DAY • HEL-EL • kah-AH-ohn!

Seventh Key

The Seventh Key is a call to carnal pleasures of the flesh and an invocation of pure lust.

The Seventh Key in English

The east is a house of harlots singing praises amongst the flames of first glory. Wherein Lord Satan hath opened his mouth, and they are become as living dwellings in whom the carnality of man rejoiceth, and they are appareled with ornaments of brightness, such as work wonders on all creatures. Whose kingdoms and continuance are as the four Queens, of the mighty tower of Lust, continual places of comfort and joy everlasting. Oh ye servants of pleasure! Move! Appear! Sing praises unto mankind, and be mighty amongst us. For to remembrance is given power, and our strength waxeth strong in the comfort of the flesh!

The Seventh Key in Enochian

Raas salman babalond oecrimi aao malprg Croodzi bvsd, qviin Helel Odo bvtmon Od z chis noas em paradial Casarmg Vgear olora chirlan; od z chis Zonac luciftian, cors ta vavl zirn tolhami; Soba londoh od miam chis ta q ziarahs, Micalz vmadea de Helel, pibliar; Moz gohed. C no qvol de qvasahi, Zacare! Zamran! Oecrimi de Helel! Omicaolz aai om; bagle papnor i dlvgam Lonshi, od vmplif vgegi blior de Helel!

The Seventh Key Enochian Intonement

RAH-ahs • EE • ZAH-luh-mahn BAH-bah-LOH-nuhd • oh-ay-kuh-REE-mee ah-AH-oh • MAH-luh-puh-ruh-jzhuh kuh-ROH-ohd-zee • BUH-vuh-zuhd kuh-VEE-een • HEL-EL • OH-doh buh-vuh-tuh-MOHN • OHD • ZEE kuh-HEES • NOH-AHS • AYM pah-RAH-dee-ahl • kuh-SAH-ruh-muhjzh vuh-GAY-ahr • oh-LOH-rah kuh-HEE-ruh-lahn; • OHD • ZEE kuh-HEES • ZOH-nahk Loo-SEEF-tee-uhn, • KOH-ruhz TAH • VAH-vuhl • ZEE-ruhn toh-luh-HAH-mee; • ZOH-bah LOH-nuh-doh • OHD • MEE-ahm kuh-HEES • TAH • KUH ZEE-ah-rahs • mee-KAH-luhts vuh-MAH-dee-ah • DAY • HEL-EL, pee-BLEE-ahr; • MAHTS • GOH-hud. KAH NOH • kuh-VOHL • DAY • kuh-VAH-sah-hee, zah-KAH-ray! ZAH-muh-rahn! oh-ay-kuh-REE-mee • DAY • HEL-EL! oh-mee-KAH-oh-luhts • ah-AH-ee • OHM; BAH-guh-lay • PAH-puh-nohr • EE duh-luh-vuh-JZHAHM • LOH-nuh-suh-hee, OHD • vuh-muh-puh-LEEF • vuh-GAY-jzhee buh-lee-OH-ruh • DAY • HEL-EL!

Eighth Key

The Eighth Key speaks of the coming of a Priest that will end the division of Satanism

The Eighth Key in English

The mid-day, is as in the Tuat of time, made of pillars of hyacinth, in whom the elders are become strong. I have prepared for my own justice! Speaketh Satan, who liveth and reign forever as a shield to the downtrodden. Rejoice! In the glory of the dragon that is triumphant and everlasting! How many are there which remain in the glory of the earth which are and shall not see death until the house doth fall and the dragon doth sink? Come away! For the thunders have roared! Come away! For the temples and robe of him that is to be, shall be crowned and are no longer divided. Come forth! Appear! Unto the terror of the Earth, and to our comfort and of such as are prepared!

The Eighth Key in Enochian

Bazm, o, i ta a at, Oln naz avabh, casarmg vran chis Vgeg ds abramg baltim goho Helel; Soba apila od bogpa gohed. Chirlan! A bvsd de vovim Ar i homtoh od gohed! Irgil chis ds paaox i bvsd De caosgo ds chis od ip Vran teloah cacrg iad gnai loncho Od fafen gnai carbaf? Niiso! Bagle avavago yor! Niiso! Bagle siaion Od mabsa de Helel trian momar Od chis ripir poilp. Niis! Zamran! Ciaofi caosgo, od bliors Od corsi ta chis abramig!

The Eighth Key Enochian Intonement

BAH-zuhm, • OH, • EE • TAH • AH DOO-waht, • OH-luhn • NAHZTS ah-VAH-buh, • kuh-SAH-ruh-muhjzh vuh-RAHN • kuh-HEES • vuh-GAYJZH DAHSS • ah-buh-RAH-muhjzh BAH-luh-teem • GO-ho • HEL-EL; ZOH-bah • ah-PEE-lah • OHD BOH-guh-pah • GOH-hud. kuh-HEE-ruh-lahn! • AH • BUH-vuh-zuhd DAY • VOH-veem • AH-ruh • EE HOH-muh-toh • OHD • GOH-hud! EE-ruh-jzheel • kuh-HEES • DAHSS pah-AH-ohx • EE • BUH-vuh-zuhd • DAY kah-OHS-suh-goh • DAHSS • kuh-HEES OHD • EEP • vuh-RAHN • tay-LOH-ah KAH-kuh-ruhjzh • ee-YAHD • guh-NAH-ee LOH-nuh-kuh-hoh • OHD • FAH-fayn guh-NAH-ee • KAH-ruh-bahf? nee-EESS-oh BAH-guh-lay • ah-vah-VAH-goh ee-YOH-ruh! nee-EESS-oh • BAH-guh-lay zee-AH-ee-ohn • OHD • MAH-buh-sah DAY • HEL-EL • tah-REE-ahn MOH-mahr • OHD • kuh-HEES • REE-pee-ruh poh-EE-luhp. nee-EESS! • ZAH-muh-rahn! KEE-ah-OH-fee • kah-OHS-suh-goh, • OHD Buh-lee-OH-rus • OHD • KOH-ruh-see • TAH kuh-HEES • ah-buh-RAH-meejzh!

Ninth Key

Is a cautionary warning against the poison of deceivers, and beckoning to return to undefiled wisdom.

The Ninth Key in English

Mighty guards of fire with two-edged swords flaming, which have vials of poison and who hath wings of wrath and wormwood and marrow of salt, have settled their feet in the south and are measured with their false ministries. These gather up the moss of the earth as the rich man doth his treasure. Cursed is he who sits on the holy throne as are his servants! Whose iniquities are in their eyes, millstones greater than the earth, and from their mouths rain seas of blood; their heads are covered with diamonds and upon their hands are marble sleeves. Happy is he on whom they frown not; For why? Satan rejoiceth in them. Come away! Leave your vials! For the time is such as requireth comfort!

The Ninth Key in Enochian

Micaolz bransg prgel Napta malpirgi, Ds brin efafafe vonpho od sobca vpaah Chis tatan od tranan balye, alar Lusda Babage od chis holq C noqvodi Mian. Vnal aldon mom caosgo Ta las ollor Gnai limlal. Amma chis idoigo Od chic noqodi! Sobca madrid chis Ooanoan, aviny drilpi caosgin, od Bvtmoni parm zvmvi cnila; daziz chis Ethamz a childao od mirc ozol chis Pidiai collal. Vlcinin a sobam vcim ip; Bagle? Helel chirlan par. Niiso! Bams ofafafe! Bagle a cocasb i Cors ca vnig blior!

The Ninth Key Enochian Intonement

mee-kah-OH-luhts • buh-RAH-nuh-suh-jzhay pah-ruh-JZHAYL • NAH-puh-tah mah-lah-pee-REE-jzhee, • DAHSS buh-REEN • AY-fah-FAH-fay VOH-nuh-puh-hoh • OHD ZOH-buh-kah • vuh-PAH-ah kuh-HEES • tah-TAHN • OHD tuh-RAH-nahn • BAH-luh-eeay, AH-lahr • luh-SUHD-ah • bah-BAH-jzhay OHD • kuh-HEES • HOH-luh-kah • KUH noh-kuh-VOH-dee • MEE-ahn. vuh-NAHL ah-luh-DOHN • MOHM • kah-OHS-suh-goh TAH • LAHSS • oh-luh-LOH-ruh guh-NAH-ee • LEEM-uh-LAH-luh. AH-muh-mah • kuh-HEES • ee-YAH-doh-EE-goh • OHD • kuh-HEES noh-KOH-dee! • ZOH-buh-kah mah-duh-REED • kuh-HEES oh-oh-AH-noh-ahn, • ah-VEE-neen-yuh duh-REE-luh-pee • OHD buh-vuh-tuh-MOHN-ee • PAH-ruhm kah-OHS-suh-jzheen, • zuh-vuh-muh-VEE kah-NEE-lah; • DAH-zeets • kuh-HEES ay-tah-HAH-muhts • AH kuh-HEE-luh-DAH-oh • OHD • MEE-ruhk OH-zohl • kuh-HEES pee-dee-AH-ee • koh-luh-LAHL. vuh-luh-KEE-neen • AH • ZOH-bahm vuh-KEEM EEP; • BAH-guh-lay? HEL-EL • kuh-HEE-ruh-lahn PAH-ruh. • nee-EESS-oh • BAH-muhs oh-FAH-fah-fay! • BAH-guh-lay • AH KOH-kuh-suhb • EE • KOH-ruhz • KAH vuh-NEE-jzhay • buh-lee-OH-ruh

Tenth Key

The Tenth Key is a curse used when the wrongs of others have gone beyond the normal. It is dangerous to employ wantonly, and is called a *Random Lightning Bolt*.

The Tenth Key in English

The thunders of judgment and wrath are numbered and are harbored In the South. In the likeness of an oak whose branches are nests ablaze with lamentation and weeping laid up for which burn night and day, and vomit out the heads of scorpions, and vial sulphur mingled with poison. These are the thunders that roar with a hundred mighty earthquakes and a thousand times as many surges, which rest not, nor know any echoing time. Here one rock bringeth forth a thousand even as the heart of man does his thoughts. Woe! Woe! Woe! Aye Woe be to all the earth for the pain of my vengeance. Great shall calamity be unto this iniquity until it is suffocated. Come away! But not your mighty sounds!

The Tenth Key in Enochian

Coraxo chis cormp od chis blans De babage. Aziazior paeb soba lilonon Chis virq eophan od raclir maasi Bagle iad od noqodi, ds ialpon Dosig od basgim, od oxex daziz siatris, Od salbrox cynxir faboan. Vnal chis Const ds yor eors vohim gizyax Od matb cocasg plosi molvi, Ds page ip, larag om droln Matorb cocasb. Emna l patralx Yolci matb Nomig monons Olora gnay angelard. Ohio! ohio! ohio! noib ohio! Bolp idoigo madriax! Bagle iad Madrid I, zirop od chiso drilpa. Niiso! Crip ip micalz apah

Tenth Key Enochian Intonement

koh-RAHK-soh • kuh-HEES • KOH-ruh-muhp OHD • kuh-HEES • buh-LAH-nuhs • DAY bah-BAH-jzhay. • ah-zee-AH-zee-ohr pah-AYB • ZOH-bah • LEE-loh-nohn kuh-HEES • VEE-ruhk • EE-oh-puh-hahn OHD • rah-kuh-LEE-ruh • mah-AH-see BAH-guh-lay • ee-YAHD • OHD noh-KOH-dee, • DAHSS • ee-AH-luh-pohn DOH-see-jzhuh • OHD • BAH-suh-jzheem, OHD • ohks-AYKS • DAH-zeets zee-AH-tuh-reess, • OHD • Zah-luh-buh-ROHKS SEE-nuhk-see-ruh • FAH-boh-ahn. vuh-NAHL • kuh-HEES • KOH-nuh-suht DAHSS • ee-YOH-ruh • AY-oh-ruhz voh-HEEM • JZHEE-zee-ahks • OHD MAH-tuhb • koh-KAH-sah-jzhay • puh-LOH-see MOH-luh-vee, • DAHSS • pah-JZHAY EEP, • lah-RAHJZH • OHM duh-ROH-luhn • MAH-toh-ruhb KOH-kuh-suhb. • AY-muh-nah • Luh pah-tuh-RAH-luhks • ee-OHL-kee MAH-tuhb • NOH-meejzh • moh-NOH-nuhs oh-LOH-rah • guh-NAH-ee-ay ah-nuh-GAY-lah-ruhd. • oh-HEE-oh! oh-HEE-oh! • oh-HEE-oh! • NOH-eeb oh-HEE-oh! • BOH-luhp • ee-YAH-doh-EE-goh mah-duh-REE-ahks! • BAH-guh-lay ee-YAHD • mah-duh-REED • EE, ZEE-rohp • OHD • kuh-HEES-oh duh-REE-luh-pah. • nee-EESS-oh! kuh-REEP • EEP • mee-KAH-luhts • AH-pah!

Eleventh Key

The Eleventh Key is a funerary call, used to herald the coming of the dead and to beckon the Satanist from mourning.

The Eleventh Key in English

The mighty seat groaned aloud and to the east were five thunders, and the eagle spake and cried with a loud voice: Come away from the house of death! And they gathered themselves together and became those of whom it is measured; The undying ones, who ride the whirlwinds. Come Away! For I have prepared a place for you. Move therefore and appear! Open the mysteries of your Creation! Be friendly unto me! For I am the servant of the same! The true worshipper of the flesh that liveth eternally.

The Eleventh Key in Enochian

Oxiayal holdo od zirom Q coraxo od vabzir camliax Od bahal: Niiso salman teloch! Od par aldon od noan Casarman holq; Gohed saga do zildar zong. Niiso! Bagle abramg pi noncp. Zacare ca od zamran! Odo cicle qaa! Zorge! Zir noco! Hoath Helel Bvfd lonsh londoh babage

Eleventh Key Enochian Intonement

ohk-see-AH-ee-ahl • HOH-luh-doh OHD • ZEE-rohm • KUH koh-RAHK-soh • OHD VAH-buh-zee-ruh • kah-muh-LEE-ahks OHD • bah-HAHL: • nee-EESS-oh ZAH-luh-mahn • tay-LOH-kuh! OHD • PAH-ruh • AH-luh-dohn OHD • NOH-ahn • kuh-SAH-ruh-mahn HOH-luh-kuh; • GOH-hud • ZAH-gah, DOH • ZEE-luh-dahr • ZOHNJZH. nee-EESS-oh! • BAH-guh-lay ah-buh-RAH-muhjzh • PEE NAH-nuh-kuh-puh. • zah-KAH-ray KAH • OHD • ZAH-muh-rahn! OH-doh • KEE-kuh-lay • KAH-ah! ZOR-ruh-jzhay! • ZEE-ruh • NOH-koh! hoh-AH-tuh-huh • HEL-EL BUH-vuh-fuhd • LOH-nuh-suh LOH-nuh-doh • bah-BAH-jzhay

Twelfth Key

The Twelfth Key is a call to the armies of Hell to bring misery, wrath, and sorrow upon the foes of Satan.

The Twelfth Key in English

O you that reign in the South and bear the lanterns of sorrow, bind up your girdles and visit unto us. Beckon forth your armies, that the Lord of the Infernal may be magnified; whose name amongst you is wrath! Move therefore and appear! Open the mysteries of your Creation! Be friendly unto me! For I am the servant of the same! The true worshipper of the King of Hell.

The Twelfth Key in Enochian

Nonci ds sonf madriax od chis d, hvbaio tibibp Allar atraah od train Ta lolcis abai Fafen de iad! Ar Helel ovof; soba dooain Aai i vonph! Zacare ca od zamran! Odo cicle qaa! Zorge! Zir noco! Hoath Helel Bvfd lonsh londoh babage

Twelfth Key Enochian Intonement

NOH-nuh-see • DAHSS ZOH-nuhf • mah-duh-REE-ahks OHD • kuh-HEES • DAH, huh-vuh-BAH-ee-oh tee-BEE-buhp • AH-luh-lahr ah-tuh-RAH-ah • OHD tuh-REE-ahn • TAH LOH-luh-keez • ah-BAH-ee FAH-fayn • DAY • ee-YAHD! AH-ruh • HEL-EL • OH-vohf; ZOH-bah • doh-OH-ay-een ah-AH-ee • EE • VOH-nuh-puh! zah-KAH-ray • KAH • OHD ZAH-muh-rahn! • OH-doh KEE-kuh-lay • KAH-ah! ZOR-ruh-jzhay! • ZEE-ruh NOH-koh! • hoh-AH-tuh-huh HEL-EL • BUH-vuh-fuhd LOH-nuh-suh • LOH-nuh-doh bah-BAH-jzhay

Thirteenth Key

The Thirteenth Key is a conjuration of lust to the impotent.

The Thirteenth Key in English

O you swords of the South which have 42 eyes to stir up the pleasures of sin, making empty men drunken; Behold! The promise of Satan! And His power, which is called amongst those in heaven, a bitter sting! Move therefore and appear! Open the mysteries of your Creation! Be friendly unto me! For I am the servant of the same! The true worshipper of Satan in glory and power exalted in the Kingdom of Hell.

The Thirteenth Key in Enochian

Napeai babage ds brin vx ooaona Lring qvasahi de doalim, eolis ollog Orsba; micma! Isro de Helel! Od tox lonshi, ds i vmd aai priaz De madriax, grosb! Zacare ca od zamran! Odo cicle qaa! Zorge! Zir noco! Hoath Helel Bvfd lonsh londoh babage

Thirteenth Key Enochian Intonement

NAH-pay-AH-ee • bah-BAH-jzhay DAHSS • buh-REEN • VAHKS oh-oh-AH-oh-nah • luh-REE-nuh-jzhay kuh-VAH-sah-hee • DAY • doh-AH-leem, ee-OH-leess • OH-luh-lohjzh OH-ruh-suh-bah; • MEE-kuh-mah! EE-suh-roh • DAY • HEL-EL! • OHD TOHKS • LOH-nuh-suh-hee, • DAHSS EE • VUH-MUHD • ah-AH-ee puh-REE-ahts • DAY • mah-duh-REE-ahks, guh-ROH-suhb! zah-KAH-ray • KAH • OHD ZAH-muh-rahn! • OH-doh KEE-kuh-lay • KAH-ah! ZOR-ruh-jzhay! • ZEE-ruh NOH-koh! • hoh-AH-tuh-huh HEL-EL • BUH-vuh-fuhd LOH-nuh-suh • LOH-nuh-doh bah-BAH-jzhay

Fourteenth Key

The Fourteenth Key is a declaration of justice to be wrought upon those who would judge others without just cause.

The Fourteenth Key in English

O you Sons and Daughters of judgment, who sit upon 24 seats vexing the creatures of the earth. Behold! The voice of Satan! The promise of Him who is called amongst you the supreme justice! Move therefore and appear! Open the mysteries of your Creation! Be friendly unto me! For I am the servant of the same! The true worshipper of Satan, the highest King of Hell.

The Fourteenth Key in Enochian

Nore od pasbs de Helel, Ds trint mirc ol thil dods
Idoigo a madriax. Micma! Bial de Helel! Isro tox de I
vmd aai baltim! Zacare ca od zamran! Odo cicle qaa!
Zorge! Zir noco! Hoath Helel Bvfd lonsh londoh babage

Fourteenth Key Enochian Intonement

NOH-ray • OHD • PAHSS-uh-bus DAY • HEL-EL, • DAHSS tuh-REE-nuht • MEE-ruhk • OHL tah-HEEL • DOH-duhs ee-YAH-doh-EE-goh • AH mah-duh-REE-ahks. • MEE-kuh-mah! bee-AHL • DAY • HEL-EL! EE-suh-roh • TOHKS • DAY • EE VUH-MUHD • ah-AH-ee • BAH-luh-teem! zah-KAH-ray • KAH • OHD ZAH-muh-rahn! • OH-doh KEE-kuh-lay • KAH-ah! ZOR-ruh-jzhay! • ZEE-ruh NOH-koh! • hoh-AH-tuh-huh HEL-EL • BUH-vuh-fuhd LOH-nuh-suh • LOH-nuh-doh bah-BAH-jzhay

Fifteenth Key

The Fifteenth Key is a warning call to deceivers and weavers of injustice that their days are numbered, and hints that no mercy will be given.

The Fifteenth Key in English

O thou governor of the first flame, beneath whose wings weave the about the Earth with the webs of deceit, which knowest and delivereth injustice and rancor. Prepare for the reign of Satan and His Kingdom on Earth! Move therefore and appear! Open the mysteries of your Creation! Be friendly unto me! For I am the servant of the same! The true worshipper of Satan the highest King of Hell.

The Fifteenth Key in Enochian

Ils tabaan l ialprt, orocha Casarman vpaahi ds oado Caosgi vonph: ds omax od Zonrensg baltim od vooan. Abramg sonf de Helel Od londoh mirc caosg! Zacare ca od zamran! Odo cicle qaa! Zorge! Zir noco! Hoath Helel Bvfd lonsh londoh babage

Fifteenth Key Enochian Pronunciation

EE-luh-suh • TAH-bah-ahn • LUH ee-AH-luh-puh-ruht, • oh-ROH-kuh-hah kah-SAH-ruh-mahn • vuh-pah-AH-ee DAHSS • oh-AH-doh kah-OH-suh-jzhee • VOH-nuh-puh: DAHSS • OH-mahks OHD • zoh-nuh-RAY-nuh-suhjzh BAH-luh-teem • OHD • voh-OH-ahn. ah-buh-RAH-muhjzh • ZOH-nuhf DAY • HEL-EL • OHD • LOH-nuh-doh MEE-ruhk • kah-OHSSK! zah-KAH-ray • KAH • OHD ZAH-muh-rahn! • OH-doh KEE-kuh-lay • KAH-ah! ZOR-ruh-jzhay! • ZEE-ruh NOH-koh! • hoh-AH-tuh-huh HEL-EL • BUH-vuh-fuhd LOH-nuh-suh • LOH-nuh-doh bah-BAH-jzhay

Sixteenth Key

The Sixteenth Key speaks of the right of the Satanic to take what is theirs by right and conquer the world.

The Sixteenth Key in English

O thou of the second flame, the House of Hell's truth which hast their beginning in glory, that comfort the just laid low, who walkest on the earth with feet of fire. Mighty art Satan who understands the difference in all creatures! Great is thine right to seize and conquer. Move therefore and appear! Open the mysteries of your Creation! Be friendly unto me! For I am the servant of the same! The true worshipper of Satan the highest King of Hell.

The Sixteenth Key in Enochian

Ils viv malpirgi salman de Donasdogamatatastos ds Acroodzi bvsd, bliorax balit; Ds insi caosg lusdan pvrgel; Micalzo chis Helel od fafen! Zacare ca od zamran! Odo cicle qaa! Zorge! Zir noco! Hoath Helel Bvfd lonsh londoh babage

Sixteenth Key Enochian Intonement

EE-luh-suh • VEEV mah-luh-pee-REE-jzhee ZAH-luh-mahn • DAY DOH-nahss-doh-gah-MAH-tahss-tohss DAHSS • ah-kuh-ROH-ohd-zee BUH-vuh-zuhd, • buh-lee-OH-rahks bah-LEET; • DAHSS • EEN-SSEE kah-OHSSK • LUH-zuh-dahn puh-vuh-ruh-JZHAYL; • mee-KAH-luh-zoh kuh-HEES • HEL-EL • OHD FAH-fayn! zah-KAH-ray • KAH • OHD ZAH-muh-rahn! • OH-doh KEE-kuh-lay • KAH-ah! ZOR-ruh-jzhay! • ZEE-ruh NOH-koh! • hoh-AH-tuh-huh HEL-EL • BUH-vuh-fuhd LOH-nuh-suh • LOH-nuh-doh bah-BAH-jzhay

Seventeenth Key

The Seventeenth Key is a call to battle, a challenge to the enemy to face their destruction.

The Seventeenth Key in English

O thou third flame whose wings are thorns to stir up vexation. Who hath a swarm of living lamps going before thee. Whose truth is wrapped in sardonic wrath! Gird up thy loins and hearken! Move therefore and appear! Open the mysteries of your Creation! Be friendly unto me! For I am the servant of the same! The true worshipper of Satan the highest King of Hell.

The Seventeenth Key in Enochian

Ils d ialprt soba vpaah chic Nanba zixlay dodsih adohi
De madriax. Ds brint em hvbaro tastax ilsi. Aldon dax
od toatar! Zacare ca od zamran! Odo cicle qaa! Zorge!
Zir noco! Hoath Helel Bvfd lonsh londoh babage

Seventeenth Key Enochian Intonement

EE-luh-suh • DAH • ee-AH-luh-puh-ruht ZOH-bah • vuh-PAH-ah • kuh-HEES NAH-nuh-bah • zeeks-LAH-yee doh-duh-SEE-huh • ah-DOH-hee DAY • mah-duh-REE-ahks. DAHSS bah-REEN-uh-tuh • AYM huh-vuh-BAH-roh TAH-suh-tahks • EE-luh-ssee. ah-luh-DOHN • DAHKS • OHD toh-AH-tah-ruh! zah-KAH-ray • KAH • OHD ZAH-muh-rahn! • OH-doh KEE-kuh-lay • KAH-ah! ZOR-ruh-jzhay! • ZEE-ruh NOH-koh! • hoh-AH-tuh-huh HEL-EL • BUH-vuh-fuhd LOH-nuh-suh • LOH-nuh-doh bah-BAH-jzhay

Eighteenth Key

The Eighteenth Key is noted as a blessing to comfort and protect.

The Eighteenth Key in English

O thou mighty light and burning flame of comfort which unveiled the glory of Satan unto the center of the earth, in whom the great secrets of truth have their abiding that is called in thy kingdom strength through joy and is not to be measured. For thou art a window of comfort unto me. Move therefore and appear! Open the mysteries of your Creation! Be friendly unto me! For I am the servant of the same! The true worshipper of Satan the highest King of Hell.

The Eighteenth Key in Enochian

Ils micaolz olpirt od malprg bliore Ds odo bvsd de Helel ovoars caosgo, Casarmg micaolz cicles vooan brints Cafafam ds i vmd a q londoh vgear de Moz od maoffas. Bolp como bliort pambt. Zacare ca od zamran! Odo cicle qaa! Zorge! Zir noco! Hoath Helel Bvfd lonsh londoh babage

Eighteenth Key Enochian Intonement

EE-luh-suh • mee-kah-OH-luhts OH-luh-PEE-ruh-tuh • OHD MAH-luh-puh-ruh-jzhuh • buh-lee-OHR-ay DAHSS • OH-doh • BUH-vuh-zuhd DAY • HEL-EL • oh-voh-AH-ruh-suh kah-OHS-suh-goh, • kah-SAH-ruh-muhjzh mee-kah-OH-luhts • KEE-kuh-lays voh-OH-ahn • buh-REE-nuh-tuhs kah-fah-FAHM • DAHSS • EE VUH-MUHD • AH • KUH LOH-nuh-doh • vuh-GAY-ahr DAY • MAHTS • OHD mah-OH-fuh-fahss. BOH-luhp KOH-moh • buh-lee-OH-ruh-tuh PAH-muh-buh-tuh. zah-KAH-ray • KAH • OHD ZAH-muh-rahn! • OH-doh KEE-kuh-lay • KAH-ah! ZOR-ruh-jzhay! • ZEE-ruh NOH-koh! • hoh-AH-tuh-huh HEL-EL • BUH-vuh-fuhd LOH-nuh-suh • LOH-nuh-doh bah-BAH-jzhay

Nineteenth Key

The Nineteenth key is the final truth. A clarion call to the Satanic to take the earth once more and bring about a dominion of Satan. To lay bare the sanctimonious, the unjust, and expose the deceivers of truth. It is both a call to action and a warning to the enemies of Hell.

Nineteenth Key in English

O you Demons who dwell upon and are mighty governors of the Earth, who execute the judgment of Satan! To you it is said: Behold the face of Satan, the beginning of comfort, whose eyes are the brightness of the stars; who provided you for the government of the Earth, and her variety, furnishing you with a power of understanding, to dispose all things according to the providence of he who reigns on the Throne of Hell and rose up in the beginning, saying: the Earth, let her be governed by her parts. The course of her, let it run with pleasure, and as a handmaid let her serve Satan.

Of the seasons, let them confound one another; and let there be no creature upon or within her the same. All her members, let them differ in their qualities; and let there be no one creature equal with another. The reasonable creatures of the Earth, let them vex and weed out one another; and the dwelling places. Let the works of the followers of deception and their pomp, be defaced. The buildings of he who sits upon the holy throne Heaven, let them become caves for the beasts of the field; and their iniquities be known.

O you sons and daughters of Satan, Arise! Let those in the kingdom of heaven serve you. Govern those that govern; Cast down unjust, and bring forth justice and destroy the rotten. No place let it remain in number. Add and diminish, until the stars be numbered. Arise, move! Appear before Satan! He has sworn unto us his justice. Open the mysteries of your creation, and make us partakers of undefiled truth.

Nineteenth Key in Enochian

Ils daemons ds praf od chis micaolz Artabas de caosgo, ds fifis balzizras De Helel! Nonca gohvlim: Micam adoian de Helel, acroodzi Bliorb, soba ooaona chis luciftias Aoiveae; das abraasa noncf Netaaib caosgi, od tilb damploz, Tooat noncf g micalz oma, lrasd tolglo Marb yarry de tox bogpa oxiayal londoh babage od torzulp acroodzi, gohol: Caosga, tabaord saanir. Elzap tilb, Parm gi qvasahi, od ta qvrlst Booapis Helel. L nimb, ovcho symp; Od christeos ag toltorn mirc q tiobl lel. Ton paombd, dilzmo aspian; od christeos Ag l toltorn parach a symp. Cordziz dodpal od fifalz l smnad; od fargt, a va de fafen de Jehova od avavox, tonvg. Orsca de idigo, Noasmi tabges levithmong; madrid trian oman. Bagle? Moooah qaan. Nore od pasbs De Helel, torzu! Priaz adohi de madriax, Aboapri. Tabaori Priaz ar tabas; Adrpan cors ta dobix; yolcam balit od qvasb Qting. Ripir paaoxt saga cor; vml od prdzar, Cacrg aoiveae cormpt. Torzu, zacar! Zamran aspt Helel! Surzas tia baltan; Odo cicle qaa, od ozazma plapli vooan.

Nineteenth Key Enochian Intonement

EE-luh-suh • DAY-mohns • Dahss puh-RAHFF • OHD • kuh-HEES mee-kah-OH-luhts • ah-ruh-TAH-bahss DAY • kah-OHS-suh-goh, • DAHSS FEE-feess • bah-luh-ZEE-zuh-rahs DAY • HEL-EL! • NOH-nuh-kah goh-huh-vuh-LEEM: • mee-KAHM ah-DOH-ee-ahn • DAY • HEL-EL, ah-kuh-ROH-ohd-zee • buh-lee-OH-ruhb, ZOH-bah • oh-oh-AH-oh-nah • kuh-HEES loo-SEEF-tee-ahs • ah-oh-EE-VEE-ah-ee; DAHSS • ah-buh-RAH-AH-sah NOH-nuh-kuhf • nay-tah-AH-eeb kah-OHS-sah-jzhee, • OHD • TEE-luhb DAH-muh-puh-lohts, • toh-OH-aht NOH-nuh-kuhf • GAH • mee-KAH-luhts OH-mah, • luh-RAH-zuhd TOH-luh-guh-loh • MAH-ruhb YAH-ruh-ruh-ee • DAY • TOHKS BOH-guh-pah • ahks-EE-ah-ee-ahl LOH-nuh-doh • bah-BAH-jzhay • OHD toh-ruh-ZOO-luhp • ah-kuh-ROH-ohd-zee, goh-HOH-luh: • kuh-OHS-suh-gah, tah-bah-OH-ruhd • zah-ah-NEE-ruh. ay-luh-ZAHP • TEE-luhb, • PAH-ruhm JZHEE • kuh-VAH-sah-hee, • OHD TAH • KUH-vuh-ruh-luh-suh-tuh boh-OH-ah-pees • HEL-EL. LUH • NEE-muhb, • OH-vuh-kuh-hoh ZEE-muhp; • OHD kuh-REE-suh-tay-ohs AH-jzh • LUH • toh-luh-TOH-ruhn pah-RAH-kuh • AH • ZEE-muhp. kuh-ROH-ohd-zee, • DOH-duh-pahl OHD • FEE-fah-luhz • LUH suh-muh-NAHD; • OHD • FAH-ruh-guht, AH • VAH-vuhl • DAY • FAH-fayn DAY • jah-HOH-vah • OHD ah-VAH-vohks, • TOH-nuh-vuhjzh. OH-ruh-suh-kah DAY • EE-dee-goh, noh-AH-suh-mee • tah-buh-JZHAY-suh LAY-vee-tuh-huh-MOH-nuhjzh; mah-duh-REED • tah-REE-ahn • OH-mahn. BAH-guh-lay? • moh-OH-oh-ah • KAH-HAN. NOH-ray • OHD • PAHSS-uh-buhs DAY • HEL-EL, • TOH-ruht-soo! puh-REE-ahts • ah-DOH-hee • DAY mah-duh-REE-ahks, • ah-boh-AH-puh-ree. tah-bah-OH-ree • puh-REE-ahts • AH-ruh tah-BAHSS; • ah-duh-ruh-PAHN • KOH-ruhz

TAH • DOH-beeks; • ee-OH-luh-kahm bah-LEET • OHD • kuh-VAH-suhb kuh-TEE-nujzh. • REE-pee-ruh pah-AH-ohks-tuh • ZAH-gah KOH-ruh; • vuh-MAHL • OHD puh-ruh-duh-ZAH-ruh, • KAH-kuh-rahjzh ah-oh-EE-VEE-ah-ee • KOH-ruh-muhp. TOH-ruht-soo, • ZAH-kahr! • ZAH-mah-rahn AH-suh-puht • HEL-EL! • ZOO-ruh-jzhahs TEE-ah • BAH-luh-tahn; • OH-doh KEE-kah-lay • KAH-AH-AH, • OHD oh-ZAH-tsuh-mah • puh-LAH-puh-lee voh-OH-ahn.

A Final Word

So it is, I have at last come to the ultimate conclusion of this project. Well for now at least. Who knows what the future may hold? Perhaps in 10, 20, or even 30 years from now, I may make a new 4th edition of this book. But for now, I draw this project to a close, and turn my attention to other works.

In writing this Testament of mine I have found myself grown beyond my wildest dreams. My understanding of not only Satanism and its world views, but more importantly myself, has exponentially expanded to a measure beyond expectation.

It is perhaps, a curse, or maybe even a boon, that writing ones first book, almost never seems complete. I started this project in 2009 as a way to document my feelings and beliefs surrounding my faith in the Satanic Religion and the occult path it represented to me. It was essentially MY Satanic Bible. Now over a decade and 3 editions later, I am moved by how many people have taken it to their own hearts as such too. Some even comparing it to Anton LaVey's seminal work itself. Certainly, I could never have foreseen that. No matter what sort of prophetic abilities I have been accused of having.

And so I would like to close this with a few sayings I said when I first sat down to begin this project so long ago.

To all the naysayers, bull shitters, hypocrites, fools, and so called "authorities" who laughed at the concept of me writing a book. And to those who have trodden the dark paths of the occult to light the way. Thank you all for being inspirations.

I am simply one man. A true Satanist flying in the face of established thought and those who would hamper its growth. This is, MY Testament to the shunned and feared religion.

Take as you will, or leave it!

About the author
Lucifer LeGivorden

Lucifer LeGivorden, sometimes known as Alexandrue Lucifer Ravensloft LeGivorden. Or just simply Luc or Legi to his friends, family, and peers. Is an accomplished Warlock, and the founder of the Satanic Thulian Society.

Having suffered a near death experience as a small child, LeGivorden developed a fixation with religious studies and the occult arts. By his late 20s he had taken on the mantle of Satanist and became ordained as a Satanic Priest.

Over the years LeGivorden has been a very outspoken voice in the argument against Atheism in Satanism, Abortion in Satanism, and The Satanic Temple, and has brought forth many forgotten texts to prove his points.

This has garnered him a mixed reputation with his contemporaries. Some love him while others despise his habit of rocking the proverbial boat.

LeGivorden currently resides in South Carolina in his 130 year old manor house lovingly named Firethorne Manor. He lives with his fiancé, son, and their menagerie of furry and scaly children.

www.ingramcontent.com/pod-product-compliance
Lightning Source LLC
Chambersburg PA
CBHW020306010526
44107CB00001B/5